The Testimony
of Two Nations

The Testimony of Two Nations

How the Book of Mormon Reads, and Rereads, the Bible

MICHAEL AUSTIN

UNIVERSITY OF
ILLINOIS PRESS
Urbana, Chicago, and Springfield

Library of Congress Cataloging-in-Publication Data
Names: Austin, Michael, 1966– author.
Title: The testimony of two nations : how the Book of
    Mormon reads, and rereads, the Bible / Michael Austin.
Description: Urbana : University of Illinois Press, [2024] |
    Includes bibliographical references and index.
Identifiers: LCCN 2023015919 (print) | LCCN
    2023015920 (ebook) | ISBN 9780252045356
    (cloth) | ISBN 9780252087479 (paperback) | ISBN
    9780252054952 (ebook)
Subjects: LCSH: Church of Jesus Christ of Latter-
    day Saints—Sacred books. | Book of Mormon—
    Relation to the Bible. | Book of Mormon—Criticism,
    interpretation, etc. | Mormon Church—Sacred books.
Classification: LCC BX8627 .A97 2024 (print) |
    LCC BX8627 (ebook) | DDC 289.3/22—dc23/
    eng/20230627
LC record available at https://lccn.loc.gov/2023015919
LC ebook record available at https://lccn.loc.gov/2023015920

For Jim Fleetwood
a good bishop and a good friend

Contents

Acknowledgments

The ideas in this book have been bouncing around my head, and my conversations with friends, colleagues, and mentors, for decades, and my list of collaborators is long. Many of them were worked out in a series of posts that I wrote for the By Common Consent blog in 2016 and published together as a stand-alone book, *Buried Treasures: Reading the Book of Mormon Again for the First Time*, in 2020. Countless readers of these posts, in either blog or book form, have improved my ideas by challenging, refining, and arguing with me about them. I am grateful to Blaire Hodges for suggesting that I write a more academic book about these same ideas and to Brian Haglund for publishing my first attempt to write about the Book of Mormon and the Bible in the *Journal of Book of Mormon Studies*.

Along the way, I talked to a lot of very smart, very knowledgeable people and shared portions of the manuscript with them. My profound thanks go to Eric Huntsman, David Bokovoy, Becky Roesler, Colby Townsand, Joseph Spencer, Dayna Kimball Brown, Chris Thomas, Tony Beavers, Chris Kimball, and Rachel Meibos Helps for reading portions of the manuscript, offering advice, talking over key points, and otherwise keeping me on the right track while I was writing this book.

William L. Davis read the entire manuscript and made game-changing recommendations, as did David Gore and an anonymous reviewer for the University of Illinois Press. My father, Roger Austin, was the first, and, I suspect, the best of my readers, and I am grateful for his constant (and very long-term) support of my academic efforts, along with those of my mother, Linda Austin, who first read the stories of the Bible and the Book of Mormon to me when I was unable to read anything myself.

Allison Syring, my editor at the University of Illinois Press, could not have been more professional, encouraging, knowledgeable, and helpful to me from the earliest days of this project until its final publication.

Thanks, love, and my deepest appreciation go to my wife, Karen D. Austin, for her constant support of this and so many other projects.

The Testimony
of Two Nations

Introduction

Book of Mormon stories that my teacher tells to me
Are about the Lamanites in ancient history.
Long ago their fathers came from far across the sea,
Giv'n the land if they lived righteously.

Lamanites met others who were seeking liberty,
And the land soon welcomed all who wanted to be free.
Book of Mormon stories say that we must brothers be,
Giv'n the land if we live righteously.
— "Book of Mormon Stories," *LDS Children's Songbook*

Like Mormon children everywhere, I grew up singing "Book of Mormon Stories" nearly every week, with its percussive piano chords designed to simulate an indigenous dance and the accompanying hand gestures that made it more of a game than a song. It was a great adventure for someone not yet five years old.

Later, we would learn that the Book of Mormon contained much more than stories. We learned that it articulated vital doctrines and testified clearly of Jesus Christ and his infinite atonement. It was theology, history, prophecy, and evidence of Joseph Smith's prophetic calling. And many of us also discovered some of the problems. We learned that the story of Lamanites being cursed with dark skin was based on racist folk etiologies common in early America and that nineteenth-century polemics against Catholics, Masons, and Universalists found their way into the Book of Mormon's religious doctrines in incongruously modern ways. And we learned that almost nobody outside the church thought it likely that Hebraic colonists from the time of the Babylonian conquest came to the New World and founded a thousand-year civilization that collapsed in the fifth century CE, with its remnants becoming the ancestors of pre-Columbian Americans.

But first we learned the stories: Nephi breaking his bow and constructing a new one while his grumpy brothers just complained; Enos going on a hunting trip and praying all day and all night; Abinadi standing in the fire and preaching to the evil King Noah; Ammon making himself a servant to the Lamanite king and cutting off the arms of the robbers trying to steal his flocks; and Helaman leading the two thousand young Lamanite soldiers into a battle that they all survived because of the great faith their mothers had taught them. We also learned the stories from the Bible, but those were different because everybody else knew them, too. The Book of Mormon's stories belonged to us. They told us things that other people didn't know, and they laid the early foundations of our faith.[1]

When I sang "Book of Mormon Stories" as a child, I had no idea how vital stories would become for me. I did not know that I would one day write a dissertation, and later a book, about the way British writers of the seventeenth and eighteenth centuries interacted with biblical narratives in their own work, or that I would write another book about the evolutionary and cognitive value of storytelling. And I could not have guessed that I would spend much of my career teaching the classics of world literature to college students. I didn't realize that stories would become some of the most important things in my life.

Christians (including Latter-day Saints) and Jews are almost alone in the world in having sacred texts that consist mainly of narratives. The Qur'an, the Upanishads, the Analects of Confucius, the Tao Te Ching, and the Discourses of the Buddha all contain narrative elements, but they are all primarily built on direct instruction. The Bible and the Book of Mormon both contain elements of direct instruction, but they are built mainly on narratives. They tell stories, and they develop their most important ideas through the interpretation of stories presented often, but not always, as historical narratives. We learn the importance of faith through the story of Abraham, the value of endurance through the story of Job, and the importance of having a written record through the story of Nephi killing Laban in order to possess the brass plates. And because the instruction depends on interpretation, we can derive other lessons from these stories as well. Stories are more fluid, more nuanced, and more open to interpretation than the direct instruction that constitutes the bulk of most sacred texts.

Narratives are also easy to connect to other narratives in ways that create connections between works. Christians call the Hebrew Bible "The Old Testament" because the New Testament connected itself to many of its major narratives and converted them into symbolic prophecies of Christ. In this book, I argue that the Book of Mormon does the same thing with the Christian Bible using many of the same tools. I also argue that the Christian Bible—both the Old and the New Testaments—provides a context in which the Book of Mormon can be interpreted: the canonical context, which in-cludes the Bible, the Book of Mormon itself, and, depending on the branch of the Restoration, other writings and revelations that have been elevated to scriptural status.[2] I focus on how the Book of Mormon connects itself to the Christian Bible to form a new canon and then uses that canonical relation-ship to reframe or reinterpret the biblical narrative. This canonical context, I argue, is a legitimate primary interpretive context for the Book of Mormon.

The proper interpretive context for the Book of Mormon has been the sub-ject of intense debate since its first publication in 1830. Latter-day Saints and other Restoration adherents have always approached the Book of Mormon as an ancient document with Hebraic origins that was composed between 600 BCE and 400 CE, redacted in the fourth century CE, and translated into English from an unknown language called "Reformed Egyptian" in the early nineteenth century. The original records are not available for examina-tion, nor do we have any surviving records in Reformed Egyptian to compare with the Book of Mormon. Latter-day Saints accept these facts as a matter of faith, not scholarship, and much (but by no means all) of the academic work conducted from this perspective aims to support these truth claims rather than illuminate the text.[3] Nearly all scholars who are not Mormon, and an increasing number who are, approach the Book of Mormon as a nineteenth-century American text that responds to religious, social, and political considerations in Jacksonian America.[4]

Most attempts to bridge the context gap take a four-corners approach that is sometimes called "bracketing" because it places the question of proper historical context in brackets. This produces something like what literary critics call "formalism" or "New Criticism," which treats literary texts as self-contained units of meaning that can be understood without reference to any external context.[5] This bracketing maneuver has produced a number of solid readings of the Book of Mormon and at least one outstanding book, Grant Hardy's *Understanding the Book of Mormon: A Reader's Guide*. Bracketing, though, has recently come under sharp criticism from academic quarters. Yale University professor R. John Williams has argued that bracketing the Book of Mormon's historical claims is both ill-advised and impossible—ill-advised because the questions that end up in brackets are precisely the questions that need to be asked, and impossible because it presupposes "the possibility of isolating the 'text' of *The Book of Mormon* as a unified, hermeneutically contained object in the first place, which . . . it can never be."[6]

Canonical analysis offers a fourth interpretive context—not to discount or try to supplant any of the others, but to bring one more critical lens to a rap-idly growing academic discussion. The canonical context can support either an ancient or a nineteenth-century provenance for the Book of Mormon, just as it can support either a human or a divine theory of authorship—and it can also support all the gradients in between these extremes. All we must accept is that the author or authors of the Book of Mormon intended it to stand with the Christian Bible as a deeply interconnected scriptural text. This is no more than the text claims for itself, but it has profound implications for the way we interpret both the Bible and the Book of Mormon. Many of the tools we need to explore these implications have been worked out by biblical critics in a critical methodology called "canonical criticism," which "insists that authority resides only in the full canon, which is the context in which every biblical text finally must be read."[7]

Canon as Context

In *Reading the Old Testament*, the eminent Oxford University theologian John Barton proposes a thought experiment to demonstrate the interpretive importance of scriptural canons. He asks us to imagine what would have happened if "the book of Ecclesiastes had been lost from all copies of the Bible . . . and were then discovered among the Dead Sea scrolls as a 'non-canonical' text."[8] In such a case, he suggests, Ecclesiastes would probably not be seen as a book that had much to do with the Bible. Its author is pessimistic to the point of nihilism, unsure about God's goodness, and uninterested in religious obligations. He repeatedly says that death makes everything meaningless, so the best that human beings can do is seek pleasure wherever they can find it. Ecclesiastes gives us the common phrase "eat, drink, and be merry," which, it argues, is the closest we can get to happiness in life (Eccl 8:15). These are hardly sentiments that accord with either the Old Testament's understanding of a people's covenant with God or the New Testament's themes of atonement and grace. If Ecclesiastes had not been part of the Bible when we found it, there would be few reasons for anyone to think that it ever belonged there.

But Ecclesiastes *was* part of the Bible when we found it, and this had profound implications for its interpretation. When we interpret Ecclesiastes as part of the biblical canon, Barton writes, "we are bound to read it so as to mitigate [its] extremes of advice, and to integrate it into its biblical framework in such a way that both hedonism and skepticism are held in check by religious faith."[9] Interpreted in this context, Ecclesiastes becomes an extreme example of Hebrew skepticism that clarifies the context of other expressions of doubt in the Bible,[10] a dialogue between a heterodox voice and a prophetic voice that contradicts it,[11] or a book that requires us to give up hope in everything else so that we can ultimately place our hope in Christ.[12] The canonical context is so important that it overrides anything we know or might deduce about the author's intentions or the original meaning of the text. "The meaning of a text inheres in the text, or in the setting within which it is read, not in the intentions of those who wrote it," Barton argues. "To insist on the 'original' meaning is to wrest the work from its context; it is to refuse to take seriously that, whatever it may have been once, we encounter it now only as part of Scripture."[13]

When a text appears within a scriptural canon, as Frank Kermode explains, it acquires a privileged relationship with every other text in the same canon. All of the texts "are held to be inspired and interrelated like the parts of a single book," he argues, and "their relations with 'outside' books are of a different order."[14] When we interpret the book of Job and the book of Luke as parts of the Christian Bible, we consider them to have far more to do with each other than either has to do with much more similar texts that are not part of the canon. Job is not the only wisdom dialogue that came from the ancient world, nor is Luke's the only biography of a religious figure to come from the early days of the Roman Empire. Though the original book of Job was part of a context that included such Mesopotamian poems as "A Sufferer's Salvation" and "A Dialogue Between a Man and His God," it has continued to be read and thought about for 2,500 years as part of several scriptural canons. These other works have largely vanished from sight and are now read only by a few highly specialized scholars of the literatures and cultures of the ancient Near East.[15]

The interpretive approach that Barton seeks to illustrate through this thought experiment been called, variously, "canonical criticism," "final-form criticism," or the "canonical approach."[16] This critical methodology grew from the work of Yale theology professor Brevard S. Childs, whose 1970 book *Biblical Theology in Crisis* argued that biblical interpretation had fixated on the wrong contexts. Historical scholars, he felt, spent too much time studying the original contexts of specific texts, ignoring the way the texts combined to create a theologically significant whole. Progressive theologians, on the other hand, tended to read the Bible in a modern context—as a volume designed to address contemporary social problems such as poverty, racism, and international conflict. Childs maintained that neither of these interpretive contexts—that of original meaning or that of contemporary reception—can explain why the Bible has been important to Christian believers for almost two thousand years. In place of these contexts, or at least in addition to them, Childs suggested that "the Canon of the Christian Church is the most appropriate context from which to do Biblical Theology."[17]

Childs' "canon-as-context" approach has been the subject of vigorous debate among theologians, many of whom consider the approach too narrow.[18] As a purely literary slant, though, it barely goes beyond first principles. We must always consult the larger narrative when interpreting a text, even if it originally came from a different context altogether. We must read the tender love sonnets that Don Quixote sends to his Lady Dulcinea differently as part of the Quixote satire than we would read them as part of a collection of love poems—and we would have to do so even if we discovered that they were originally composed by someone else for an entirely different purpose. We know beyond any doubt that Shakespeare did not write *King Lear* for the Beatles, but when fragments of the fourth act appear in "I Am the Walrus," we must interpret Shakespeare's words in a context that also includes egg men and yellow matter custard. Context always matters, and when the context of interpretation changes, the meaning of a text can change dramatically. But when the stakes include the correct interpretation of scripture—texts that, for those who believe them, convey the mind and will of God—finding the right context becomes a matter of eternal significance.

For an example of how the canonical context shapes the meaning of scriptural texts, let us consider four possible interpretations of the story of Adam, Eve, and the serpent in Genesis 3, one of the most important and well-known religious stories in the world. Each interpretation flows logically from the interpretive context created by associating this story with other texts.

- If the text of Genesis 3 had been completely forgotten by the ancient world and rediscovered in a twentieth-century archaeological dig, it would fit nicely into the trickster folk narrative tradition. Talking animals acting as tricksters appear in cultures all over the world doing very similar things: Anansi the spider, Sun-Wukong the monkey king, Coyote, Raven, Reynard the Fox, and Br'er Rabbit, to name just a few. Tricksters frequently move between gods and humans, tricking both equally or pitting them against each other. They frequently steal power from the gods—fire, magic spells, sacred stories, talismans, elixirs of immortality—and give it to humans in order to blur the boundaries between the human and the divine (i.e., "ye shall be as the gods"). And one of the trickster's main narrative functions is to introduce chaos into an otherwise stable system in order to make things happen. In nearly every one of these particulars, the story of Adam, Eve, and the serpent, once removed from the context of any sacred canon, reads like a typical folk creation story.[19]
- As part of the Hebrew *Tanakh*, the story of Adam and Eve works with dozens of other accounts of God's interactions with human beings to

draw contrasts between Yahweh and other Near Eastern deities. As Stephen Greenblatt has recently suggested, one of the major functions of the stories in Genesis and elsewhere in the Hebrew Bible was to distinguish between Yahweh and the morally capricious gods of the Babylonians, whose destruction of Jerusalem was a major shaping event for the entire Hebrew canon. For example, although the story of the great flood in Genesis has many similarities with the flood story in the *Epic of Gilgamesh*, there is one important difference: In *Gilgamesh*, the gods decide to destroy humanity because humans are making too much noise, a selfish and morally capricious motivation. In the Bible, Yahweh destroys the world because humans have become wicked. One can certainly argue with God's moral reasoning in this case, but the point of the story is that Yahweh does use moral reasoning.[20] We see this in the story of Adam and Eve, as well. God does not act capriciously when he kicks our first parents out of the garden. He states his expectations clearly and, when Adam and Eve violate those expectations, he responds proportionately. He exiles them from their home. This exact dynamic becomes the major theme of the Deuteronomic History, in which post-exilic scholars framed Israelite history as a long period of disobedience to God's laws and rejection of his prophets. In response, God exiled the Jews from their homeland.[21]

- In the Christian tradition, the book of Genesis shares the canonical stage with the story of Christ's temptation in the wilderness (Matt 4:1–11; Luke 4:1–13) and with a brief reference to God's primordial battle with Satan in the book of Revelation (Rev 12:7–9). With these other narratives as part of the interpretive context, Christians began to read the serpent in Genesis not as a trickster or as a talking animal but as Satan, who, after being cast out of heaven, determined to destroy God's new creatures by tempting them to their destruction. This interpretation turned the story of Adam and Eve's fall into the first act in a great drama that spans all of human history. By an initial act of disobedience, Adam and Eve brought death into the world and cursed their descendants with the stain of original sin. By obedience, Christ brings resurrection and atonement for sin. "For as in Adam all die, even so in Christ shall all be made alive" (1 Cor 15:22). In the hands of one of the world's greatest poets, the story of Adam and Eve succumbing to Satan's temptation in the Old Testament becomes *Paradise Lost* and the story of Christ resisting Satan's temptation in the New Testament becomes *Paradise Regained*—two incomplete narratives that have to be understood as halves of one coherent whole.[22]

- The meaning of the text changes yet again when we place it in a canon that includes the Book of Mormon and other Restoration scriptures. As we will see in Chapter 2, the Book of Mormon rejects the idea that the fall of Adam and Eve was a tragedy or that their partaking of the forbidden fruit was a sin in any but the most technical of terms. In a blessing given to his son Jacob, the Book of Mormon prophet Lehi explains that the first parents were unable to progress or have children in Eden and that they had to eat the fruit in order to progress. "Adam fell that men might be," Lehi explains, "and men are, that they might have joy" (2 Ne 2:22–25). The Book of Mormon rejects the Christian response to the choice offered by God: Stay in the Garden of Eden and never progress or procreate, or eat the fruit and become fully human, with all of the joy and sadness that humanity entails. In the Book of Moses—Joseph Smith's revision of the first six books of Genesis—Eve comes to realize that the consequences of eating the fruit were actually divine rewards: "Were it not for our transgression," she tells Adam, "we never should have had seed, and never should have known good and evil, and the joy of our redemption, and the eternal life which God giveth unto all the obedient" (Moses 5:11). The Adam and Eve of Mormon scripture are moral heroes who are given an impossible test with conflicting instructions and still manage to make the right choice.

Each of these interpretations makes perfect sense in the right interpretive context—and very little sense outside of it. This is how canons work. They construct the big story that makes sense of all the smaller stories. The three religious canons in the example above—the Hebrew *Tanakh*, the Christian Bible, and the Restoration canon—provide three different, often mutually exclusive contexts on the basis of which to interpret their stories. It would be a mistake to treat these as multiple iterations of a single canon, a perpetually expanding corpus of sacred works that occasionally makes room for an entirely new volume of scripture that clarifies misconceptions while remaining 100 percent true to the original meaning. That is not how canons work. Although 75 percent of the Christian Bible comes from the Hebrew *Tanakh*, and a similar proportion of the Restoration canon comes from the Christian Bible, the three canons create three very different interpretive contexts in which the exact same words can mean very different things.

How the Book of Mormon Approaches the Bible

From the very beginning, readers were intended to see the Book of Mormon as something like the Bible. The first edition of the Book of Mormon in 1830 was designed to mirror the binding and lettering of the most widely distributed Bible of its day,[23] and subsequent editions have increased these similarities in format and typesetting styles.[24] And the text of the Book of

Mormon mimics both the language and the cadences of the King James Bible, from which it also directly quotes hundreds of passages and nearly two dozen whole chapters.[25] The Book of Mormon presupposes a high degree of familiarity with the Bible. Its readers are expected to understand, among other things, the story of Adam and Eve, the Tower of Babel, the Abrahamic covenant, the Hebrew Exodus, the Mosaic law, the Davidic monarchy, the writings of Isaiah, the prophecies of Jeremiah, the Babylonian captivity, and the birth, crucifixion, and resurrection of Jesus Christ. These are the starting points for both the story and the doctrine of the Book of Mormon, which cannot be understood or interpreted correctly without the Bible.

And yet the first author of the Book of Mormon—an ancient prophet named Nephi whose family escaped from Jerusalem before the Babylonian invasion early in the sixth century BCE—prophetically identifies two short-comings in the future Christian Bible. In the first book of his record (1 Ne 11–14), Nephi has a panoramic vision featuring the descendants of the Jews he left in Jerusalem and the colony he establishes in the New World. With the guidance of an angel, Nephi sees the birth and ministry of Jesus Christ and the coming forth of the Bible. The vision in First Nephi leaves us with the impression that the Bible was once a complete and easily understandable record of God's dealings with humanity. It would "go forth from the Jews in purity unto the Gentiles, according to the truth which is in God" (1 Ne 13:25). Over time, however, the Bible would be corrupted by a "great and abominable church, which is most abominable above all other churches" that would intentionally remove from the Bible "many parts which are plain and most precious; and also many covenants of the Lord [will they take] away" (1 Ne 13:26). The book that Nephi's descendants will create, the Book of Mormon, will restore what has been lost. "For, behold, saith the Lamb," the angel tells Nephi, quoting Christ himself, "I will manifest myself unto thy seed, that they shall write many things which I shall minister unto them, which shall be plain and precious" (1 Ne 13:35).

Later in his life Nephi suggests that, even if the Bible had been preserved perfectly, the Book of Mormon would still be necessary because no single record from one part of the world can encompass all of God's words. Nephi prophesies that God will bring forth a new work of scripture based on the "the words of your [Nephi's] seed" (2 Ne 29:2) and that this scripture will be rejected by foolish Gentiles who say, "A Bible, a Bible, we have got a Bible! And there cannot be any more Bible" (2 Ne 29:3). The remainder of the chapter constitutes an elaborate argument against the idea of a closed scriptural canon, one that contains a strong universalist contention that God loves all people equally:

Know ye not that there are more nations than one? Know ye not that I the Lord your God have created all men and that I remember they which are upon the isles of the sea and that I rule in the heavens above and in the earth beneath and I bring forth my word unto the children of men, yea, even unto all the nations of the earth? Wherefore murmur ye because that ye shall receive more of my word? Know ye not that the testimony of two nations is a witness unto you that I am God, that I remember one nation like unto another? Wherefore I speak the same words unto one nation like unto another; and when the two nations shall run together, the testimony of the two nations shall run together also. (2 Ne 29:7–8)

Thus, the two most salient shortcomings of the Christian Bible, as presented through Nephi's prophecies hundreds of years before Christ, are (1) that it will be deliberately altered by enemies of God to remove its original clarity, and (2) that it will be a regional and partial record focusing on only one of the peoples God interacts with, rather than a universal and complete record of God's dealings with human beings. The first of these characteristics represents a problem with the Bible's text, which, Nephi claims, will be inaccurate. The second represents a problem with the biblical canon, which will be incomplete. The very existence of the Book of Mormon argues against the Bible's being a closed canon or a complete repository of God's word. The two primary canonical objectives that Nephi creates for the Book of Mormon, then, are (1) to restore the Bible's original clarity and (2) to create a new, expanded, and open canon of scripture to stand along with the Bible and any other scriptures that God chooses to send into the world.

Along with looking and sounding like the Bible, the Book of Mormon narrative mirrors the overall structure of the Bible. Both scriptures, as Laurie Maffley-Kipp observes, "contained sweeping historical accounts of communities led by prophets who cajoled their people to follow the ways of a loyal but sometimes judgmental God, and both culminated with the death, resurrection, and appearance of Jesus Christ to loyal believers."[26] In this book I focus on the larger narrative patterns that define both books and give structure to the entire canon. Specifically, I examine the following narrative patterns that apply equally to the Bible and the Book of Mormon:

1. Near the beginning of the narrative, we find a story about a tree and a fruit that people find desirable. The original ancestors in each story partake of this fruit, and, in doing so, dramatically change their lives and the lives of their descendants.
2. Most of the narrative is framed as the story of the descendants of a single family that has a unique relationship with God. The original ancestor is a righteous patriarch with a younger son who becomes

his spiritual heir, despite the efforts of his jealous older brothers, who try to take his life. Events in the lives of the original family members become etiological tales to explain the world of the text's primary authors.

3. The Lord leads a select group of people out of a great city and requires them to wander for a time in the wilderness to prepare them for a promised land that he has prepared for them.

4. After they inherit the promised land, the chosen people break into two separate societies, each of which traces its origins back to the original family. In each case, one of the two societies is destroyed, while the other becomes a "saving remnant" that will perpetuate the unique relationship to God.

5. A significant portion of the narrative consists of the writings of prophets, who speak in a voice of warning to the people and are frequently persecuted by unbelievers.

6. About three fourths of the way through the text, the story is permanently and drastically changed by the appearance of Jesus Christ.

7. The narrative ends with a cataclysmic event that fundamentally alters the society that it depicts.

These are all big narratives, or narrative frames, that become settings for the smaller stories. These big narratives provide the structure and logic of the overall text—and much of the glue that creates a consistent story across different books that were not originally created to accompany each other. Many of these same plot elements recur within the texts of a single book, such as the story of the righteous younger brother, which occurs seven times in the book of Genesis alone.[27] Or the story of God leading his people out of danger in an established city and to a promised land, which we see seven different times in the Book of Mormon.[28] By incorporating most of the Bible's narrative frames into itself, the Book of Mormon makes the case, not simply that it is the same kind of story that the Bible is, but that it and the Bible are part of the same story and have always belonged together. And we know that they are part of the same story because they have been constructed from the same narrative building blocks.

But connection is only half of the game. The New Testament didn't merely forge connections between itself and the Hebrew scriptures. It used those connections to reinterpret the *Tanakh* and turn it into the Old Testament. The Book of Mormon does something similar with the Christian Bible. As Elizabeth Fenton has written, the Book of Mormon's interactions with the Bible often "take the form of repetition with a difference."[29] This is true of many of the specific narratives that the two books share. Fenton, for example, notes the similarities between Nephi finding his enemy, Laban, asleep and helpless and delivered into his hands (1 Ne 4:4–18) and David finding his enemy, Saul, asleep and helpless and delivered into his hands (1 Sam 24:1–7). The stories are clearly connected, but the Book of Mormon uses the connection to revise the original text. Its version of the story "carries the trace of the older text while simultaneously overmatching it."[30] The same thing, I argue, happens with the larger patterns and narrative arcs that the two volumes share. Consider how each of the structural similarities above has a corresponding structural difference:

1. In Genesis, God commands Adam and Eve not to eat the fruit, and the adversary convinces them that they should. They eat and are (rightly) ashamed. In Lehi's Tree of Life Dream, the God-figure invites him to eat the fruit, and he invites his wife and children to do the same. The adversaries (the people in the Great and Spacious Building) try to convince people not to eat the fruit and to be (wrongly) ashamed if they do.

2. Unlike the etiologies in Genesis, the primary etiological narrative in the Book of Mormon—the curse of Laman and Lemuel—does not create permanent ancestral categories, nor do the resulting groups correlate consistently with God's favor.

3. The biblical exodus ends with the conquest of Canaan and the genocidal slaughter described in the books of Joshua and Judges, and the text presents the bloodshed through which the Israelites obtain the promised land as the will of God. In the Book of Mormon, the exodus of Lehi's family from Jerusalem ends not in conquest but with the Lehites occupying a land that the text presents as empty. Or does it?

4. In the Bible, the Israelites who remain after the Northern Kingdom of Israel is destroyed are the ones who create the final form of the Hebrew Bible for their community. In the Book of Mormon, the Nephite recordkeepers are destroyed, and Lamanite survivors, who do not create a record, become the saving remnant. The text specifically acknowledges that the final form of the Book of Mormon was created by the Nephites for the benefit of the Lamanites.

5. The Bible generally presents prophets as outsiders who warn both political and religious leaders to repent. Two of the prophets in the Book of Mormon fit this model (Abinadi and Samuel the Lamanite), but most of the other prophets hold significant ecclesiastical and political authority themselves. They are kings (Benjamin and Mosiah), high priests (Alma and Alma the Younger), generals (Helaman, Mormon, and Moroni), and chief judges (Alma the Younger and Helaman the Younger). Unlike the Bible, the Book of Mormon frequently presents prophecy as a function of institutional leadership.

6. The Jesus of the New Testament is a mortal teacher who is despised by the religious figures in his community and executed by the state. The Jesus of the Book of Mormon comes as a resurrected and immensely powerful deity who always commands the chastened people's respect.
7. The cataclysm that ends the Bible—the devastation described in the book of Revelation—is presented as prophecy, something that will happen in the future. The cataclysm that ends the Book of Mormon—the destruction of the Nephites and the end of the sacred record—is presented as history, something that has already happened, more than once, in the past, and will continue to happen in the future.

These seven broad areas of similarity and difference form the basic outline of this book. The first chapter explores the nature of typology and proposes a vocabulary for examining typological connections between the Bible and the Book of Mormon. Each of the seven subsequent chapters examines one of the issues listed above, using analytical tools drawn from the disciplines of biblical and literary criticism.

The primary units of analysis in this study are the stories of the Bible and the Book of Mormon. Narrative scriptures are actually quite rare in the world of sacred texts and, as Grant Hardy observes, almost unheard-of in the past thousand years. Most of the world's scriptures "consist of commandments, devotional poetry, doctrinal expositions, community regulations, scriptural commentary, or prophecy." Both the Bible and the Book of Mormon contain these elements too, but it is the stories that people remember the most. Our cognitive architecture is built on an innate understanding of narrative patterns such as temporal sequence, spatial sequence, and cause and effect. We think in stories, and we gravitate toward information that takes a narrative form.[31] This is why most children who go to a Sunday school can retell the stories of Adam and Eve, Joseph, Moses, Jonah, and the baby Jesus, while most adults who have gone to church all of their lives have no idea what might be in the book of Leviticus. The narrative nature of the Book of Mormon and the Bible offers the opportunity to create powerful connections between the two texts by making their stories part of the larger narrative shared by the two volumes of scripture. These connections, and the stories that make them possible, are the main characters in the chapters that follow.

Some Choices Explained

Writing anything involves choices, and when writing about ideas that are sacred to millions of people, those choices can have unfortunate, if unintended, consequences. Consistency is important. Below, in no particular order, are some of the choices and distinctions that I have made throughout this book, along with my reasoning for making them:

- One of the most difficult issues to navigate has been the distinction between "the Hebrew Bible" and "the Old Testament"—terms that define the same group of texts but which do so from very different religious perspectives. I use "Hebrew Bible" or *Tanakh* to refer to the collection of law, history, prophecy, and literature that was assembled during the Babylonian captivity and the Second Temple period and has become the canonical scripture in Judaism. I use "Old Testament" to describe that same collection of texts as interpreted through the New Testament and incorporated into the Christian canon.

- The Church of Jesus Christ of Latter-day Saints, the largest of the denominations tracing back to the Smith-Rigdon Restoration movement, currently discourages the use of the terms "Mormon" and "Mormon Church."[32] I use "the Church of Jesus Christ of Latter-day Saints" to describe this church, its structure, and its scriptures. However, the name cannot be properly applied to other denominations that fall under the Restoration umbrella, nor does it adequately describe the religious tradition tracing back to Joseph Smith that reads and values the Book of Mormon. I will continue to use the term "Mormon" to refer to the spiritual and scriptural tradition to which members of this church belong but do not completely define.

- I use the term "Restoration canon" to refer to the canon of scripture that includes the Bible and the Book of Mormon and—in varying degrees among the different Restoration traditions—the revelations contained in the Doctrine and Covenants and in the LDS Pearl of Great Price (the books of Moses, Abraham, Joseph Smith—Matthew, and Joseph Smith—History). Because different denominations accept different texts outside the Bible and the Book of Mormon as scripture, there are, strictly speaking, multiple Restoration canons. In much the same way, Catholics, Protestants, and various Orthodox groups accept different texts as part of their canons, resulting in multiple versions of the Christian Bible. Yet we can still speak productively about a Restoration canon and a Christian Bible by focusing on the similarities at the core of these canons rather than the differences around the edges.

- Throughout the book, I refer to both the Bible and the Book of Mormon as though they were individual authors with purpose and agency (e.g., "the Bible suggests X, but the Book of Mormon wants us to understand Y"). This is a convention of the critical vocabularies that I am employing to study these texts. It acknowledges the fact that, while authorship in both texts is contested and convoluted, the purposes of my study are not served by lengthy digressions discussing the original authorship of any particular passage.

- I treat the historical claims of both the Bible and the Book of Mormon as part of the texts themselves and of the larger canons of which they are both a part. No text can proclaim itself historical with absolute finality, since the claims themselves are part of the text and may be—as they were in such books as *Robinson Crusoe* and *Gulliver's Travels*—a part of the fiction. But the Restoration canon includes external texts that assert the historicity of the Bible and the Book of Mormon, such as the Joseph Smith—History contained in the Pearl of Great Price, which canonizes Joseph Smith's origin story for the Book of Mormon. I believe, therefore, that historical truth claims in the Bible and the Book of Mormon must be taken seriously when interpreting the texts. Taking historical claims seriously as a matter of interpretation, though, is not the same as endorsing or accepting those claims in the world outside the text. Beyond acknowledging the reality that these claims have for the characters in the texts, and for many of the people who consider these texts sacred, I take no position on whether any of the events described in either the Bible or the Book of Mormon actually occurred.
- I will not always assume that the narrators of these stories are acting in good faith or communicating all of the relevant information. Treating historical claims seriously does not mean accepting everything that a narrator says at face value. History always comes to us through unreliable narrators—observers who lacked all the facts, partisans who had motives to slant the presentation, actors who were too close to the events to describe or evaluate them correctly, and so on. For example, to suggest that Alma the Younger gave a complete and unbiased account of the trial of Nehor—which he presided over as both the chief judge of the Nephite state and as the head of the church that Nehor opposed (Alma 1:1–15)—is to claim a truth status for contemporary reporters of historical events that can only be called ahistorical. Such unity and certainty are the provinces of fiction.
- A number of the names in the Book of Mormon repeat at different times. There are three Nephis and three Helamans, two Mosiahs, Almas, Moronis, and Lehis. A recent scholarly convention uses subscript numerals to distinguish between the figures: $Nephi_3$ $Moroni_1$, $Alma_2$, and so forth. I adopt this convention very selectively in *The Testimony of Two Nations* and only when, in my judgment, the correct figure cannot be immediately identified by the context.
- All citations from the Book of Mormon come from Royal Skousen, ed., *The Book of Mormon: Earliest Text*, 2nd ed. (Yale University Press, 2022). This version of the text coordinates the two handwritten manuscript versions of the text with its earliest published edition to produce

a critical edition that recaptures, as well as anybody can, the original version of the manuscript before any editorial changes. I have noted in endnotes the few instances in which changes in the modern LDS edition of the Book of Mormon alter the meaning of the text in significant ways.

- All citations from the Christian Bible will be from the King James Bible, a Protestant version that was in common use in America in the early nineteenth century. This is the version of the Bible that Joseph Smith and the first generation of Mormon readers read, and it is the version that the Book of Mormon acknowledges through frequent quotation and allusion. The canon of scripture that the Book of Mormon creates includes the English-language King James Version of the Bible as its authoritative biblical text.[33]

- All quotations or references to the Bible and the Book of Mormon are cited in parentheses in the text. All other references are cited in endnotes.

- I imagine two primary audiences for this book. The first consists of readers and scholars familiar with both the Bible and the Book of Mormon who are unfamiliar with the vast body of critical and scholarly work on the Hebrew and Christian Bibles. The second audience consists of scholars who are familiar with the Bible and its critical and scholarly traditions but have little experience with either the Book of Mormon or with Mormonism generally. While there is some overlap between these groups, it is quite small. Terms and concepts that are very familiar to one group will be just as unfamiliar to the other. In order to address this, I spend some time providing basic definitions of terms and concepts that will seem elementary to one group of readers in the hope that they will prove useful to the other.

CHAPTER ONE

A Theory of Types

Typology is a figure of speech that moves in time. . . .
What it both assumes and leads to, is a theory of history,
or more accurately of historical process: an assumption
that there is some meaning and point to history, and
that sooner or later some event or events will occur
which will indicate what that meaning or point is, and so
become an antitype of what has happened previously.
—Northrop Frye, *The Great Code*

Here is a story about a book that changed the world.

This book started its life with the bold claim that it was both equal to and inseparably part of the most famous and most sacred book ever written (which was really two distinct books that had long been bound together as a single text by those who saw it as divinely inspired). Even more audaciously, this book claimed to reopen a canon that had been closed for hundreds of years and to give new revelations about groups of people who featured in the established narratives.

This new book begins in the same city where many events in the other book took place, right before that city was destroyed and its inhabitants were either killed or taken captive into foreign lands. It begins with the story of one small group of people, all connected to the family of a pious man, who were saved by divine intervention in the form of a dream warning the man to take his family and flee into the wilderness. This group eventually built a ship and sailed to a new land—a land of promise and infinite potential. Once there, they built a great civilization that endured for more than a thousand years.

Most of this book is set in the New World; it even gives the native inhabitants of that world a sacred pedigree and an Old World genealogy. Thus, it fulfilled an important cultural purpose: It wrote the new nation into the sacred history that most of its citizens believed in, but which they always saw as a foreign import. As the new nation grew more powerful, the book's importance increased, structuring the belief and directing the worship of millions of people in the new land—and, eventually, throughout the world. Today, many people see this book as a vital cultural touchstone and a work of great inspiration and power. Even people who do not accept its religious and historical claims see it as an important piece of literature. It routinely ranks along with the Bible and the works of Shakespeare as one of the most influential books ever written.

* * *

The book that I refer to, of course, is the *Aeneid* by Publius Vergilius Maro—usually referred to in English as Virgil (or Vergil)—who borrowed heavily from both the *Iliad* and the *Odyssey* to construct a mythology of the Roman people.[1] These earlier works had long been attributed to Homer, the mysterious blind bard who lived sometime in the seventh or eighth century BCE. Over time, the two books of the Homeric canon became the most important cultural and religious texts in the Greek world, and they served as the basis for much of the mythology and culture of classical Athens.

Eight hundred years later, when Augustus Caesar emerged from the civil wars as the first emperor of Rome, the new empire had a problem. Greek culture and mythology dominated Roman life. Although Rome's military had conquered Greece more than a hundred years earlier, the cultural conquest went in the other direction. As Horace said, "Captive Greece took her uncultured captor captive."[2] Educated Romans spoke Greek, read Plato and Aristotle, and thought of their own gods and goddesses largely in forms drawn from the Greek myths. The immense influence of Greek culture was at odds with the narrative of Roman exceptionalism that Augustus championed. And he relied on the great poets of the age who competed for his favor—Horace, Ovid, and especially Virgil—to make the Greek myths more Roman.

Virgil came through magnificently with the *Aeneid*, his epic poem about the founding of Rome. Since he could not minimize the importance of Greek culture in Roman life, he instead gave the Romans a new genealogy that made them part of the Greek story all along. In order to do this he turned the central events of the *Iliad* into an origin story for the Roman people. As the Greeks were sacking Troy, the story goes, Venus (whom the Greeks called Aphrodite) led her son Aeneas and his family out of the city. Aeneas built a fleet of ships and wandered around the Mediterranean for a while, having adventures and wooing the mighty queen Dido. He even takes a trip through the underworld (as all epic heroes must) before landing in Latium, the settlement that will eventually become Rome.

In structural terms, the *Aeneid* is modeled on both the *Iliad* and the *Odyssey*. The first half of the epic (books 1–6), like the first half of the *Odyssey*, consists of a sea journey with many stops and adventures along the way. The second half (books 7–12), much like the *Iliad*, consists of a series of epic battles that Aeneas fights to establish the colony that will one day produce Romulus and Remus and the other mythic ancestors of the Roman people. According to Virgil, Romans were actually Trojans, the most famous enemies of the Greeks, who could only defeat them by shameful trickery. And Virgil incorporates many recognizable elements from Homer in his own story, which makes perfect sense. He is trying to write himself and his culture into a canon that already exists.

But Virgil also changes the meaning of Homer's stories in ways that his readers would read back into the Homeric canon. Consider one of the most famous scenes in the *Odyssey*, in which Odysseus must sail his ship through a treacherous strait, with the six-headed monster Scylla on one side of the strait and the sea-demon Charybdis on the other. Trying to avoid Scylla would nearly guarantee destruction by Charybdis, so the only way through the pass was to hug the shore and sacrifice six men to the monster. The witch Circe explains all of this to Odysseus before he heads out:

> The other crag is lower—you will see, Odysseus—
> though both lie side-by-side, an arrow-shot apart.
> Atop it a great fig-tree rises, shaggy with leaves,
> beneath it awesome Charybdis gulps the dark water down.
> Three times a day she vomits it up, three times she gulps it down,
> that terror! Don't be there when the whirlpool swallows down—
> not even the earthquake god could save you from disaster.
> No, hug Scylla's crag—sail on past her—top speed!
> Better by far to lose six men and keep your ship
> than lose your entire crew.[3]

Odysseus protests that there should be some way to fight both monsters and save all of his men, but Circe just laughs at him, reminds him that Scylla and Charybdis are both immortal, and tells him that he will have to "bow to the deathless gods themselves." Odysseus does as she advises and sacrifices six men to Scylla.

The Scylla-Charybdis scene in the *Aeneid* is much different. Like Odysseus, Aeneas learns of the dangers in advance. After wandering around the Mediterranean, Aeneas discovers that his friend Helenus, the Trojan prince and son of King Priam, has become the king of the land of Buthrotum (in present-day Albania), where he was originally taken as a slave after the fall of Troy. Helenus has the gift of prophecy, and he tells Aeneas that, in order to fulfill his destiny and travel to Italy, he will first have to go through the underworld. But Helenus makes it clear that Aeneas should sail all the way around Sicily rather than attempt to pass through the strait between Scylla and Charybdis.[4] Helenus's suggestions add about two hundred miles, or six days of traveling time, to Aeneas's journey from Buthrotum to Latium, but it is well worth the extra time to avoid the monsters:

> But now Scylla to starboard
> blocks your way, with never-sated Charybdis off to port—
> three times a day, into the plunging whirlpool of her abyss
> she gulps down floods of sea, then heaves them back in the air,
> pelting the stars with spray. Scylla lurks in her blind cave,
> thrusting out her mouths and hauling ships on her rocks.
> She's human at first glance, down to the waist a girl
> with lovely breasts, but a monster of the deep below,
> her body a writhing horror, her belly spawns wolves
> flailing with dolphins' tails. Better to waste time,
> skirting Sicily then in a long arc rounding Cape Pachynus,
> than once set eyes on gruesome Scylla deep in her cave,
> her rocks booming with all her sea-green hounds.[5]

Aeneas takes Helenus's advice, but the winds blow him toward Scylla and Charybdis anyway. He escapes by rowing furiously in the other direction.

There are some surface similarities in these two scenes beyond the fact that they both deal with Scylla and Charybdis. They both feature a wandering hero trying to sail to a home (a remembered home for Odysseus and a prophesied home for Aeneas), and both heroes are warned by wise, prophetic individuals about the dangers of the same patch of ocean. But the morals of the two stories could not be more different. Circe tells Odysseus that he has to choose Scylla or Charybdis—six guaranteed deaths or the high possibility of total ruin. He must also accept that his fate is controlled by the gods and that he can't fight or trick his way out of every dilemma. The comparable scene in the *Aeneid*, though, suggests that both Circe and Odysseus were wrong. With careful planning and patience, Aeneas manages to avoid the no-win situation that traps Odysseus (or, more specifically, Odysseus's sailors). Virgil's version of the scene refutes Homer's fatalistic message while writing his nation into Homer's story. As it does, it showcases traditional Roman values such as prudence and industry. The *Aeneid* is both an unauthorized sequel to, and a partial rebuttal of, the work of Homer.

The central question of the present book, of course, is not "How does the *Aeneid* read the *Iliad* and the *Odyssey*?" It is, "How does the Book of Mormon read the Bible?" But the two questions have similar answers. When Joseph Smith published the Book of Mormon in the early days of the American republic, he was grappling with many of the same issues that Virgil encountered at the dawn of the Roman Empire: Most Americans were Christians and were deeply familiar with the narratives of the Bible—from their own reading, if they were literate, or from the deeply Christian, deeply narrative sermon culture of the early nineteenth century.[6] Nonetheless, the Bible was a foreign story from an old world that seemed to have nothing to do with the spaces that Americans inhabited. The Book of Mormon made America theologically important by injecting its land into the biblical narrative and giving its native inhabitants a biblical genealogy. It said that the prophets of the Old World knew about the New World and made references to it in their prophecies that nobody had ever understood before. And it said that Jesus Christ not only knew about the people of the Americas, he came and visited them after his crucifixion and resurrection in the Old World. As the *Aeneid* did with Rome and Romans, the Book of Mormon wrote America and Americans into a sacred story that they already believed but did not yet consider part of their nation's history. The Book of Mormon and the *Aeneid* used the same narrative strategies to read themselves into previous stories. They are the same strategies that the New Testament used to read itself into the Hebrew Bible. These strategies can collectively be called "typology."

In narrative theory, a "type" is a symbol that works in reverse—an allusion to something that hasn't happened yet. The discourse of typology emerged in late antiquity as a strategy for reading the two Testaments of the Christian Bible in relation to each other. Over the course of two millennia, typology has become a powerful strategy for connecting literary and polemical works to the Bible's rhetorical authority. As Northrup Frye explains, the essential argument of intertestamental typology is that "everything that happens in the Old Testament is a 'type' or adumbration of something that happens in the New Testament."[7] The typological association of Christ with the Old Testament is not something that later Christians imposed on the New Testament. New Testament writers quote the Hebrew Bible nearly three hundred times, and these direct citations constitute only a fraction of its typological references.[8] "Much of the NT abounds with references to the OT that have little resemblance to the exact wording," writes Leonhard Goppelt in his monumental study *Typos*. "Continual allusions to Scripture are found in the exposition of the writers as well as in the actions of Christ and his Church.

They did not regard this as a collection of proof texts, but as a word that was living in their hearts and minds and was intended for their time."[9]

Christian literature since the New Testament contains plentiful examples of authors using typology to connect themselves to the rhetorical power of their culture's most sacred text. We find it in the poems of Dante and Milton, the novels of Bunyan, Defoe, and Richardson, the sermons of Cotton Mather and Jonathan Edwards, and the speeches of Abraham Lincoln and Martin Luther King Jr. The typological imagination embeds assumptions about history, theology, and language that were vital for the Puritans who settled the American Northeast.[10] And they were almost universally accepted by Christians during the first part of the nineteenth century.[11] Much of the power that this book had for its first readers came from the way it deployed familiar typologies to narrate their new nation into a sacred story that they had always accepted but never really felt part of before.

Typology and Type-scenes

To the nonbeliever or to the believer in different things, typology is a mode of rhetoric, a narrative strategy that speakers and writers use to connect their words to larger, more popular, or more persuasive ideas. To the believer, however, typology is a mode of history. It proceeds from the assumption that the events we experience or read about are manifestations of deeper truths and historical patterns that are part of the fabric of reality itself. Thus, the *Akedah*, the Old Testament story of Abraham binding Isaac on the altar (Gen 22:1–14), can be the straightforward story of a man choosing to obey God by sacrificing his son and, at the same time, represent eternal and always-present truths about men, sons, obedience, and sacrifice. These truths will continue to surface in different historical events precisely because they are truths. And since God is the ultimate eternal and ever-present truth, the story of Abraham's near-sacrifice of Isaac must also be connected to God's sacrifice of his son, Jesus Christ.

In order to accept the theological claims of typological interpretation, one must abandon the dichotomy between history and allegory and agree that a single text can serve both functions at once. Typological interpretation of this sort can also be called "figural interpretation" (Greek *typos* = Latin *figura*), and one of the most important essays ever written about it is Eric Auerbach's "Figura" (1944), first published in English in the 1959 book *Scenes from the Drama of European Literature*. "Figural interpretation," he explains, "establishes a connection between two events or persons, the first of which signifies not only itself but also the second, while the second encompasses or fulfills the first."[12] In theological and historical terms, typological interpretation asserts the literal truth of both the type (the Old Testament figure) and the antitype (the New Testament fulfillment). Auerbach believes that this kind of interpretation was vital to the early diffusion of Judeo-Christian religion:

> The figural interpretation changed the Old Testament from a book of laws and a history of the people of Israel into a series of figures of Christ and the Redemption. . . . In this form and in this context, from which Jewish history and national character had vanished, the Celtic and Germanic peoples, for example, could accept the Old Testament; it was part of the universal religion of salvation and a necessary component of the equally magnificent and universal vision of history that was conveyed to them along with this religion. In its original form, as a law book and history of so foreign and remote a nation, it would have been beyond their reach.[13]

Typology supports, and is supported by, a view of history that sees events as linked not by cause and effect but by recurring patterns of prophecy and fulfillment. There could be no "New Testament" without such an assumption because, without these recurring patterns, nothing connects the stories of Jesus to an "Old Testament" for the New Testament to be newer than. For the Hebrew Bible to become the Old Testament, we must read it as fundamentally about the same thing that the New Testament is about. And even though the New Testament writers didn't know that they were contributing to a future anthology, they knew that they had to connect the story of Jesus to the texts that they, along with most of their original audience, considered sacred. And they did this right from the start. The first chapter of Matthew begins, "The book of the generation of Jesus Christ, the son of David, the son of Abraham" (Matt. 1:1)—a formulation that, together with the genealogy that follows, ties the hero of the New Testament to two of the most important figures of the Hebrew Bible.

But Matthew is not simply trying to show that Jesus was a descendent of Abraham and David (which would have made him no different than everybody else who was in Bethlehem for the census). He was trying to show that Jesus was a figure who fulfilled a series of ancient Hebrew prophecies—and that the writers of the Hebrew scriptures knew that he was coming. Toward the end of chapter 1, Matthew makes it clear that Jesus was born of a virgin because Isaiah prophesied that "a virgin shall be with child, and shall bring forth a son, and they shall call his name Emmanuel". (Matt 1:23, quoting Isa 7:14). And nearly everything that Matthew relates about Jesus's birth and early life in his second chapter is designed to attach Christ to the Hebrew understanding of the Messiah. The reason that Matthew (and Luke) have to spend so much time getting Mary and Joseph to Bethlehem is that there is a prophecy to be fulfilled (Mic 5:2). Not long after Jesus is born, Mary and Joseph must take him to Egypt so that "it might be fulfilled which was spoken of the Lord by the prophet, saying, Out of Egypt have I called my son" (Matt 2:15, quoting Hos 11:1). While the Holy Family was in Egypt, Herod orchestrated the despicable massacre of the innocents, once again, to fulfill "that which was spoken by Jeremiah the prophet" (Matt 2:17, referring to Jer 31:15). And when they return from Egypt, they settle in the village of Nazareth "that it might be fulfilled which was spoken by the prophets, He shall be called a Nazarene" (Matt 2:23).[14]

Matthew employs another narrative strategy to connect Christ's birth to the events of the Hebrew Bible without making the connection explicit. The first story that we encounter in the New Testament (assuming we start with Matthew) is that Herod orders the murder of all Hebrew males less than two years old when the wise men tell him that a king has been born in Bethlehem (Matt 2:1–18). This story repeats most of the structural elements of the Pharaoh's massacre of Hebrew children in the first chapter of the story of Moses (Exod 1:22). This part of the story, notes R. T. France in his commentary on Matthew, "could hardly fail to remind a Jewish reader of the Pharaoh at the time of Moses's birth whose infanticide threatened to destroy Israel's future deliverer." France argues further that this connection "sets up the typological model for the newborn Messiah to play the role of the new Moses, who will also deliver his people."[15]

Matthew's story of the massacre of the innocents is a typological reference because it repurposes an ancient narrative and presents it as a pre-figuration of Christ. But it is also another kind of device that narrative theorists call a "type-scene." A type-scene is not quite the same thing as a typological reference, though both devices are built on the presence of recurring events. The first significant study of type-scenes as a narrative device came from studies of classical Greek rather than biblical Hebrew. In 1933 a German classicist named Walter Arend published the book *Die typischen Scenen bei Homer* (Type-scenes in Homer).[16] For Arend, type-scenes are "recurrent block[s] of narrative . . . whose elements consistently appear in the same order."[17] Type-scenes occur within and across different kinds of narratives in all kinds of interesting ways. In early cultures, they most often occurred within long oral narratives, where they functioned as a mnemonic device to help storytellers keep track of a large number of details. Type-scenes also allowed early poets to compress their narratives by invoking all of the elements of a well-known scene by associating it, however briefly, with another narrative known to the audience—much as a modern playwright might, simply by having a character glance at a human skull sitting on a mantel and say "alas," incorporate all of Hamlet's "Alas, poor Yorick" speech into a new work.

As an example of this kind of type-scene, consider the well-known adventure scenes of Homer's *Odyssey*—all of the experiences that Odysseus and his men had after they left Troy and sailed for home (books 9–12). Perceptive readers have noted that the nine adventure stories reduce to three basic scenes: (1) stories about inhospitable monsters who kill Odysseus's men (the Cyclops, the Laestrygonians, and Scylla and Charybdis); (2) stories about external agents who delay the journey by manipulating their sensual pleasures (Circe, the Lotus Eaters, and the Sirens, who correspond, very roughly, to sex, drugs, and rock & roll); and (3) stories of foolish actions that the sailors are driven to by their own greed and short-sightedness (the raid on the Ciccones, Aeolus's bag of winds, the Island of Hyperion's cattle). Each of these type-scenes occurs once as a detailed narrative that takes up the bulk of a book (The Cyclops, Circe, and Hyperion's Cattle) and twice in a much briefer form clearly intended to invoke the more detailed version. These type-scenes turn the apparent chaos of Odysseus's return into manageable—and therefore memorizable—blocks of narrative.[18]

Type-scenes were also important to the oral narratives that constituted the earliest biblical texts, as Robert Alter explains in his groundbreaking book *The Art of Biblical Narrative*. Perhaps the most famous example from Alter's work is the betrothal-at-the-well type-scene that we first see in Genesis. Alter explains the basic narrative block as follows:

> The betrothal type-scene, then, must take place with the future bridegroom, or his surrogate, having journeyed to a foreign land. There he encounters a girl—the term *"na'arah"* invariably occurs unless the maiden is identified as so-and-so's daughter—or girls at a well. Someone, either the man or the girl, then draws water from the well; afterward, the girl or girls rush to bring home the news of the stranger's arrival (the verbs "hurry" and "run" are given recurrent emphasis at this junction of the type-scene); finally, a betrothal is concluded between the stranger and the girl, and in the majority of instances, only after he has been invited to a meal.[19]

The first and most elaborate example of this type-scene occurs in Genesis 24, with Isaac (through a servant) and Rebekah. It recurs in a somewhat shorter form in Genesis 29 with Jacob and Rachel and as an extremely compressed scene in Exodus 2 with Moses and Zipporah. Each time it recurs, the scene requires less detail because the author assumes that the reader will remember and import the details from earlier stories into the most recent one. Over the many years of the Hebrew Bible's composition, type-scenes formed a set of narrative building blocks available to authors at different times. They function as a kind of shorthand capable of invoking an entire narrative with just a few words—as the author of the book of Ruth invokes the betrothal-at-the-well type-scene by having Boaz instruct Ruth to "drink of that which the young men have drawn."[20] A compressed version of this type-scene also occurs in the New Testament when Jesus meets the Samaritan woman at the well, and, through the logic of figuration, all of the themes and nuances of the other type-scene become part of the New Testament story (John 4:1–19).[21]

In this book, my interest lies in the type-scenes and typological narratives that connect the Bible to the Book of Mormon. These stories, like Matthew's story about Herod's massacre of the Jewish children, serve a connective purpose. They give shape to the new canon by demonstrating that all of its parts belong to the same master narrative. Some of these type-scenes are easy to see and have been the subject of much comparative discussion, such as the conversion stories of Saul in the book of Acts and of Alma the Younger in the book of Mosiah, both of whom persecute the Church until they are converted by a heavenly being and then spend the rest of their lives building it up.[22] Others are harder to see, such as the Garden of Eden story in Genesis and the tree of life dream in 1 Nephi, which contain the same structural elements in very different contexts and in a slightly different order.[23] It is to these type-scenes—and to the ways in which typological reasoning and figural logic are deployed throughout the Book of Mormon—that we now turn.

Typology and Type-Scenes in the Book of Mormon

The word "type" itself appears nine times in the Book of Mormon. The references vary in purpose from King Benjamin's exposition of the law of Moses and the "many types and shadows" that the Lord showed the Jews concerning the coming of Christ (Mosiah 3:15) to Alma's rhetorical question to Helaman, describing the Liahona that their forefathers used in the wilderness, "Is there not a type in this thing?"—which leads to a comparison between the Liahona and the words of Christ: "Just as surely as this director did bring our fathers, by following its course, to the promised land, shall the words of Christ, if we follow their course, carry us beyond this vale of sorrow into a far better land of promise" (Alma 37:45).[24]

The Book of Mormon is also explicit when it uses typology as an internal narrative device rather than a symbol of the coming Christ. The most instructive reference comes from the prophet Abinadi, who, when he is arrested by the wicked King Noah, says, *"What you do with me after this shall be as a type and a shadow of things which are to come"* (Mosiah 13:10). Rather than explaining what such a thing might mean, Abinadi uses his prediction as a springboard for discussing the way the law of Moses—which the priests of Noah had asserted in defense of their own righteousness—relates typologically to the prophesied Messiah:

> Therefore there was a law given them, yea, a law of performances and of ordinances, a law which they were to observe strictly from day to day to keep them in remembrance of God and their duty towards him. *But behold, I say unto you, that all these things were types of things to come.*
> . . .
>   For behold, did not Moses prophesy unto them concerning the coming of the Messiah and that God should redeem his people? Yea, and even all the prophets which have prophesied ever since the world began, have they not spoken more or less concerning these things? Have they not said that God himself should come down among the children of men and take upon him the form of man and go forth in mighty power upon the face of the earth? (Mosiah 13:30–31; 33–34, emphasis mine)

In this discourse, Abinadi uses his own life and impending death as part of a lesson in typology. He begins with the prediction that his fate will be a type of things to come and then goes on to use the same words to describe the relation of the law of Moses to the coming Messiah. When Abinadi is put to death by fire (Mosiah 17:20), followed two chapters later by King Noah's being put to death by fire (Mosiah 19:20), the sermon on typology seems complete. The mode of Noah's death gives the original audience a very clear example of how an event can be both itself and a recurrence of a type, and the audience seems to get the message. After their king is killed by fire and their land invaded by Lamanites, Noah's people ask, "Are not the words of Abinadi fulfilled which he prophesied against us—and all this because we would not hearken unto the words of the Lord and turn from our iniquities?" (Mosiah 20:21).

But the Book of Mormon has more to say about the typology of Abinadi's death. (One can never be done with typology, really, because one of its core assumptions is eternal recurrence.) The story is told again in the book of Alma. It is important to note that the original story of Abinadi and King Noah comes from the portion of the book of Mosiah known as the Record of Zeniff,[25] which means that it has a different narrator than the rest of Mosiah and the subsequent books of Alma, Helaman, and 3 Nephi, which are narrated primarily by the redactor Mormon, who lived hundreds of years after the events that he describes. So, when Mormon retells the story of Abinadi in Alma, he does so to show how its typology was actually fulfilled by the descendants of Amulon and Noah's other priests, leading to a minor civil war between the descendants of Noah's priests and the newly Christianized Lamanites. Mormon presents this as a fulfillment of Abinadi's prophecy:

> And it came to pass that those rulers which were the remnant of the children of Amulon caused that they [Lamanite converts to Christianity] should be put to death, yea, all those that believed in these things. Now this martyrdom caused that many of their brethren should be stirred up to anger. And there began to be contention in the wilderness, and the Lamanites began to hunt the seed of Amulon and his brethren and began to slay them; and they fled into the east wilderness. And behold they are hunted at this day by the Lamanites.
>
> Thus the words of Abinadi [were] brought to pass which he said concerning the seed of the priests, which caused that he should suffer death by fire. For he said unto them: What ye shall do unto me shall be a type of things to come. (Alma 25:7–10)

Mormon here subtly nudges our understanding of Abinadi's earlier typological prophecy, and he has to apply a bit of rhetorical legerdemain to make it work. In his speech from the fire, which comes four chapters after the initial "type of things to come" prophecy, Abinadi makes several more predictions about the priests of Noah. He says that their seed would cause others to be put to death by fire (which is, indeed, fulfilled in Alma), but he also makes several statements that appear to be about the priests themselves: that they "shall be afflicted with all manner of diseases," that they "shall be smitten on every hand and shall be driven and scattered to and fro," and that, "in that day ye shall be hunted, and ye shall be taken by the hand of your enemies. And then ye shall suffer as I suffer the pains of death by fire" (Mosiah 17:16–18).

Mormon's re-narration of Abinadi's prophecies requires us to amend the original text. Specifically, he reports Abinadi's speech in Mosiah 17:15–18 as follows:

> And he said unto the priests of Noah that their seed should cause many to be put to death in the like manner as he was, and that they should be scattered abroad and slain, even as a sheep having no shepherd is driven and slain by wild beasts. And now behold, these words were verified, for they [the descendants of Amulon] were driven by the Lamanites, and they were hunted and they were smitten. (Alma 25:12)

Mormon transforms a prophecy about *both* the descendants of the priests and the priests themselves into one that is entirely about the descendants.

This interpretation is defensible. It is possible to read Abinadi's use of "ye" as referring to whole families, but the words themselves are directly addressed to individuals, which appears to be how they were originally understood.

More significantly, Mormon labels the action of Amulon's descendants as the fulfillment of the type of Abinadi's death, or as what Abinadi meant when he said "What ye shall do unto me shall be a type of things to come." Without Mormon's insertion, readers would be almost forced to read King Noah's death as the antitype of Abinadi's death—it is the only thing in the original narrative that really works. But this is not how Mormon explains it. Rather, he says, it is the burning to death of the Lamanite Christians that fulfills Abinadi's typological pronouncement.

This reframing has profound consequences for how we understand the underlying theology. When King Noah is put to death by fire the same way Abinadi was, we are tempted to feel that the wicked king got his comeuppance and good riddance—much as we feel at the end of an action movie when the villain dies a gruesome and humiliating death while trying to kill the good guy. This is a very human feeling, but it is not very good theology. God's job is not to facilitate emotionally satisfying revenge plots that cause us to cheer when someone dies a painful and horrible death. We aren't supposed to glory in the suffering of any human being, even a nasty one like King Noah. Mormon subtly corrects Zeniff's narrative and proposes a different reading of the typology, one that sees the continuing persecution of believers, rather than tit-for-tat retribution, as the recurring type. In the process, he connects Abinadi and the Lamanite converts to a host of other heroes condemned to die by fire for their beliefs, including Shadrach, Meschach, and Abednego; the early Christian martyrs; and Joan of Arc.

I bring this up not to disparage Mormon, or Zeniff, or Abinadi, or anybody else, but to show how typology can be both connective and corrective at the same time. Because typology works backward—with the later text determining the meaning of its connection to the earlier one—it always contains the possibility of revision. The later text can always correct its predecessor in ways that make the correction a part of the overall narrative. Remember that the ultimate purpose of typological interpretation is not to explain the meaning of either the type or the antitype. Each recurrence of the type clarifies this deeper truth and helps us incorporate the sacred texts into our own lives as these realities continue to manifest in new situations and contexts. And the deeper meaning can always be revisited, reframed, and revised by a new manifestation of the type.

Subversive Sequels in the Book of Mormon

Type-scenes work internally to connect ideas, themes, and patterns within a single narrative, but they can also work externally to connect one text retroactively to another. When Virgil composed the *Aeneid*, he could draw on type-scenes to create hundreds of connections between his own work and Homer's. When readers of the *Odyssey* encounter Aeneas in the company of Dido, the beautiful queen of Carthage, they have no trouble equating this to Odysseus's dalliances with Circe and Calypso—and realizing that the hero's sexual desire has temporarily overcome his sense of purpose and destiny.[26] And when Matthew shows the tyrant Herod murdering Hebrew children, his audience can immediately incorporate the story of Moses and appreciate that the child spared from the massacre will become a great religious hero.

Type-scenes work as a connection strategy between different texts because of the way narratives are constructed. Any story can be broken down into its structural elements, represented by small bits of narrative. Once we do this, it is easy to see how different stories can be built with the same structural building blocks. For example, "young hero is called to adventure by the search for his heroic father" can describe *Hamlet*, the *Odyssey*, *Sohrab and Rostam*, and *Star Wars*, while "young woman must prevent her community from spiritual pollution and physical disaster" might describe Antigone, Esther, Scheherazade, or Wonder Woman. Bits of one narrative embedded in another create connections that work in both directions simultaneously. The later work can influence our perception of the former. Once someone figures out that the 1956 science fiction film *Forbidden Planet* incorporates a number of scenes from *The Tempest*, for example, they may never be able to watch the Shakespeare play again without thinking of the ways in which Caliban resembles Robbie the Robot.[27]

Biblical scholars have only recently started to examine the way differences in type-scenes operate across biblical texts. Judy Klitsner's 2008 book *Subversive Sequels in the Bible* is a groundbreaking study in this regard. Klitsner reads the original Hebrew texts carefully to uncover layers of connection between stories whose messages seem at odds with each other. She has coined the phrase "subversive sequel" to describe a biblical narrative that intentionally incorporates elements of an earlier story and "questions and overturns the assumptions and conclusions of the [earlier] narrative."[28] Subversive sequels allowed later biblical writers to reverse or reinterpret earlier narratives in light of new or different understandings. The type-scene then becomes much more than a mnemonic device or a framing strategy; it becomes a way to correct a perceived error in the earlier text.

As Klitsner reads it, the first chapter of Job, in which all of Job's children are killed in rapid succession, is a subversive sequel to the story of Abraham binding Isaac in Genesis 22. In these stories, Klitsner argues, "some basic similarities are obvious, such as the featuring of God-fearing men who face a mortal threat by God to their offspring."[29] And the connections go much deeper. Both Abraham and Job are called "God-fearing," for example, but the story of Abraham ends with this designation, whereas the book of Job begins with it, "suggesting the presence of a sequel in that the Book of Job begins where the story of the *Akedah* ended." And a number of personal names in the Abraham story reappear as place names in Job.[30] Both the thematic and the linguistic connections suggest that we are dealing with a type-scene in which God demands the sacrifice of a righteous man's child or children as an ultimate test of righteousness. But the reactions of the two men could not be more different. In one, God demands an unjust sacrifice from Abraham and then prevents it from occurring, leading the subject of the test to praise his mercy. In the other, God determines to test Job and simply kills not one, but ten children, leaving Job to make accusations of injustice.

> These differences lead to the most striking point of contrast between the two stories, which is Abraham's silent compliance with God's cruelty as opposed to Job's outspoken objections to God's injustice. Abraham proved his ability to call God to task in Sodom when he boldly insisted that a just God must act justly (Gen. 18:25). But in the *Akedah*, Abraham's assertive stance gives way to unquestioning compliance with God's morally perplexing decree. In the end, God is pleased with Abraham's willingness to obey him (22:12) and seemingly with Abraham's silence, as well. In contrast, as Job's life is unjustly shattered, the hero rejects all attempts to justify God's actions and instead demands answers from God with ever-increasing audacity. Yet despite his contentious words, so antithetical to the wordless obedience of Abraham, God upholds Job's responses over those of his friends, God's apologists. God instructs Job's friends to bring sacrifices and to have Job pray for them, "since you have not spoken to Me correctly as did My servant Job" (42:8). In this, the subversive sequel to the narrative of the binding of Isaac, being God's beloved servant no longer requires voiceless acceptance of all God's actions and decrees. A faithful servant can also protest God's injustice and demand a quality of life commensurate with one's deeds.[31]

What Klitsner points to is a different use of typology than scholars of the Hebrew Bible normally discuss, but one that will be crucial to my analysis of typology in the Book of Mormon. As a Jewish scholar, she confines her analysis to the Hebrew Bible. But the notion of a subversive sequel works just as well with intertestamental typology and with the ways in which type-scenes connect across narratives. And this will be my fundamental argument about typology in the Book of Mormon: As "another Testament of Jesus Christ," it presents itself as a narrative capable of constraining and correcting the ways we interpret the Bible by using typology and shared type-scenes to retroactively revise the biblical narrative.

A Theory of Types: Naming the Tools

Narrative theory has developed a rich vocabulary for talking about how type-scenes relate to each other and to the larger narratives of which they are a part. I want to define four terms from this field of study that can help us understand the different levels at which typological discourse functions. Together, these terms provide a framework that can be used to analyze the Book of Mormon with reference to the way it shares figural representations with the Bible and with other texts. All four words are slippery, though, and they can all be used in different contexts with very different meanings. Here I define them as I intend to use them in the remainder of this book:

Type: A type is the first occurrence of a concept that points to (or is read as pointing to) another narrative that will occur later, as Abraham's binding of Isaac points to God's sacrifice of his only begotten son. According to the special logic of typology, the type is simultaneously real in every way in which the later narrative is real and, at the same time, a reference to the later narrative, which will, when it occurs, clarify its meaning.

Antitype: The antitype is the fulfillment of a type, or the later narrative to which the type points. In the Christian typological tradition, Jesus Christ is the universal antitype, which means that nearly every narrative in the Old Testament is read by that tradition as pointing to something in the life or ministry of Jesus Christ. In other contexts, the antitype can simply be a narrative that incorporates elements of an earlier narrative, the way *The Lion King* incorporates elements from *Hamlet*.

Neotype: The term "neotype" was coined in 1972 by literary historian Steven Zwicker to explain the way John Dryden's poetry functioned during the political battles of seventeenth-century England. A neotype is an extension of biblical typology to the present historical situation, based on the belief that the scriptures were explicitly written to address our day.[32] For Zwicker, this means that a poem such as Dryden's "Absalom and Achitophel"—which used the Old Testament narrative of Absalom's rebellion against David as a framing device to discuss the Duke of Monmouth's rebellion against Charles II—presented a contemporary event as the literal fulfillment of a biblical type. Even in the time of King David, Dryden argued, God knew about the coming perfidy of the Earl of Shaftsbury.[33] The concept of neotypes had a special importance to the New England Protestant culture into which the Book of Mormon was first translated. As Sacvan Bercovitch has demonstrated, this culture was deeply infused with a typological understanding of its own mission.[34]

Archetype: Those who study myth and folklore have long observed similarities in the sacred stories of different cultures. Stories of floods, elixir thefts, journeys to the underworld, tricksters, and heroes exist in nearly all cultures, even those that do not appear to have had contact with each other. This has led many to speculate that there are even older stories behind these ancient tales—stories that stretch far back into human history and penetrate deep into the human mind. These "stories behind the stories" are called "archetypes." The term is often associated with Carl Jung, who believed that archetypes come from a universal store of memories called the "collective unconscious." But that is just one explanation for the phenomenon. Others have attributed the presence of archetypes to real events that actually happened, to a level of cultural diffusion beyond what we normally assume, or to very sophisticated instincts honed by millions of years of evolution mapped onto cognitive processes that rely on narrative to process information.[35]

When we add the Book of Mormon into the mix with the Old Testament, the New Testament, the nineteenth century, and the present day, we get a lot of interesting permutations in the possible interactions between types, antitypes, neotypes, and archetypes. Not only does the Book of Mormon add a third "testament" to the scriptural canon that incorporates narratives from the other two, but the drama of its coming forth in the latter days played out on a typological stage. Joseph Smith and his companions saw nearly every aspect of the Restoration movement as the fulfillment of either biblical or Book of Mormon prophecy, and this understanding influenced the way in which they acted their parts. They perceived their story as part of a sacred narrative that stretched backward to the Garden of Eden and forward to the Second Coming.

To get a sense of how all of these different elements can work together in the Bible–Book of Mormon canon, let us consider one more example from the Book of Mormon—a brief passage from 2nd Nephi in which Lehi, coming to the end of his life, blesses his son Joseph:

And now Joseph, my last-born, whom I have brought out of the wilderness of mine afflictions, may the Lord bless thee forever, for thy seed shall not utterly be destroyed. For behold, thou art the fruit of my loins, and I am a descendant of Joseph, which was carried captive into Egypt. And great were the covenants of the Lord which he made unto Joseph.

Wherefore, Joseph truly saw our day, and he obtained a promise of the Lord that out of the fruit of his loins the Lord God would raise up a righteous branch unto the house of Israel, not the Messiah, but a branch which was to be broken off, nevertheless to be remembered in the covenants of the Lord, that the Messiah should be made manifest unto them in the latter days in the spirit of power unto the bringing of them out of darkness unto light, yea, out of hidden darkness and out of captivity unto freedom. (2 Ne 3:3–5)

Here we have two characters named Joseph who are connected by patrilineal descent and by their participation in a shared type-scene. The original type occurs in Genesis 49, when the patriarch Jacob gives his dying blessing to each of his twelve sons. Joseph, as the favorite son and recipient of the birthright, receives the most elaborate blessing (though all of them are fairly short):

> **Joseph is a fruitful bough, even a fruitful bough by a well; whose branches run over the wall:** The archers have sorely grieved him, and shot at him, and hated him: But his bow abode in strength, and the arms of his hands were made strong by the hands of the mighty God of Jacob; (from thence is the shepherd, the stone of Israel:) Even by the God of thy father, who shall help thee; and by the Almighty, who shall bless thee with blessings of heaven above, blessings of the deep that lieth under, blessings of the breasts, and of the womb: The blessings of thy father have prevailed above the blessings of my progenitors unto the utmost bound of the everlasting hills: they shall be on the head of Joseph, and on the crown of the head of him that was separate from his brethren. (Gen 49:22–26)

The Book of Mormon establishes deep typological connections between the Lehi and Jacob stories. Both fathers have led their families on long migrations and have established them in a new land. Both assemble their sons on their deathbeds to pronounce blessings that are at once directive and prophetic. And, of course, they both have a son named Joseph. Most important, the Book of Mormon presents Lehi and his family as the fulfillment of the prophecy that the branches of Joseph will "run over the wall"—an association that Lehi draws specifically in this blessing.[36] This is a near-perfect example of a type-scene in which the antitype—directly and explicitly—provides an interpretation of the type that fundamentally alters the way readers must interact with the text.

But the narrative is not done with Josephs. Lehi states that the ancient Joseph saw a vision of the last days and prophesied that "a seer shall the Lord my God raise up, which shall be a choice seer unto the fruit of thy loins" (2 Ne. 3:6).[37] This seer, we learn, will also be named Joseph, as will his father (2 Ne. 3:15), and he "shall write, and the fruit of the loins of Judah shall write" and the two writings "shall grow together, unto the confounding of false doctrines and laying down contentions" (2 Ne. 3:12). These prophecies leave little doubt that the "choice seer" should be interpreted as Joseph Smith or that the writing in question is the Book of Mormon, the very volume in which this prophecy occurs. It also invokes the prophecy in Ezekiel that the sticks of Judah and Joseph will one day be joined together (37:15–16). By using language that is almost identical to Ezekiel's but makes it clear that the "sticks" are actually writings, Lehi's blessing constrains the interpretation of a second biblical passage by rewriting its predecessor and connects them both to Joseph Smith, the nineteenth-century neotype who brought forth the Stick of Joseph.

And there is more going on still, as Lehi's blessing, like Jacob's, is part of a much larger narrative tradition of dying fathers assembling their sons to impart a final blessing. This is part of a larger archetypal pattern of interaction between fathers and sons. Most world cultures share stories of father-son interaction that emphasize (1) the son's need to receive the father's wisdom, status, and other resources that will help him make his way in the world and (2) the young man's need to break ties with the father and create his own identity. Paradoxically, the son must both embrace and reject the father in order to become an adult. Freud invoked this general tension in his theory of the Oedipus complex, in which a child fantasizes about killing his father and sexually possessing his mother—and then feels immense guilt for daring to think such horrible things. Jung invoked a different archetype to account for this tension: the "Wise Old Man" who invariably appears as part of a young hero's journey to adulthood.[38] This figure (think: Gandalf, Dumbledore, and Obi-Wan Kenobi) provides both temporal assistance and spiritual guidance to the hero, but he must die or be otherwise removed from the narrative before the hero faces the ultimate test. The hero cannot fully individuate while the father figure is still alive. The whole point of these stories (according to Jung) is to dramatize, through myth, that children cannot become functioning adults until they leave their parents' spheres of influence.

All of these typologies interact with each other through this single passage in 2 Nephi, which (under the definitions I have suggested) occupies the position of the antitype. It changes our understanding of the original type by portraying the biblical Joseph as a prophet whose prophecies of the last days, omitted from the biblical text, were restored in this portion of the Book of Mormon.[39] It also reaches forward to the neotype and encourages us to see Joseph Smith and the Restoration as part of a recurring typological pattern that was understood by key figures in both the Bible and the Book of Mormon. And it reaches upward, to the archetype, and incorporates prophecy into the set of gifts that fathers give their sons to prepare them for adulthood. This all works because, according to the logic of typology that the passage employs, all four versions of the story are connected to each other in such a way that our interpretation of one affects our understanding of all the others.

This is just a brief example of how a single typological connection can reframe a text on multiple levels. The Book of Mormon's narrative claims to represent a recurrence of a pattern established in the first book of the Bible, and it reframes the logic of that first occurrence so that we read the Bible and the Book of Mormon and apply them to the contemporary world that we inhabit. The vocabulary of typology gives us a powerful set of tools for examining the ways both works connect to each other as narratives. This, in turn, allows us to study the way both books merge together at the narrative level to form a single canon of interconnected sacred stories.

CHAPTER TWO

Stories of the Fall

> As for mankind, although born of a corrupted and
> condemned stock, he still retains the power to form and
> animate his seed, to direct his members in their temporal
> order, to enliven his senses in their spatial relations, and
> to provide bodily nourishment. For God judged it better to
> bring good out of evil than not to permit any evil to exist.
> — St. Augustine, *Enchiridion on Faith, Hope, and Love*

> The Lord said to Adam that if he wished to remain as he
> was in the garden, then he was not to eat the fruit, but if he
> desired to eat it and partake of death he was at liberty to
> do so. So really it was not in the true sense a transgression
> of a divine commandment. Adam made the wise decision,
> in fact the only decision that he could make.
> — Joseph Fielding Smith, *Answers to Gospel Questions*

Saint Augustine thought it very important for everybody to understand that Adam and Eve could have had sex in the Garden of Eden if they had wanted to. Had they done so, then "without any restless fever of lust, without any labor and pain in childbirth, offspring would [have been] brought forth from their sowing." The children of Adam and Eve, he continued, would grow to adulthood and remain in their prime—never aging and needing only the fruit of the tree of life for nourishment—until the earth reached an ideal population. As new children came into the world, those who lived honorable lives would have been "converted without dying into something of a different kind and be entirely at the beck and call of the spirit governing them. All of this, Augustine believed, would have been the natural state of humanity "if the transgression of the commandment had not earned the punishment of death."[1]

The question of prelapsarian procreation takes up most of book 9 in Augustine's twelve-book treatise *The Literal Meaning of Genesis,* the longest and most significant of the five commentaries that he wrote about the biblical creation story.[2] Augustine articulated several arguments against those who held that sex and reproduction could not occur in an unfallen world. In the first place, he argued, if God had not intended Adam to reproduce in the garden, he never would have given him a woman as a companion. Adam had no need to till the earth, and, even if he had, "a male would have made a better help." This is also true of companionship. "How much more agreeably, after all, for conviviality and conversation would two male friends live together on equal terms than man and wife?"[3] Augustine also objected to the view that sexuality was inherently sinful or that the fruit in the Eden story symbolized sexual experience. It was the lust that drove sexual excess, not the act, that constituted the sin, and without lust, there would have been no moral reason for Adam and Eve not to have sex.[4] "Why should we not suppose," he asked, "that before sin those two human beings were able to control and command their genital organs the same way as their other limbs, which the soul moves for all kinds of action without any trouble or any sort of prurient itch for pleasure."[5]

But Augustine's most urgent argument—the one that he could not see any way around without shaking the foundations of the Christian faith to their core—was this: if Adam and Eve could not procreate in their unfallen state, then God's commandment to them to "multiply and replenish the earth" would have been impossible to fulfill without disobeying another commandment. To doubt that Eve was given to Adam for the express purpose of populating the earth without disobeying God, he insisted, "is to undermine the foundations of everything we believe."[6] If God placed Adam and Eve in the Garden of Eden and told them, on one hand, to "multiply and replenish the earth," and on the other hand, to avoid the fruit of the tree of knowledge of good and evil, then there must have been a way for them to do both. Otherwise, God's commands would have been contradictory and, therefore, imperfect. And that was something that Augustine could not allow.

Augustine's view of the Fall, on which much of the Christian tradition rests, holds it impossible for God to require incompatible things. Since God would not set his creations up to fail, and since he would never have given Adam anything as impractical as a woman if he did not intend for them to mate, we can only conclude that God fully intended for Adam and Eve to remain in the garden and procreate. Their disobedience was a terrible sin that saddled all of humanity with a share of the guilt, but it did not frustrate God's plans. God's great foresight and goodness allowed him to turn even the horror of the Fall into something ultimately beneficial through the redemption that Jesus Christ would eventually effect. In the same way that one man's disobedience cursed the human race, one man's perfect obedience would bless all of humanity and save us from the effects of the original sin. This was what Augustine made of St. Paul's statement that, "as in Adam all die, even so in Christ shall all be made alive" (1 Cor. 15:22).[7]

Augustine's formulation of the Adam and Eve story in Genesis has come to be known in theology and history as the *felix culpa*, or "fortunate fall." When Latter-day Saints hear this phrase, they often imagine that it describes an area of agreement between their doctrines and those of historical Christianity. It does not. For Augustine and those who followed him, the "fortunate fall" meant that God's goodness and perfection were so absolute that he could take the most awful catastrophe imaginable and still arrange for things to turn out for the best through the atonement of Christ. The "happy" part refers not to the Fall itself, which was incalculably sad and tragic, but to the benevolence and omnipotence of God. The actual phrase *felix culpa* comes from words in a hymn in the Roman Catholic Easter Mass *Exsultet*: *O felix culpa quae talem et tantum meruit habere redemptorem*, "O happy fault that earned for us so great, so glorious a Redeemer."

Latter-day Saints believe not so much in a fortunate fall as in a necessary fall—an event that had to happen because, they believe, Augustine was wrong about sex in paradise. The Book of Mormon is crystal clear on this point in the opening chapters of 2 Nephi, when Lehi explains to his son Jacob that it was only by eating the fruit and disobeying one command that Adam and Eve could multiply, replenish the earth:

> And now behold, if Adam had not transgressed, he would not have fallen, but he would have remained in the garden of Eden; and all things which were created must have remained in the same state in which they were after that they were created. And they must have remained forever and had no end, and they would have had no children. Wherefore they would have remained in a state of innocence, having no joy, for they knew no misery, doing no good, for they knew no sin. (2 Ne 2:22–23)

Humanity, then, never could have existed without the Fall. Had Adam and Eve declined the forbidden fruit, all of God's plans for humanity would have been frustrated. And thus, as Terryl Givens writes, the Book of Mormon makes "what Christians had called 'the greatest catastrophe in human history' into an occasion for rejoicing."[8]

The Mormon view of the Fall leads directly to the rejection of the concept of original sin as articulated in the Second Article of Faith: "We believe that men will be punished for their own sins, and not for Adam's transgression." This formulation, for all of its simplicity and intuitive appeal, places Mormon belief outside the boundaries of Catholic and Protestant orthodoxy. "Repudiation of original sin is perhaps the earliest major divergence from creedal Christian doctrine (other than the act of the Book of Mormon itself as canon-disruptive) that Mormonism unambiguously asserts," writes Givens.[9] And the twentieth-century theologian Sterling McMurrin adds that "to fail to recognize that at its foundations Mormon theology is essentially a rebellion against especially the orthodox Protestant dogma of original sin, and the negativism implied by it for the interpretation of the whole nature and life of man, would be a failure to discern not only the distinctive character of Mormon doctrine, but also of the Mormon religion itself."[10]

In order to appreciate how completely Latter-day Saint doctrine rejects the traditional Christian view of the Fall, we must also understand the Mormon concept of pre-existence. Latter-day Saint scriptures, especially the Pearl of Great Price, hold that all humans who have ever been born were first created as spirits and lived in a spirit world with God. Spiritual progress required both corporeal existence and distance from God, which, in turn, required mortality. The Eden story is, in the context of Mormon belief, an analog to the pre-existence. Adam and Eve had to "fall" into mortality for the same reason our pre-existent spirits had to leave a comfortable environment and assume corporeal shape. Learning and growth require challenges, and progression in a physical world requires mastery of a material form. As Lehi tells Jacob in his final blessing, "It must needs be that there is an opposition in all things. If not so . . . righteousness could not be brought to pass, neither wickedness, neither holiness nor misery, neither good nor bad" (2 Ne 2:11). The need for both Adam and Eve's fall and Christ's atonement were established in the pre-existence and were part of God's design from the very start.[11]

Latter-day Saints are hardly alone in seeing the narrative of the Fall as something other than a treatise on original sin. Over the course of three millennia, the core narrative of Adam and Eve has supported an enormous range of meanings and conclusions. It has been proposed to explain, among other things, why we are subject to death, how sin came into the world, and why we must suffer. In Christian typology, it creates the imperative for the Atonement and links Adam and Eve directly to Christ. And for those who study human universals, the story of the Fall emphasizes the need for children to separate from their fathers when they marry, the role of sexual activity in emerging adulthood, and the inherent tradeoff between innocence and knowledge. For the practical-minded, it can even serve as an eminently sensible warning to stay away from snakes.

When we break the story of the Fall into its constituent archetypes, it becomes even more pervasive and all-encompassing because its primary symbols—man, woman, serpent, garden, fruit, sacred tree—turn up in different combinations in origin myths all over the world. In Greek mythology, for example, Persephone partially forfeits her right to live on Olympus by eating a forbidden fruit, in this case pomegranate seeds, while she is in the underworld. The Sumerian hero Gilgamesh goes on an epic journey to find the elixir of eternal youth only to have immortality snatched out of his hands by a crafty serpent.[12] Paradisiacal gardens show up in the myths and legends of cultures throughout human history: Among the more famous are the Garden of Hesperides in Greek mythology, the Babylonian Garden of the Gods, and the Persian "walled garden," or *pairi-daeza*, which gives us our root word for "paradise." The sacred tree is one of the most common and important archetypes across human cultures and is found throughout the world's creation stories.[13]

The Book of Mormon does not have a clear narrative parallel to the Eden story, but it does use nearly all of the archetypes from that story in its descriptions of a dreamlike vision sent to the prophet Lehi while he and his family are in the wilderness. Like the story of Adam and Eve, the dream involves people being tempted, eating the fruit of a special tree, and feeling great shame after they do. The Book of Mormon presents and explains Lehi's dream to us in three distinct stages. First, Lehi narrates the dream to his family (1 Ne 8). Second, Nephi prays to understand his father's vision and has an elaborate, panoramic vision of the Messiah and of the future of his own descendants (1 Ne 11–14). And third, after his extensive vision, Nephi interprets the dream for his brothers as a harsh warning against sinful behavior (1 Ne 15).

Edenic Typology in Lehi's Dream

In an essay originally published in 1977, Brigham Young University English professor Bruce W. Jorgensen offered Lehi's tree of life dream as the key to understanding the typological unity of the Book of Mormon.[14] The vision, he argues, establishes a narrative pattern that becomes important throughout the Book of Mormon. "Call it quest or conversion," he writes, "at bottom the pattern is a simple transformation: from dark and barren waste by means of the Word to a world fruitful and filled with light. And the transformation is enacted again and again in the Book of Mormon at both the individual and communal levels."[15] Jorgensen sees this as the basic typological pattern repeated in the stories of Enos, Alma the Elder, and Alma the Younger, each of which repeats the basic transformation from desolation to light through the vehicle of the word of God.

If we simply read the pattern that Jorgensen identifies in reverse—as the transformation from a fruitful world to a lonely and desolate one—we arrive back in Eden with Adam and Eve, which is precisely the story of how humanity moved from a blessed paradise to a lone and dreary world. And once we reverse the direction this way, we can see all the other things that the two narratives have in common. They are both stories about eating the fruit of a specific tree, for one thing, and the term "tree of life" appears in both.[16] Both stories also include specific references to shame, enemies of God trying to convince others to disobey him, and a mention of a "dreary wilderness" or "dreary world."[17] Other than the serpent, all of the typological and symbolic elements from the Garden of Eden appear in Lehi's dream, only they appear in a slightly different order, which makes sense typologically, as the Book of Mormon uses this typology to reverse an interpretation of the Eden narrative that has prevailed for more than fifteen hundred years among those who accept the Christian canon.

The dream begins with Lehi in a "dark and dreary wilderness" (1 Ne 8:4) when he sees a man in a white robe who leads him to a large field with a single tree:

> And it came to pass that I beheld a tree whose fruit was desirable to make one happy. And it came to pass that I did go forth and partook of the fruit thereof and beheld that it was most sweet, above all that I ever before tasted. Yea, and I beheld that the fruit thereof was white to exceed all the whiteness that I had ever seen. And as I partook of the fruit thereof, it filled my soul with exceeding great joy. Wherefore I began to be desirous that my family should partake of it also, for I knew that it was desirous above all other fruit. (1 Ne 8:10–12)

As he surveys the scene Lehi sees that his family, along with many other people, is far away from the tree. In order to reach it, they must follow a "straight and narrow path." As people try to navigate the path, dark mists arise and make it impossible for anyone stay on the path unless they hold fast to the "rod of iron" that runs beside it (2 Ne 8:19–20). Many people lose their way because they do not hold to the rod, and many others reach the tree and partake of the fruit only to be mocked by naysayers in a great and spacious building. "After that they had tasted of the fruit," Lehi reports, "they were ashamed because of those that were a scoffing at them, and they fell away into forbidden paths and were lost" (1 Ne 8:28). Only the most valiant, including Sariah, Nephi, and Sam, partake of the fruit and experience the joy that it brings, precisely because they do not feel the shame that the others feel about eating the fruit. Others are lost in the mist, drowned in the nearby river, or absorbed into the cynicism of the great and spacious building.[18]

When we strip Lehi's dream and the story of Adam and Eve to their most important narrative elements—recognizing that this will remove shades of meaning and distinctions that are important to the way we read both stories—we can identify four principal archetypes that they share: Both narratives speak of the *fruit* of a specific tree, both associate that fruit with *shame*, both contain one setting that we can consider a *paradise*, and both contain a second setting described as a dreary *wilderness*. In Genesis, these elements combine in a straight line to produce a bare-bones narrative something like this:

PARADISE → FRUIT → SHAME → WILDERNESS.

1 Nephi 8, on the other hand, starts in the lone and dreary wilderness and essentially moves backward through the same symbols:

WILDERNESS → FRUIT → (NO) SHAME → PARADISE.

The order of the archetypes has profound consequences for how we read the common story. If we read the Book of Mormon version in isolation, we may conclude that it is a simple reversal of the text (eating the fruit is not a bad thing; it is a good thing). Or we could just chalk it up to an issue of obedience (Adam and Eve disobeyed God, and Lehi obeyed God, and that makes all the difference). But when we read Lehi's dream as something like a sequel to the story in Genesis, an even more interesting story starts to take shape.

In essence, we have one story about human beings being thrust out of paradise followed by a second story in which they find their way back in. *Paradise Lost* is followed by *Paradise Regained*, though not quite in the way that Milton imagined it. Here, the way out and the way back follow the same symbolic path, and both go through the symbolic act of eating the fruit of a tree. Furthermore, those who decline to eat the fruit experience the same consequences in Lehi's dream that Adam and Eve experience in Genesis: They are (or, at least, Lehi fears they will be) "cast off from the presence of the Lord" (1 Ne 8:36). As Matthew Bowen has aptly noted, "Adam and Eve's choice to partake of the fruit of the tree of the knowledge of good and evil had enduring consequences for themselves and their posterity. Similarly, Laman and Lemuel's choice not to partake of the tree of life resulted in long-lasting bitter consequences for themselves and their posterity. In both instances, the consequence of the decision was being "cut off" or "cast off" from the presence of the Lord."[19]

An equally important shift in the underlying archetype has to do with shame. In the Genesis story, we are told that Adam and Eve, before eating the fruit, "were both naked . . . and were not ashamed" (Gen 2:28). After they ate the fruit, they "sewed fig leaves together, and made themselves aprons" because they were ashamed to be naked (Gen 3:7). The clear implication is that the fruit made them capable of shame because it made them natural human beings, and human beings naturally feel shame when they are naked. In Lehi's dream, the shame is weaponized by the unrighteous people in the great and spacious building:

> And it was filled with people, both old and young, both male and female, and their manner of dress was exceeding fine. And they were in the attitude of mocking and pointing their fingers towards those which had come at and were partaking of the fruit. And after that they had tasted of the fruit, they were ashamed because of those that were scoffing at them, and they fell away into forbidden paths and were lost. (1 Ne 8:27)

As in Genesis, shame follows the eating of the fruit, but only for a certain category of people—those who care more about the world's opinion than God's. And only those who can ignore the voices from the great and spacious building can experience the paradise that comes with partaking of the fruit. Shame in the biblical account comes from within Adam and Eve and is presented by the text as a proper response, if not to their nudity, then to their sinfulness. In the Book of Mormon, shame comes entirely from the outside and becomes an impediment to happiness in the kingdom of God.

The stories also differ substantially in their presentation of cause and effect, one of the basic patterns in human narrative. The transition from paradise to wilderness in Genesis is a *punishment for* eating the fruit, whereas the transition from wilderness to paradise in Lehi's dream is a *consequence of* eating the fruit. This is much more than a semantic difference; it signals that the two stories operate on different systems of moral reasoning. The Garden of Eden—at least in the way that it has traditionally been understood in the Christian tradition—operates on a system of regulative commands enforced by rewards and punishments. The one prohibition, eating the fruit of the tree of knowledge of good and evil, is wrong because God says it is wrong. When Adam and Eve break the commandment, God punishes them by casting them out of paradise. Lehi's dream, on the other hand, describes a moral situation governed not by rewards and punishments but by choices and consequences. The God-figure in Lehi's dream, the man in the white robe, does not command him to eat, or not to eat, the fruit; he simply leads Lehi out of the dreary wilderness and shows him the tree. Lehi intuitively understands that the fruit of the tree "was desirable to make one happy." The light and joy that constitute Lehi's paradise come entirely from the act of eating the fruit.

After showing Lehi the tree the God-figure disappears from the dream, and everything else is motivated by the logic of choices and consequences. Those who choose to eat the fruit and remain near the tree experience the peace and happiness that the tree of life brings. Those who do not partake of the fruit do not experience peace and happiness. And those who partake and become ashamed—roughly the actions of Adam and Eve as represented in Genesis—no longer remain in paradise. They are not cast out, though; they leave of their own accord and choose loneliness and darkness over fellowship and light. Nothing in the narrative hints at divine reward or punishment. People simply make choices and experience the consequences inherent in the choices they make.

When we read the moral logic of Lehi's dream back into the Genesis account, we get something very much like the Book of Mormon's understanding of the Fall of Adam. We need not speculate about how Joseph Smith might have revised the opening chapters of Genesis to make them more consistent with the Book of Mormon. He produced precisely such a revision, which now constitutes the book of Moses in the Pearl of Great Price.[20] God's instructions to Adam and Eve in the book of Moses sound very different than they do in Genesis:

> And I, the Lord God, commanded the man, saying: Of every tree of the garden thou mayest freely eat, but of the tree of the knowledge of good and evil, thou shalt not eat of it, nevertheless, thou mayest choose for thyself, for it is given unto thee; but, remember that I forbid it, for in the day thou eatest thereof thou shalt surely die. (Moses 3:16–17)

The wording here much more closely resembles the consequence-based moral universe of Lehi's dream than the transactional commandments of Genesis. Under such a reading, God did not punish Adam and Eve for disobeying him; he gave them a choice—a choice between staying in the garden and never having children but living forever or eating the fruit, peopling the earth, and becoming mortal. The consequences of each choice inhered in the structure of the decision itself. When they chose their action, they also chose the consequences, and God gave them the moral agency to make either choice and accept either set of consequences.

The interpretation that these sources lead to is not new, nor is it prohibited by the Genesis text. In Augustine's time, a British monk named Pelagius gained a large following by teaching a doctrine of the Fall with many similarities to the one developed in the Book of Mormon—including a denial of the concept of original sin.[21] But Pelagius was condemned as a heretic and excommunicated, in part through Augustine's efforts, and Pelagianism has been considered a heresy for fifteen centuries by nearly all Christian denominations. It is the post-Augustinian interpretive tradition, rather than the text of the Bible itself, that the Book of Mormon disputes. The revision of the Eden typology in Lehi's dream accomplishes typologically what other passages in the Book of Mormon accomplish theologically: Taken together, they constrain the interpretation of the Genesis narrative within the larger Restoration canon of which both books are a part.

Nephi's Vision and the Condescension of God

One of the most important functions of Lehi's dream is to introduce Jesus Christ into the Book of Mormon narrative—not by his name, which (in modern editions) will not be given until the second book of Nephi—but by his function.[22] After Lehi narrates the specifics of his dream to his family, he does not try to interpret it for them. Rather, he reiterates his previous prophecies about the destruction of Jerusalem and then launches into the first explicitly messianic prophecy of the Book of Mormon:

> Yea, even six hundred years from the time that my father left Jerusalem—a prophet would the Lord God raise up among the Jews, yea, even a Messiah, or in other words, a Savior of the world. And he also spake concerning the prophets, how great a number had testified of these things, concerning this Messiah of which he had spoken, or this Redeemer of the world. Wherefore, all mankind were in a lost and in a fallen state and ever would be save they should rely on this Redeemer. (1 Ne 10:4–6)

Lehi moves quickly from narrating his vivid dream to prophesying about a Messiah. He continues to give some loosely connected facts about the Messiah: that another prophet would prepare his way (1 Ne 10:7), that this prophet would baptize him, that the Messiah would be "the Lamb of God, which should take away the sins of the world" (1 Ne 10:10), that the Jews would be scattered, and the gospel of the Messiah would go to the Gentiles (1 Ne 10:11), and that the Messiah would be the Son of God (1 Ne 10:17).

We miss the radical nature of Lehi's revelations when we read them through two thousand years of Christian thought and practice. Most of what Lehi tells his family would have been incomprehensible to any group of Jews born during the reign of King Josiah and raised during an intense religious revival driven by Yahwist prophets (including Lehi).[23] And what little they could have comprehended would have seemed dangerously blasphemous. As we interpret these passages, we must keep in mind that Nephi and his family have been away from Jerusalem for a few years at most, and they are hearing, for the first time, things that most modern readers of the Book of Mormon have known about all their lives. And they are also getting this information in a sequence that does not make intuitive sense. Lehi begins his discourse by explaining his dream about a tree and then moves, with no clear transitions, into messianic prophecies that go well beyond anything in the Hebrew scriptures. The next five chapters consist of different explanations of Lehi's dream to the confused members of his audience. Chapters 11–14 present the expansive vision that Nephi experiences in response to his prayer to understand his father's dream, and Chapter 15 narrates Nephi's conversation with his brothers, who have been trying in vain to understand the words of their father.

Nephi responds to the confusion caused by his father's dream and subsequent discourse by praying fervently to "behold the things which [his] father saw" (1 Ne 11:3). This is part of the remarkable vision sometimes called "Nephi's Apocalypse," in which he is "caught away in the Spirit of the Lord, yea, into an exceeding high mountain" where he sees a vision of his own (1 Ne 11:1).[24] The vision is framed as a conversation between Nephi and several divine interlocutors, beginning with "the Spirit of the Lord," who "spake unto me as a man speaketh with another." When the spirit shows him a vision of the tree that his father saw, Nephi asks "to know the interpretation thereof" (1 Ne 11:11). In response, the second interlocutor, an angel, appears and shows Nephi the birth of the Messiah:

> And it came to pass that I saw the heavens open, and an angel came down and stood before me. And he saith unto me: Nephi, what beholdest thou? And I saith unto him: A virgin most beautiful and fair above all other virgins. And he saith unto me: Knowest thou the condescension of God? And I said unto him: I know that he loveth his children; nevertheless I do not know the meaning of all things. And he saith unto me: *Behold, the virgin whom thou seest is the mother of God after the manner of the flesh.*
>
> And it came to pass that I beheld that she was carried away in the spirit. And after that she had been carried away in the spirit for the space of a time, the angel spake unto me, saying: Look! And I looked and beheld the virgin again, bearing a child in her arms. And the angel said unto me: *Behold the Lamb of God, yea, even the Eternal Father!* Knowest thou the meaning of the tree which thy father saw? (1 Ne 11:14–21, emphasis mine)

These opening lines of Nephi's vision follow the same trajectory as Lehi's earlier discourse. It begins with a tree—the same tree that Lehi saw—and when Nephi asks what the tree means, an angel appears and shows Nephi an image of a virgin and her child, calling her "the mother of God" and the child "the Eternal Father." We can have little doubt that the angel's question, "Knowest thou the meaning of the tree which thy father saw?" is intended to equate the tree with the incarnation of God, "even the Eternal Father," as an infant.[25] Nephi answers the angel by saying that the tree represents "the love of God, which sheddeth itself abroad in the hearts of the children of men; wherefore it is the most desirable above all things" (1 Ne 11:22). This is technically correct—the incarnation was an act motivated by love—but Nephi completely misses the significance of God himself becoming an infant child and mingling with human beings. Unsatisfied with Nephi's response,[26] the angel tries again:

> And after that he had said these words, he said unto me: Look! And I looked and I beheld the Son of God a going forth among the children of men. And I saw many fall down at his feet and worship him. And it came to pass that I beheld that the rod of iron which my father had seen was the word of God, which led to the fountain of living waters, or to the tree of life, which waters are a representation of the love of God. And I also beheld that the tree of life was a representation of the love of God. And the angel said unto me again: Look and behold the condescension of God! (1 Ne 11:24–26)

After uttering the phrase "condescension of God" a second time, the angel goes on to show Nephi scenes from Christ's life and ministry: being baptized, calling the twelve apostles, healing, casting out devils, being crucified for the sins of the world, and being resurrected (11:27–12:6). All of this, the vision says, is what the tree means, because all of it is what the love of God means.

The phrase "condescension of God" is a translation of the Latin *dignatio Dei*, which has been used for centuries to describe the virgin birth and phenomenon of God taking a human form.[27] In colonial America the term appeared regularly in religious writings such as Jonathan Edwards's well-known sermon "The Excellency of Christ" (1738), in which he describes the paradox of Christ's essence as "infinite highness and infinite condescension":

> Yea, so great is His *condescension*, that it is not only sufficient to take some gracious notice of such as these, but sufficient for everything that is an act of *condescension*. His *condescension* is great enough to become their friend; to become their companion, to unite their souls to Him in spiritual marriage.
> . . . And what act of *condescension* can be conceived of greater? Yet such an

act as this, has His *condescension* yielded to, for those that are so low and mean, despicable and unworthy![28]

By the 1830s, the phrase "condescension of God" was used regularly in sermons, hymns, and theological writings to describe the virgin birth and the mortal life of Jesus Christ. Most Protestant hymnbooks at the time incorporated some version of Isaac Watts's rendering of the psalms, which included some form of "the condescension of God" as a recurring theme in its descriptions.[29] For the Book of Mormon's first readers, the term would have immediately invoked the Christian doctrine of the Incarnation, in which God became human and was born to the Virgin Mary.

Nephi's vision moves quickly into a sweeping view of the future, with symbols from Lehi's dream becoming starting points for much more expansive conversations. In order to explain that the tree of life represents "the love of God," the angel shows Nephi the things that God did because of his love: He became a mortal human being, called disciples, healed the sick, cast out devils, and was ultimately "lifted up upon the cross and slain for the sins of the world" (1 Ne 11:25–33). To show how the great and spacious building represents "the pride of the world," the angel shows the wars and the destruction that the Nephites would experience because of their pride (1 Ne 11:36, 12:1–4). By the end of the vision, Nephi has seen the appearance of Christ in the New World, and he learns that his descendants will eventually be overcome by the descendants of his brothers (1 Ne 12:19–20).[30] He also sees the development of a "Great and Abominable Church" that will lead people astray and learns how the Book of Mormon will come forth in the last days to steer people back onto the straight and narrow path.

If we use Nephi's vision as a key to interpreting the symbols in the Eden story—on the assumption that the two trees and their fruits are connected through a common typology—we get a dramatic extension of the text's already explicit argument against original sin. We have already seen that the Book of Mormon frames the choice to partake of the fruit as both necessary and correct because Adam and Eve cannot remain in Eden and also fulfill God's command to multiply and replenish the earth. Their transgression was a lesser evil because they disobeyed a lesser command in order to obey a greater one. If we equate the tree with God's love, though, and with the very person of Jesus Christ, then we must see the choice to eat the fruit, not as an evil of any kind, but as a positive moral good. Refusing to do so would have been tantamount to rejecting Christ and would have deprived Adam and Eve of the joy that comes with God's gifts. This is precisely how Joseph

Smith reworks the Eden story in the book of Moses, which portrays Adam and Eve after the Fall reflecting on their transgression:

> And in that day Adam blessed God and was filled, and began to prophesy concerning all the families of the earth, saying: Blessed be the name of God, for because of my transgression my eyes are opened, and in this life I shall have joy, and again in the flesh I shall see God. And Eve, his wife, heard all these things and was glad, saying: Were it not for our transgression we never should have had seed, and never should have known good and evil, and the joy of our redemption, and the eternal life which God giveth unto all the obedient. (Moses 5:10–11)

In this version of the text, both Adam and Eve use the word "joy" to describe the consequences of eating the fruit. This directly echoes the way Lehi describes eating the fruit in his dream: It filled his soul "with exceedingly great joy" (1 Ne 8:12). And it also echoes the language of the angel who announces Christ's incarnation to the shepherds: "Fear not: for, behold, I bring you good tidings of great joy, which shall be to all people" (Luke 2:10). Across all three texts, the presence of joy reliably indicates God's love, because God wants humans to have joy. For Nephi, joy is the purpose of human existence, and it could not be had in the Garden of Eden (2 Ne 2:2). This is the reason that Mormon theology sees Adam and Eve as heroes and not as original sinners. "Considering our full knowledge of the purpose of the plan of salvation, and the reason for placing Adam and Eve on earth, the apparent contradiction in the story of the 'Fall' vanishes," wrote Mormon apostle John A. Widtsoe in his book *Evidences and Reconciliations*. "God's command is qualified by his great purpose to bless his children. Adam and Eve rise to the position of helpers in initiating the divine purpose on earth. They become partners with the Lord in making eternal joy possible for the hosts of heaven."[31]

Teaching His Brothers About the Vision

The third iteration of Lehi's dream occurs when Nephi returns to his father's tent to find his brothers arguing over various things that their father had said. He has a productive conversation with them about some of Lehi's teachings about the restoration of Israel, and they "did humble themselves before the Lord" (1 Ne 15:20). When they start talking about the dream, they show genuine interest and ask what it means, giving Nephi a rare moment of connection with his normally recalcitrant brothers. In quick order, Nephi defines the tree as "a representation of the tree of life" (1 Ne 15:22), the rod of iron as "the word of God" (1 Ne 15:24), and the river of water as "filthiness" (1 Ne 15:27) before going on to warn his brothers about the fires of hell awaiting them if they disobey God's commandments:

> But behold, I say unto you that the kingdom of God is not filthy, that there cannot any unclean thing enter into the kingdom of God. Wherefore there must needs be a place of filthiness prepared for that which is filthy. And there is a place prepared, yea, even that awful hell of which I have spoken, and the devil is the preparator of it. Wherefore the final state of the souls of man is to dwell in the kingdom of God or to be cast out because of that justice of which I have spoken. Wherefore the wicked are separated from the righteous and also from that tree of life, whose fruit is most precious and most desirable of all other fruits; yea, and it is the greatest of all the gifts of God. (1 Ne 15:34–36)

The difference between what the angel showed Nephi when he asked about his father's vision, and what Nephi told his brothers when they asked the same question, could not be starker. Nephi has been blessed with a panoramic vision that explains how the fruit of the tree of life, as a symbolic representation of God's love, represents the embodiment of that love in the person of Jesus Christ. Nephi's vision was long and complicated and dealt with thousands of years of future history. But when his brothers ask him what the vision means, he makes no mention of the Messiah or the doctrine of atonement. He doesn't talk about the future that he saw or the fate of his descendants. He doesn't even mention that the fruit of the tree represents God's love. Instead, as Grant Hardy notes, "he introduces a harsher, more judgmental reading of the allegory."[32] Hardy offers several reasons why Nephi might have shifted his emphasis so dramatically. He could have been "devastated by his discovery that his descendants would be destroyed by the Lamanites" and preemptively took his anger out on his "stubborn, rebellious brothers." Or perhaps Nephi determined that Laman and Lemuel were more motivated by the threat of punishment than by the promise of reward, and Nephi, concerned for their welfare, felt that a threat would be more effective than a moral plea.[33]

Both of Hardy's scenarios are plausible, but neither justifies Nephi's most glaring omission. When his brothers ask what the tree in Lehi's dream represents—exactly the same question that he asks the spirit of God at the beginning of his vision (1 Ne 11:9–11)—he answers with a single short sentence: "And I said unto them: It was a representation of the tree of life" (1 Ne 15:22). It would be hard to imagine a less helpful answer to the question, since "the tree of life" is the metaphor that Nephi's brothers want to know the meaning of. And Nephi knows a simple answer. One of the first things he learned was that "the tree of life was a representation of the love of God" (1 Ne 11:25). He also knows the much more complicated answer: that the tree of life represents the fact that God loves humanity so much that he will one day become human in order to redeem us. Nephi does not say any of these things to his brothers.

A likely reason for Nephi's answer is that, when he talks to his brothers, he still is working within the theological framework that he had before his transformative vision. It takes time to transform one's understanding of the universe. Nephi has just learned that God himself—Yahweh, the Lord of armies who drowned Pharaoh's soldiers and shook the walls of Jericho to the ground—will one day allow himself to be born to an unmarried peasant woman from a little village called Nazareth.[34] It will take him years of reflection to understand everything that the angel showed him. We know that he will spend many years of his life studying passages from Isaiah that relate specifically to the birth of the Messiah, and he will demonstrate his intellectual debt by copying sixteen full chapters into his own record. But Nephi's conversation with his brothers occurs just moments after he sees a vision that destabilizes everything that he thought he knew about God. He will need time before he can give a good answer to a question like, "What meaneth the things which our father saw in a dream? What meaneth the tree which he saw?" (1 Ne 11:21).

Conclusion

After reading both Lehi's dream and Nephi's vision, readers should understand that four recurring elements of the Book of Mormon narrative—the fruit of the tree of life, God's love, the condescension of God, and the birth of the Messiah—all mean the same thing. Because of God's infinite love for humanity, he descended from his eternal throne to be born to a virgin and live among human beings and die to atone for our sins. We accept God's gift of atonement when we "repent and come unto him" (1 Ne 10:18). This is the meaning of the tree that Lehi sees in his dream and the fruit that he wants his family to eat. The theology of Lehi's dream, as interpreted through Nephi's vision, does not depart in any meaningful way from the standard Christian understanding of the Incarnation except that it comes six centuries before the birth of Christ. However, when we acknowledge the typological connection between Lehi's dream and the Genesis creation story, the picture changes considerably. Lehi's dream redeploys the symbols from Genesis to create a counternarrative that challenges the orthodox Christian understanding of the Fall.

Through Lehi's dream and Nephi's vision, the Book of Mormon also reframes the New Testament's typology of Adam and Christ. In his letter to the Romans, Paul specifically calls Adam "the figure of him that was to come" (Rom 5:14), but the figuration works differently with Adam than it does with any other Old Testament Christ type. Normally, typological connections works through similarities. But Adam typifies Christ entirely through contrasts. "As in Adam all die, even so in Christ shall all be made alive," Paul writes in his first letter to the Corinthians," and then "the first man Adam was made a living soul; the last Adam was made a quickening spirit" (1 Cor 15:22, 45). Adam and Christ are related to each other, as one German theologian writes, "as a photographic negative to its positive print or as a mold to the plastic shaped by it."[35] The New Testament presents Christ as the second Adam, who healed the wounds inflicted by the first. Adam subjected all people to the curse of death, and Christ gave all people the gift of resurrection. Both acted as representatives of the human race in the moral choices they made. And, as James Dunn writes, "Adam represents humankind through life to death, so Christ represents humankind through death to life."[36]

The Book of Mormon tells a different story, and it tells it consistently in both straightforward passages and typological symbols. In this version, Adam and Christ have been part of the plot from the very start. Adam and Eve were placed in a superficial paradise: a garden in which everything they needed was instantly provided for them. They could not experience opposition, so they did not grow. They did not understand good and evil, so they could not exercise moral reasoning. They could never die, but they could never have children. Until they ate the fruit, they could not progress, which is how Mormon theology defines "damnation."[37] God did not give them a prescriptive commandment not to eat the fruit; he simply explained the consequences of their doing so—that they would become subject to death—and allowed them to make the choice. In order to fulfill the greater commandment, to multiply and replenish the earth, Adam and Eve ate the fruit and accepted mortality and everything that comes with it, including death and sin and separation from God. Their actions allowed humanity to exist, and, even before they acted, the incarnation and atonement of Jesus Christ had already been foreordained and built into God's plan for the world.

CHAPTER THREE

Curses from God

> Tradition has it that his God. . . . had made him both
> far-reaching and tightly circumscribed promises to the
> effect that not only would he, the man of Ur, become a
> nation numberless as sand and stars and a blessing to all
> nations, but also to the effect that the land in which he
> now dwelt as a stranger and to which Elohim had led him
> out of Chaldea would be given to him and his seed as an
> eternal possession in all its parts — whereby the God of
> gods must have expressly listed . . . all those whom God
> clearly intended be subjugated and reduced to servitude
> in the interest of the man of Ur and his seed.
>
> —Thomas Mann, "Descent into Hell," prelude to
> *Joseph and His Brothers*

Thomas Mann wrote *Joseph and His Brothers*, the series of four novels that he considered his greatest masterpiece, over the course of sixteen years, between 1924 and 1942, when both his own life and the world were in near-constant turmoil. He began the series in Germany, continued it while exiled in Switzerland, and published the final volume while living in Los Angeles. During this time he won the Nobel Prize for Literature and became a prominent and outspoken opponent of the Nazi regime. In the preface to the first English translation of *Joseph and his Brothers*, Mann wrote that the work was "my refuge, my comfort, my homeland, a symbol of stability, the guarantee of my own steadfastness amidst a storm of change."[1]

The novels in the tetralogy—*Stories of Jacob, Young Joseph, Joseph in Egypt*, and *Joseph the Provider*—take the bare scaffolding of the patriarch's narratives in Genesis and spin them into a sprawling multigenerational saga exploring the invention of monotheism in the god-soaked worlds of Late Bronze Age Mesopotamia and eighteenth-dynasty Egypt. Mann's work came at a time when mythology had become intensely political. The fascist regimes of Hitler and Mussolini aggressively coopted myths to serve their overtly nationalist agendas, while academic theologians such as Rudolf Bultmann wanted to "demythologize" the Bible by naturalizing the supernatural parts and separating its edifying moral teaching from its unsupportable historical claims.[2] In the tetralogy, notes a German literary critic, Mann "opposes not only reactionary attempts to restore myth but also modernist attempts to eliminate it."[3] Rather, Mann proposed to read myths of Genesis as myths, and he realized just how powerful and transformative myths can be.

The key to the success of *Joseph and His Brothers* lies in Mann's ability to combine a deep appreciation of the universal elements in the Genesis stories with a constant awareness of how differently Bronze Age cultures understood and crafted stories about their world. Neither side of the equation can be ignored. Mann presents the accounts of Abraham, Isaac, Jacob, and Joseph as profoundly important stories that establish key human truths—to treat them otherwise would diminish the role that these stories had in moving the world toward war and genocide. But he also recognizes that they are narratives by cultures that would be virtually unrecognizable to modern minds, people whose understanding of religion, history, literature, science, and nature were more alien than most of us can imagine. In "Descent into Hell," the prelude to the tetralogy, Mann meditates on this strangeness and its implications for how we understand the Bible's mythic beginnings. And one of the most important things he asks us to remember is that the stories we read now have been revised and reshaped many times by those with a strong motivation to use ancient stories for contemporary political advantages. Mann insists that elements of these stories are "late and tendentious interpolations, whose purpose is to find in God's intention from earliest times a sanction for political arrangements established much later by force of arms."[4] This does not invalidate the stories or their spiritual value, but it does mean that we have to pay special attention to the oldest biblical narratives when they seem to be taking a side in a political dispute that occurred much later in biblical history.

We see this often in stories that explain the early ancestry of Judah's Iron Age enemies. The compilers of the Hebrew Bible had a definite interest in portraying the neighboring tribes, and especially the Canaanites, as people who deserved to be conquered and enslaved. Though most archeological and genetic evidence suggests that Israelites and Canaanites—and most of the other people of the Levant—had the same Semitic ancestry (and were essentially the same people),[5] the book of Genesis posits unflattering genealogies for nearly all of them. The Moabites and the Ammonites, says Genesis, descended from the two sons born of the incestuous union between Lot and his daughters (Gen 19:37–38). The Edomites descended from Jacob's birthright-selling brother, Esau, who was also known as Edom (Gen 36:9).

And, most crucial, the Canaanites descended from Canaan, the grandson of Noah, who was cursed when his father, Ham, uncovered Noah's nakedness in the days following the great flood. The Israelites traced their ancestry to Noah's oldest son, Shem (hence "Semitic"), and they saw themselves as beneficiaries of Noah's declaration, "Blessed be the Lord God of Shem; and Canaan shall be his servant" (Gen 9:26).

We can see the same dynamic at work in the Book of Mormon simply by looking at what the text says about its own composition; it is more difficult to see only because we are less accustomed to looking for it. The Bible was composed in a knowable historical context. We can look to nonbiblical sources to learn about the Babylonian captivity or the edicts of Cyrus, and we know more about ancient Rome during New Testament times than we do about most places that have ever existed. We can check the biblical record against other sources and make allowances for the tendency of its writers to overstate the accomplishments of their own people and exaggerate the awfulness of their enemies. The Book of Mormon makes the same kinds of historical claims that the Bible does, but we have no cultural context beyond what the text itself provides. Yet the text provides enough context for us to see that, taken entirely on its own terms, the Book of Mormon has the same kinds of transmission and composition difficulties that the Bible does. It claims to be based on four different sets of metal plates in three different languages that were accumulated over a thousand years and passed on through several family lines—and through multiple migrations and civilization-ending catastrophes—to be abridged and collated into a single set of plates by one of the last leaders of the Nephite civilization.[6]

The potential difficulties with the narrative go beyond the convoluted chain of custody for its primary sources. The two final redactors, who created the document in its current, if untranslated, form, were deeply invested participants in the final days of the civilization they described. Mormon was the commanding general of the Nephite armies in the final battle that ended their civilization (Morm 6:6–15). The first sentence that he speaks in the entire Book of Mormon ends with the phrase, "Behold, I have witnessed almost all the destruction of my people, the Nephites" (W of M 1:1). His son spent most of his adult life hiding, knowing that he would be killed the instant he was discovered (Morm 8:3). When they narrate the Nephites' history, including conflicts with the Lamanites taking place over hundreds of years, they do not approach those conflicts as disinterested observers. It would go against almost everything we know about the writing of history for us to assume that the devastation they witnessed failed to color their presentation of past events.[7]

We have analogs to Mormon and Moroni in the historians of late antiquity—trained scholars such as Eunapius, Sozomen, and Orosius, who lived in the Roman Empire at roughly the same time when, according to the Book of Mormon, the Nephite civilization was coming to an end somewhere in the New World. These historians had all the benefits of a classical education and access to the Roman libraries and archives, and they are generally seen as reliable chroniclers of Rome's decline. When they wrote about the Huns, however—and other barbarian groups who were in the process of destroying the empire—their perspective reveals, as one scholar puts it, "both the ignorance of westerners of Hunnic origins and the willingness of historians to rely on mythical tales to supplement their knowledge."[8] Instead of a learned assessment of the customs and traditions of Germanic tribes, their writings are full of folktales and magical origins that no historian today takes seriously.[9] Mormon had exactly the same motivations to frame the Lamanites negatively in his story. Much as the barbarian tribes of late antiquity brought down a civilization that had endured for a thousand years, the Lamanites of Mormon's day all but destroyed the equally long-lasting Nephite civilization during his lifetime.

All of this suggests that historians rarely do a good job of describing the distant origins of their enemies. Understanding this becomes crucial as we discuss the main topic of this chapter: the racially charged, politically fraught curse narratives in the Bible and the Book of Mormon. These three type-scenes—the curse of Cain in Genesis 4, the curse of Ham in Genesis 9, and the curse of Laman and Lemuel in 2 Nephi 5—all tell the same basic story: In response to one or more acts of disobedience, God, or someone representing God, pronounces a curse on an older son and elevates the status of a younger brother in ways that affect the posterity of both siblings. These three narratives—all instances of a single type-scene—share more than a similar sequence of events. All three were put in their final form a thousand years or more after the events they describe, and all three propose unflattering etiologies for groups in conflict with the cultures of the final redactors. And all three stories survived well into the modern era as religious justifications for enslaving, conquering, colonizing, and otherwise mistreating ethnic groups that could be framed as descendants of a cursed ancestral line.

Divine Curses and Racial Etiology in the Bible

The first major division of the Bible begins and ends with God cursing the entire human race. In between these two general curses come two more specific curses of human beings who displease God for one reason or another. And, in between these individualized curses, God destroys the world with a great flood. All of this cursing comes in the short portion of Bible that scholars call the "primeval history," which consists of the first eleven chapters of Genesis, before the introduction of Abraham and the covenant line. The primeval history is the most universal part of the Old Testament.[10] Everything else presents the history, literature, law, and prophecy of a specific group of people descended from Abraham, Isaac, and Jacob. But the first eleven chapters of Genesis offer a universal history of God's earliest interactions with humanity.

As the book of Genesis presents it, the human race began with an act of disobedience and a set of curses. Before they are cast out of the Garden of Eden, Adam and Eve are not quite human, or, at least, not human in the way we understand the term, because they are not yet mortal. Through their disobedience they fall from immortality to mortality, and God curses them with statements meant to describe fundamental things about the human condition. To Eve he says, "I will greatly multiply thy sorrow and thy conception; in sorrow thou shalt bring forth children; and thy desire shall be to thy husband, and he shall rule over thee" (Gen 3: 16). To Adam he says, "In the sweat of thy face shalt thou eat bread, till thou return unto the ground; for out of it wast thou taken: for dust thou art, and unto dust shalt thou return" (Gen 3:19). The text makes it clear that these punishments—labor pain for women, labor requirements for men, and eventual death for everyone—apply to all of humankind, for whom Adam (Hebrew for "mankind") and Eve (Hebrew for "source of life") serve as proxies.

The final curse in the primeval history comes in Genesis 11, when God confounds language in response to the human attempt to build the Tower of Babel:

> And they said, Go to, let us build us a city and a tower, whose top may reach unto heaven; and let us make us a name, lest we be scattered abroad upon the face of the whole earth. And the Lord came down to see the city and the tower, which the children of men builded. And the Lord said, Behold, the people is one, and they have all one language; and this they begin to do: and now nothing will be restrained from them, which they have imagined to do. Go to, let us go down, and there confound their language, that they may not understand one another's speech. So the Lord scattered them abroad from thence upon the face of all the earth: and they left off to build the city. (Gen 11: 4–8)

As it is in the story of the Fall, God's punishment is generalized to all of humanity. Indeed, the punishment can only be understood collectively. No human being is lessened by the confounding of language, but humankind loses the ability to act collectively. And because mutually exclusive languages often delimited tribal and national boundaries, the Tower of Babel story is usually seen as an etiology of human differences—and, by extension, of the human propensity to divide into tribal, ethnic, and linguistic in-groups.[11]

These two scenes of universal punishment share several striking similarities. First, both come in response to a human threat to invade the realm of the gods—and, according to the text, God takes such threats seriously. The serpent tempts Eve to eat the forbidden fruit by saying, "Your eyes shall be opened, and ye shall be as gods, knowing good and evil" (Gen 3:22). After punishing Adam for their disobedience, God confirms that, indeed, "man is become as one of us, to know good and evil" and must be evicted from the garden "lest he put forth his hand, and take also of the tree of life, and eat, and live for ever" (Gen 3:22–23)—thus presumably erasing any distinction between the human and the divine. With the Tower of Babel, people are quite literally trying to use human technology to invade God's realm, and God appears to acknowledge that they might succeed. God, then, confounds human language for the same reason that he ejected humanity from paradise: to protect his secrets and preserve his godly prerogatives.

The chapters in Genesis that fall in between these two general curses contain two individual curses against specific human beings: Cain and Ham. These scenes, like the Tower of Babel scene, offer an etiology of human difference. They explain, or seek to explain, why some human beings are better than others—more righteous, more chosen, more blessed by God. Like all myths, they primarily reference the conditions of the world in which the stories were told, rather than the world that the stories describe, much as Shakespeare's *Hamlet* says much more about Elizabethan England than it says about medieval Denmark.[12] The main lineage traced in the primeval history—from Abraham through Isaac, Jacob, and Joseph—explains why some people, the Israelites, were favored by God. But there is a second lineage, too: that of the cursed (Cain and Ham), the unloved (Ishmael), and the despisers of their birthright (Esau). This is the lineage of the unchosen people—or, to use Thomas Mann's evocative phrase, "all those whom God clearly intended be subjugated and reduced to servitude in the interest of the man of Ur and his seed."

The first human to be cursed after the Fall is Cain, who kills his brother Abel in a dispute over religious sacrifices. The specific nature of Cain's curse both inverts and extends the punishment given to Adam. God curses Adam and his descendants by forcing them to till the earth to grow their sustenance. Cain already lives under this first punishment, and now is further cursed such that he will not be able to grow crops even if he does till the earth (Gen

4:12), giving him no role in the postlapsarian human community. Cain had one job, tilling the earth, and he can't do it anymore. Like Adam and Eve, he is cast out from the only world that he knows and cursed to become "a fugitive and a vagabond" on the earth. When he protests that "every one that findeth me shall slay me," God gives a him a special mark designed to protect him. Cain is not afraid that people will kill him because of the mark; they will kill him because he is unable to participate in the agricultural life of the community and earn his keep. The mark is a partial mitigation of that punishment and a sign that Cain, however useless and unproductive, is under God's protection (Gen 4:13–15). "In such a simple way," writes Walter Brueggemann, "the narrative articulates the two-sidedness of human life, in jeopardy for disobedience and yet kept safe. The acknowledgment of guilt and the reality of grace come together in this presentation."[13]

In the next iteration of the type-scene, Noah's son Ham was punished when he "saw his father's nakedness, and told two of his brethren without" (Gen 9:33). Once again, the text inverts an element of the Fall. Adam and Eve were punished after they saw and recognized their own nakedness and covered themselves (Gen 3:7), while Ham is punished when he uncovers his father and recognizes his nakedness. There has never been much consensus on what Ham's sin actually was. Early rabbinical debates constructed interpretations that had Ham sodomizing or castrating his father.[14] Others have argued that seeing a parent's sexual organs was an extreme cultural taboo because it equated with seeing God's phallus.[15] And still others suggest that Ham's sin was to expose his father to ridicule.[16] We do not need to know exactly what Ham did in order for us to understand the story, only that it was really bad. But it is not Ham who receives the punishment. Rather, an enraged Noah turns to Ham's son and says, "cursed be Canaan; a servant of servants shall he be unto his brethren. . . . Blessed be the Lord God of Shem; and Canaan shall be his servant" (Gen 9:25–26).

The first three stories—Adam and Eve, Cain and Abel, and Ham and Noah—have all been placed at crucial moments in the primeval history. "Each of them," Devora Steinmetz notes, "tells of an act of violation perpetrated in a new world."[17] The world, she explains, is created and destroyed three times in the first eight chapters of Genesis. As soon as the world is created as the paradisiacal Garden of Eden, Adam and Eve disobey God and are punished by being thrust into the world of thorns and thistles (Gen 3:18). And, in the first story that we read in the postlapsarian world, Cain kills Abel, and God appears again to curse a human being. But he does not curse them all, and this is the first time the human world divides into those who are, and those who are not, favored of God. In time, the unfavored dominate the world, and, once again, God destroys it and starts all over again, with Noah and his family as the only humans in the new world. Once again, humanity must start anew in a new world. And the first story told in the postdiluvian world concerns an act of disobedience and a curse. The Tower of Babel story is also set at a transition point, but it is a transition point in the narrative, not the world. At the end of Genesis 11, the entire focus of the narrative shifts to Abraham and the covenant lineage. The rest of Genesis will be a history not of the planet but of a small group of people living in the world that the cataclysms of primeval history created.

In the repetition of these type-scenes, we can see the narrative logic of figuration at work. Remember that typology arises from a view of history that sees certain types of people, situations, and sequences of events as hard-wired into the nature of reality. Types recur because they reflect unchanging truths about human beings and the way they interact with each other and with God. The same sets of circumstances always produce the same sequences of events. One of these recurring types is that, when God creates a new reality with its own rules, somebody will immediately disobey those rules, and that somebody will be cursed. This happens with Adam and Eve, Cain, and Ham in the primordial history. But it also happens nearly every time the biblical narrative shifts in a significant way: When Moses leads the Israelites out of Egypt, beginning a new chapter in the history of the covenant people, said covenant people worship a golden calf in the desert (Gen 32:1–7); when God establishes a new monarchy, Saul fails to destroy the Ammonites entirely, as God commanded (1 Sam 15:3–22); when the monarchy divides, Jeroboam sets up idols in the high places (1 Kgs 12:26–30). In each case, a major narrative transition begins with an act of disobedience and a divine punishment, culminating in the conquest of Israel in 722 BCE and the destruction of Jerusalem in 586 BCE—both, according to the cause-and-effect logic of the Old Testament, as punishment for disobeying God and worshipping idols.

The scenes themselves also serve as etiological tales, or origin stories that describe how the world of the Israelites got to be the way it is. We see this most clearly in the Tower of Babel story, which purports to explain why human beings, who all descended from the same Mesopotamian family, spoke so many mutually unintelligible languages. The story of the Fall, too, has etiological significance; it explains how death, labor pains, and the requirement to work came into the world. The other two curse narratives—Cain and Ham—worked as a pair to create the idea of different genealogical lines with different destinies and different relationships with God. It is no accident that Ham's sin caused a son named Canaan to be cursed. "Canaan stands for the Canaanite people," writes Steven L. McKenzie. "The point of the story is to show that Israel's conquest of the land of Canaan and subjugation of its inhabitants was justified because of the curse of slavery that Noah imposed upon Ham's son Canaan."[18]

Much later, as Christianity rose to power in the West, the narratives of Cain and Canaan became part of the biblical justification for slavery and conquest. Scholars such as David Goldenberg and Stephen R. Haynes have traced the evolution of the curse narratives of Ham and Cain through Second Temple Judaism and early Christianity into the modern era, when they became the rationalization for chattel slavery in Europe and America.[19] Goldenberg explains that such a justification required Christians to conflate the curses of Cain and Ham into a single narrative because each story contains something that the other lacks. The story of Cain and Abel allows for a physical mark of God's curse that could be interpreted as dark skin, but it says nothing about slavery. The story of Ham specifies slavery as part of the curse but says nothing about any physical mark. Only a mashup of the two stories produced a rationale for enslaving those with dark skin.[20] We should not be surprised that these two versions of the same type-scene came to be associated with each other in this way. That is how typology works. It allows elements from one narrative to be read into another simply because, according to the logic of figuration, they are the same story, or at least the repetition of the same cause-and-effect patterns hard-wired into the nature of reality.

All of this historical and theological speculation was part of the world into which Joseph Smith published the Book of Mormon. Nearly all of the doctrines and biblical narratives that Latter-day Saints would eventually invoke to defend policies denying priesthood ordination and temple ordinances to Black people—that the mark of Cain was part of the curse (rather than a sign of God's protection), that the mark was black skin, that the lineage of Cain came through the great flood because Ham's wife was a descendant of Cain, and that anybody with black skin or African descent was a doubly cursed descendant of both Cain and Ham—were regularly taught by American Protestants well before the Book of Mormon appeared.[21] Smith did not create these misreadings of the biblical record, but he did insert them into the Mormon scriptural canon in several different places, making them difficult for church leaders to disown in the modern era, when they proved to be scientifically groundless and theologically incoherent.[22]

This is all part of the context that we must consider when trying to interpret the Book of Mormon's version of the curse type-scene in 2 Nephi 5, when God curses Laman, Lemuel, and all of their descendants with "a skin of blackness" (2 Ne 5:21). This scene marks the first narrative transition in

the Book of Mormon, when the family of Lehi splits into the two civilizations—the Nephites and the Lamanites—whose interactions with each other
structure the remainder of the Book of Mormon.

Races and Curses in the Mormon Canon

Few things embarrass even modestly progressive Latter-day Saints more
than the just-mentioned passage in 2 Nephi. The verse seems to embody
everything that open-minded religious people don't want to associate with
their sacred texts: openly racist equation of sinfulness and dark skin, nineteenth-century hysteria about miscegenation, and simplistic folk etiologies of
race. For the past fifty years or so, Mormon historians and theologians have
worked hard to reframe, reinterpret, recontextualize, and apologize for this
passage. Latter-day Saint scholars defending the Book of Mormon against
charges of racism or of nineteenth-century sensibilities have argued that
"blackness" should not be read as describing skin color, that a contemporary
etiology of Native Americans would have used "red" instead of "black" to
describe skin color, that the darkening of skin was a gradual process caused by
intermarriages with Amerindian natives external to the Nephite population,
and that there is a difference between the "curse" and the "mark," making
the dark skin not part of the curse and, therefore, presumably, not a sign of
spiritual deficiency.[23]

With no prejudice to any of these readings, I suggest that we cannot
understand the Lamanite curse narrative fully unless we see it as a type-
scene that shares its narrative sequence with the curse scenes in Genesis 4
(Cain) and Genesis 9 (Ham). As nearly all of the Book of Mormon's shared
type-scenes do, the curse scene in Nephi has both connective and corrective
properties. It connects the Book of Mormon to the Bible in ways that had
a special resonance in the racial discourse of the nineteenth century. At the
same time, though, it changes the underlying typology of divine curses in
ways that affect how all three stories should be read and understood in the
expanded canon.

The Book of Mormon is not the only work in the Mormon canon that
connects to the curse narratives in Genesis. Several passages in the Pearl of
Great Price, the shortest and least unified of Mormonism's four standard
works, address and adjust these narratives directly in ways that anticipate
the Book of Mormon's version. The book of Moses in the Pearl of Great
Price is a rewritten and expanded version of the first six chapters of Genesis
meant to be part of Joseph Smith's "inspired revision" of the Bible.[24] The
Cain and Abel story in Moses is much longer than the version in Genesis,

and it makes Cain a much more sinister character. Rather than killing Abel in the heat of passion, Cain conspires with Satan to become the master of a great secret and makes a pact to kill Abel as a part of his Faustian bargain:

> And Satan said unto Cain: Swear unto me by thy throat, and if thou tell it thou shalt die; and swear thy brethren by their heads, and by the living God, that they tell it not; for if they tell it, they shall surely die; and this that thy father may not know it; and this day I will deliver thy brother Abel into thine hands. And Satan sware unto Cain that he would do according to his commands. And all these things were done in secret. And Cain said: Truly I am Mahan the master of this great secret, that I may murder and get gain. Wherefore Cain was called Master Mahan, and he gloried in his wickedness. And Cain went into the field, and Cain talked with Abel, his brother. And it came to pass that while they were in the field, Cain rose up against Abel, his brother, and slew him. And Cain gloried in that which he had done, saying: I am free; surely the flocks of my brother falleth into my hands. (Moses 5:29–33)

The great secret Cain introduces into the world—that one can "murder and get gain"—plays a major role in the later part of the Book of Mormon, where it becomes the ideology of the Gadianton robbers, who emerge in Nephite society in the book of Helaman (Hel 2:4) and eventually surpass the Lamanites as the Nephite civilization's principal enemy (4 Ne 1:42–46). In a stark digression in the book of Helaman, Mormon tells us that "those secret oaths and covenants did not come forth unto Gadianton from the records which were delivered unto Helaman; but behold, they were put into the heart of Gadianton by that same being who did entice our first parents to partake of the forbidden fruit—yea, that same being who did plot with Cain that if he would murder his brother Abel, it should not be known unto the world" (Hel 6: 26–27). Crucially, though, the original robbers were Nephites, not Lamanites (Hel 1:7–11), and they eventually become a superordinate group made up of both Nephites and Lamanites, capable of fielding an army against either or both groups (3 Ne 2:11–12). There is no indication in the text that they come from any specific ancestral lineage.

In the seventh chapter of Moses—as part of a vision given to Enoch, an antediluvian prophet who builds a city so righteous that its inhabitants were taken up to heaven without tasting death—God shows a future in which "a blackness came upon all the children of Canaan" (Moses 7:8) and in which all of the descendants of Adam were gathered together, "save it was the seed of Cain, for the seed of Cain were black, and had not place among them" (Moses 7:22). The mystery of how the seed of Cain could exist after the great flood, which killed all but eight of the people in the world, is addressed elsewhere in the Pearl of Great Price in the book of Abraham, which gives a name and a canonical shape to the popular nineteenth-century speculation that a descendant of Cain married Ham and carried the cursed lineage through the flood:

> The land of Egypt being first discovered by a woman, who was the daughter of Ham, and the daughter of Egyptus, which in the Chaldean signifies Egypt, which signifies that which is forbidden; When this woman discovered the land it was under water, who afterward settled her sons in it; and thus, from Ham, sprang that race which preserved the curse in the land. (Abr 1:23–24)

This passage does more than canonize the link between Cain and Ham, though; it also changes the terms of Ham's punishment. In Genesis, only Canaan's line is cursed. The book of Abraham expands this to all of Ham's children, who, as descendants of Cain, carry the initial curse through the flood and into the future, substantially expanding the number of people in the world who must live under a primal curse.[25]

The reframing of the biblical curse narratives in the Pearl of Great Price adds three elements to the stories that we do not find in the Genesis accounts. First, they tie the "mark of Cain" to a physical skin color. Second, they establish the heritability of Cain's curse and the accompanying mark. And finally, they tie the stories of Cain and Ham together as narratives about the same divine curse that was preserved from the flood in the person of Egyptus.[26] None of these innovations originated with Joseph Smith or the Pearl of Great Price. The stories of Cain and Ham had already been yoked together in the American mind and offered as a biblical justification for conquest and slavery and complete disregard for the humanity of anyone with black skin or African descent.[27] Smith simply put into the biblical text the story that most Americans assumed had been there all along.

The curse narrative in 2 Nephi matches its two biblical predecessors on many points, but it matches Joseph Smith's revisions of these stories in the books of Moses and Abraham on nearly every point. The mark of the curse is clearly stated to be "a skin of blackness," and the heritability of both the curse and the mark, and their extension to anybody who marries into the cursed line, are also clearly established:

> Wherefore, the word of the Lord was fulfilled which he spake unto me, saying that inasmuch as they will not hearken unto thy words, they shall be cut off from the presence of the Lord. And behold, they were cut off from

his presence. And he had caused the cursing to come upon them, yea, even a sore cursing because of their iniquity. For behold, they had hardened their hearts against him, that they had become like unto a flint. Wherefore as they were white and exceedingly fair and delightsome, that they might not be enticing unto my people, therefore the Lord God did cause a skin of blackness to come upon them. And thus saith the Lord God: I will cause that they shall be loathsome unto thy people save they shall repent of their iniquities.

And cursed shall be the seed of him that mixeth with their seed, for they shall be cursed even with the same cursing. And the Lord spake it, and it was done. And because of their cursing which was upon them, they did become an idle people, full of mischief and subtlety, and did seek in the wilderness for beasts of prey. (2 Ne 5:20–24)

The Lamanite curse scene combines elements from stories of both Cain and Ham to produce a version of the myth that was in line with both the Pearl of Great Price and the nineteenth-century American public sphere. Most of the narrative building blocks come from the story of Cain and Abel in Genesis 4. In both stories, the curse comes in response to the mistreatment of a more favored brother (Cain killed Abel; Laman and Lemuel attempted to kill Nephi); both come with a physiological marker; both cause the subjects of the curse to be physically unattractive to others; and both affect the subjects' ability, or willingness, to participate in the agricultural life of the community: Cain's curse makes him unable to till the ground, while the Lamanites, "because of their cursing," become idle hunter-foragers who "seek in the wilderness for beasts of prey." The one important detail from Ham's story that is not part of Cain's curse in the text, though it has been read into that story for thousands of years, is the heritability of the curse. Noah does not curse Ham; he curses Ham's son, Canaan, and by extension, all of the Canaanites. The story of Ham's curse was designed to be a racial (or, at least, a national) etiology; the story of Cain's curse became one only when its report a physiological mark became necessary to the prevailing narrative.

The Book of Mormon's version of the curse scene contains one element that the biblical texts do not, one that dramatically revises the underlying type: The curse in the Book of Mormon is reversible and tied clearly to continuing behavior. In the Bible, God simply says to Cain, "And now art thou cursed from the earth, which hath opened her mouth to receive thy brother's blood from thy hand; When thou tillest the ground, it shall not henceforth yield unto thee her strength; a fugitive and a vagabond shalt thou be in the earth" (Gen 4:11–12). And after Ham uncovers Noah's nakedness, Noah says, "Cursed be Canaan; a servant of servants shall he be unto his brethren" (Gen 9:25). Neither curse holds out any hope of redemption.

Much as God's curse of Adam and Eve irrevocably bound all of humanity to death and sin, the subsequent biblical curse condemns Cain to a life of wandering. And though it does not condemn Cain's descendants, as later tradition would have it, the curse of Ham is pronounced against his posterity with no sunset clause for its effects. Consequently, some four thousand years later, people could still invoke the biblical curse narratives to justify conquest and slavery.

To Laman and Lemuel, however, God says, "I will cause that they shall be loathsome unto thy people *save they shall repent of their iniquities*" (2 Ne 5:22, emphasis mine). The descendants of Laman and Lemuel are specifically not cursed in perpetuity, and much later in the Book of Mormon, "those Lamanites which had united with the Nephites were numbered among the Nephites. And their curse was taken from them, and their skin became white like unto the Nephites" (3 Ne 2: 14–15). Furthermore, as Nancy Bently explains, the most significant consequences of the curse are those that the Lamanites choose themselves. "The difference in skin color between the Nephites and the Lamanites does not mark a difference between separate biological races; all are equally the 'seed' of Lehi," she argues. What sets the Lamanites apart from the Nephites for most of the Book of Mormon is their choice to live in tribal societies rather than cities and the larger political units that mark the Nephite civilization after the discovery of Zarahemla. "When the Lamanites refuse the enlightened, family-based spirituality introduced by Lehi and Nephi, they *make* themselves tribal," she notes. "Even race is a matter of choice, or rather its most visible effect."[28]

Though the Book of Mormon has been justly criticized for the overt racism in some of its passages concerning race and skin color, it also injected something genuinely new into the divine-curse-as-racial-etiology genre of scripture. Max Perry Mueller explains how thoroughly these passages reframed the discussion of curses and races in the nineteenth century:

The Book of Mormon diverges from other nineteenth-century biblical and biological beliefs by teaching that race is not destiny. When Christ comes to America, his church establishes peace and prosperity for all. The universal gospel creates a unified, just, and equitable American Christian society. There are no "rich and poor, bond and free, but they were all made free, and partakers of the heavenly gift." What's more, eventually there are even no "Lamanites, nor any manner of Ites," as Lamanites and Nephites unify to create a raceless (white), Christian people. Race is a false, or at least, an impermanent distinction, the result of human temporal, not God's eternal design.[29]

Table 1. Comparison of Curse Narratives in the Bible, the Book of Mormon, and the Pearl of Great Price

	Reason for curse	Nature of curse	Physical manifestation	Consequences for posterity	Reversibility of curse
Cain (Gen 4)	Cain was cursed for killing his brother Abel.	Cain can no longer work the ground and bring forth crops, which gives him no way to contribute to society and forces him to become a vagabond.	Cain is given a mark, not as part of his punishment, but as a way to show that he is under God's protection so that nobody will kill him.	There is no textual evidence that either the curse or the mark of Cain was passed on to his descendants.	The mark that God gives Cain mitigates the consequences of the curse, but there is no way provided to reverse the curse.
Cain (PoGP)	Cain entered into a secret combination with Satan to "murder and get gain" (Moses 5:21).	Along with being cursed with the inability to raise crops, Cain is "shut off from the presence of the Lord" and driven out of the community.	The mark becomes a sign of the curse and is carried through the flood through a descendant of Cain. The specific nature of the mark is not given in the text.	Cain's descendants all carry the mark of Cain, and several of them become masters of the "great secret that was administered unto Cain by Satan" (Moses 5:49).	The Lord renews the curse of Cain with Lamech, his descendant (Moses 5:52), and another descendant, Egyptus, becomes the wife of Ham and carries the curse through the flood. No way is provided for the posterity of Cain to remove the curse.

Table 1. continued

	Reason for curse	Nature of curse	Physical manifestation	Consequences for posterity	Reversibility of curse
Ham (Gen 9)	Ham uncovered his father's nakedness.	Noah pronounces the curse, not against Ham, but against his son, Canaan: "Cursed be Canaan; a servant of servants shall he be unto his brethren" (Gen 9:25).	No physical manifestation of the curse is mentioned in the text.	The curse is pronounced against Canaan, one of Ham's children, making it an inherited curse from the very beginning.	The text contains no statement limiting the duration of the curse.
Laman and Lemuel (2 Ne 5)	The people of Nephi and the people of Laman had already separated into two physical locations. The text states, "That they might not be enticing unto my people . . . the Lord God did cause a skin of blackness to come upon them" (2 Ne 5:21).	In the text the Lamanites are caused to have dark skin, designed to make them "loathsome" to the Nephites (2 Ne 5:22). The text also includes a punishment reminiscent of Cain: "Because of their cursing which was upon them, they did become an idle people, full of mischief and subtlety, and did seek in the wilderness for beasts of prey" (2 Ne 5:24).	The curse has a strong physical manifestation of dark skin.	Not only is the curse heritable, God specifically says that it will apply to "the seed of him that mixeth with their seed, for they shall be cursed even with the same cursing" (2 Ne 5:23).	The curse is reversible and tied specifically to unrighteous behavior. It will endure until "they shall repent of their iniquities" (2 Ne 5:22). In Third Nephi righteous Lamanites are rewarded with light skin (3 Ne 2:15).

The way in which the Book of Mormon revises the biblical curse scene is entirely consistent with the way it modifies the biblical story of the Fall. As we saw in Chapter 2, the Book of Mormon reframes Adam's original sin as the correct choice between two untenable alternatives and also reframes God's cursing of Adam and Eve as a simple explanation of the natural consequences of that choice. And Mormon orthodoxy entirely rejects the idea of original sin. The second article of faith that Joseph Smith proposed in 1842 reads, "We believe that men will be punished for their own sins, and not for Adam's transgression."[30] The idea of a permanent, irrevocable, multigenerational curse would fly in the face of the theological position that Nephi had already carefully worked out. It would make the Atonement that Nephi has already prophesied about irrelevant (1 Ne 10:4–6).

The Book of Mormon's view of the Lamanites as cursed but redeemable shaped the early church's behavior toward Native Americans. From very early on, Latter-day Saints felt a responsibility to proselytize their Indian neighbors. In September 1830, just six months after the church was established, Joseph Smith called Oliver Cowdrey and Peter Whitmer on a "mission to the Lamanites" of western Missouri, to be joined later by Parley P. Pratt, Ziba Peterson, and Frederick G. Williams. These early Mormon stalwarts embraced the task enthusiastically, knowing that "the purposes of God were great respecting that people, and hoping that the time had come when the promises of the Almighty in regard to them were about to be accomplished, and that they would receive the Gospel, and enjoy its blessings."[31] The early Mormons treated Native Americans unevenly, especially after they began to settle the Great Basin and displace the indigenous populations of the region. But there can be no doubt that the first generations of Mormons saw the American Indians as a holy people, a remnant of the house of Israel, and as part of the sacred story into which they were writing themselves.[32]

Table 1 shows the similarities and differences between the cursing of Cain in Genesis, the cursing of Cain in the Pearl of Great Price, the cursing of Canaan in Genesis, and the cursing of Laman and Lemuel in the Book of Mormon.

Reading the Lamanite Curse Narrative Today

Nothing in the text of the Book of Mormon posits the Lamanite curse as an explanation of the physical characteristics of modern American Indians.[33] But nobody in the nineteenth century could have read the text in any other way. Its close parallels to the stories of Cain and Ham—which were widely accepted as the explanation for black skin—ensured that Mormons would read the cursing of Laman and Lemuel as an explanation for the skin color of Native Americans and that non-Mormons would see it as an attempted explanation of the same. Like the biblical stories, the Lamanite curse narrative had the sort of explanatory power that people gravitate to in the absence of better explanations. In the pre-Mendelian, pre-Darwinian world that most people saw as only a few thousand years old, divine intervention and outright magic were among the few explanations available to explain phenotypical differences within the human family. Folk etiologies for skin-color differences are a human universal, found in nearly every pre-modern culture that has been studied.[34] And when folk etiologies can be drafted into the service of colonization and conquest, they stand little chance of being refuted easily.

In recent years the Church of Jesus Christ of Latter-day Saints has backed away almost entirely from presenting curse narratives as an explanation for contemporary racial characteristics. "Race and the Priesthood"—one of the Gospel Topics Essays published by the Church on its website between 2013 and 2015 in an effort to deal more directly with difficult questions—clearly and unequivocally "disavows the theories advanced in the past that black skin is a sign of divine disfavor or curse."[35] Another essay, "Book of Mormon and DNA Studies," retreats substantially from the claim that Native Americans are descendants of the Lamanites of the Book of Mormon. Acknowledging that most Native American DNA appears to have an Asian origin, the essay speculates that there were several large populations of people on the American continents other than the Nephites and the Lamanites and that "the DNA of Book of Mormon peoples likely represented only a fraction of all DNA in ancient America."[36] Given the extent to which the opinions of "living prophets" constrain canonical authority in the modern LDS Church, we can now safely say that, for adherents of Mormonism's largest denomination, the stories of Cain, Ham, Laman, and Lemuel should no longer be seen as etiologically significant for any human beings alive today.

These formal statements go a long way toward resolving these narratives' disturbing cultural and political implications, but they don't get us any closer to a useful interpretation. If these stories are not supposed to be racial etiologies, what are they supposed to be? But this is not quite the right question. These narratives *are* supposed to be racial etiologies—just not of any contemporary races. In order to interpret these stories, we must recognize that their original authors—along with the various editors, translators, abridgers, redactors, and scribes standing between the original narratives and the final canonical form—were trying to create unflattering etiologies of their enemies. And they all had strong motivation to shade their narratives to the disadvantage of their subjects. The possibility for bias comes in at every stage of the Book of Mormon narrative. Whether as an author or a translator, Joseph Smith would have been influenced by the nineteenth-century reception of the curse narratives discussed above. And we have already seen how Mormon might have allowed his own experience with Lamanites to color his historical descriptions. But the actual narration of the Lamanite curse narrative comes from a section of the Book of Mormon attributed to the "Small Plates of Nephi," which contain Nephi's words verbatim, without Mormon's editorial intervention. Nephi's motivations, and his reliability as a narrator, matter too.[37] And, as it does with Mormon, the text gives us some indications that Nephi's descriptions of Lamanite origins should be read with caution.

Nephi created the record of his family at the end of his life, many years after the events he described. "The mature Nephi," Grant Hardy writes, "is something of a tragic figure, cut off from his culture, despairing of his descendants, and alienated from his own society." As he crafts his record, "writing from the spiritual and political needs of thirty years later, [he] takes care to present his brothers in the worst light possible." Even so, readers can peek behind the scenes to construct a counternarrative "in which Laman and Lemuel's hesitancies are reasonable, their beliefs orthodox, and their actions faithful."[38] Nephi the writer is an aging political leader who has been fighting with another group of people for many years (1 Ne 5:34) and whose political legitimacy rests on his having been correct in his original decision to separate from his brothers. Attributing the original schism to a divine curse and naturalizing the results of that curse by tying it to skin color relieves Nephi from any responsibility that he may have had in the breakup of the family. This would be very human behavior, as Fatima Saleh and Margaret Olsen Hemming point out in *The Book of Mormon for the Least of These*:

> It appears that post-schism, Nephi continues to resent and fear his brothers and their families. This is understandable, as Nephi endured so much trauma at their hands and his people begin to battle with the Lamanites almost immediately after the separation. Nephi seems to be taking that lingering resentment and building a case against the Lamanites. He is reframing the narrative, attributing their behavior to skin color when his account states otherwise and pointing out every possible trait he can criticize. It's such a universal human reaction that we can understand Nephi's hurt. Nephi's vitriol reveals the grief he has never finished processing.[39]

This Lamanite curse narrative contains several other assertions that suggest that Nephi may have exaggerated in an attempt to make sure that readers understood that his brothers bore full responsibility for the split. First, he indicates that before the curse his brothers "were white, and exceedingly fair and delightsome." Such a statement almost certainly misrepresents the skin color of Lehi's children or any other inhabitant of Jerusalem in the sixth century BCE. As John L. Sorensen writes, "their typical copper-olive skins, dark hair, brown eyes, and slight build would mean that the party of Lehi would not stand out sharply in physical appearance from many Indian groups." Sorenson's analysis of likely skin color among Book of Mormon peoples concludes that "it is likely that the objective distinction in skin hue between Nephites and Lamanites was less marked than the subjective difference."[40]

Nephi also makes statements about the Lamanite's social development that conflict with the evidence in the text. Specifically, he portrays them as "an idle people, full of mischief and subtlety, [who sought] in the wilderness for beasts of prey" (2 Ne 5:24). This uncharitable formulation seems designed to present the Lamanites as less cultured and less civilized than the Nephites, though, at every stage in the Book of Mormon, these groups are shown to be at roughly the same level of social development, with the Lamanites, in every case, described as significantly more numerous.[41] Population density is a function of social organization, and it would simply not have been possible for a population of hunters and foragers to exceed, so dramatically, a population of agrarian city builders like the Nephites. Either the Lamanites very quickly overcame the idle lifestyle that Nephi attributed to them, or, more likely, he exaggerated the cultural differences between the two populations in order to cast his enemies, who were also his relatives, in a negative light.[42]

None of these arguments about Nephi's potential for bias (or Mormon's, or that of the scribes who compiled the Old Testament) requires us to reject any volume of scripture as an ahistorical document. Rather, it requires that we treat these volumes precisely as historical documents—ones that, like every other historical document ever written, contains biases, omissions, incorrect evaluations, and cultural blind spots. This is especially true when people are writing about their current enemies. We make these adjustments naturally when we read what Thucydides said about the Spartans, what Eunapius said about the Huns, or what Americans during World War II said about the Japanese. If we take seriously the notion that sacred texts are actually historical documents, we must make the same allowances for the things that Israelite writers said about the Canaanites and that the Nephite writers said about the Lamanites. And when the information we are evaluating involves the kinds of racial etiologies that were ubiquitous in the ancient world but conflict with everything we now understand about the evolution of phenotypes, we do well to exercise an even greater degree of readerly caution.

So, where does all of this leave us with the curse type-scene in the Bible+Book of Mormon canon? The three stories are clearly versions of the same underlying type: a divine curse invoked to explain both the spiritual status and the physical characteristics of a group of people. The potential for such a story to justify truly egregious behavior toward other human beings—and the long history of these three narratives doing exactly that—makes them difficult to read in any context. But the version in the Book of Mormon makes one enormous correction to the underlying type-scene that deserves much more attention than it has ever received. Divine disfavor, the Book of Mormon tells us, is not forever. Everybody can be redeemed—Cain, Ham, Laman, Lemuel. Everybody. Latter-day Saints have never been consistent about this aspect of their theology. The temple/priesthood ban was an enormous failure on the part of an institutional church to recognize the grace inherent in its own theology. But an institutional failure to grasp the implications of a sacred text does not make those implications less powerful. Though the Book of Mormon's writers don't always toe the line, and though the practices of its adherents frequently fall short of the ideal, the Book of Mormon narrative never strays far from the ideal advanced in 4 Nephi 1:17: "Neither were there Lamanites, nor any manner of -ites; but they were in one, the children of Christ, and heirs to the kingdom of God."

CHAPTER FOUR

Reimagining the Exodus

The escape from bondage, the wilderness
journey, the Sinai covenant, the promised land:
all these loom large in the literature of revolution.
Indeed, revolution has often been imagined as an
enactment of the Exodus and the Exodus has often
been imagined as a program for revolution.
—Michael Walzer, *Exodus and Revolution*

Not only does Exodus seem to blind its intellectuals
to the rights of others, it permits them to believe that
history—the world of societies and nations, made by men
and women—vouchsafes certain peoples the extremely
problematic right of "Redemption." . . . Redemption, alas,
elevates human beings in their own judgment to the status
of divinely inspired moral agents. And this status in turn
minimizes, if it does not completely obliterate, a sense of
responsibility for what a people undergoing Redemption
does to other less fortunate people, unredeemed, strange,
displaced, and outside moral concern.
—Edward Said, "Michael Walzer's *Exodus and Revolution*:
A Canaanite Reading"

It is not often that secular public intellectuals get into spats about the proper typological interpretation of an Old Testament story. It happened in 1986, though, when the high-profile political theorist Michael Walzer published *Exodus and Revolution*, in which he labels the book of Exodus "a paradigm of revolutionary politics" that develops "the idea of a deliverance from suffering and oppression: this-worldly redemption, liberation, revolution."[1] Soon after its publication, the equally high-powered literary and cultural critic Edward Said wrote a rebuttal in an article that he called a "Canaanite reading" of Walzer's book. The story of Exodus, he argues, is a story of liberation and redemption only for the Israelites. It is quite another story for the Canaanites, who were already living in the "promised land" when their distant cousins came to take possession. For them, it was a story of conquest and colonization and being on the wrong end of a divinely authorized genocide.[2]

Beneath the surface of this debate between liberal academic superstars lurked a political question more contemporary than the biblical conquest of Canaan. Walzer is a strong supporter of the modern state of Israel. Said (who died in 2003) was both a Palestinian and one of the best-known post-colonial critics of the twentieth century. Their debate about Exodus is really a debate about the modern problem of Israeli settlement, as Said himself makes clear:

> According to Walzer, we are fully entitled to reject anything about Exodus that smacks of mere territorialism, since what matters is the "deeper argument" proposing "that righteousness " is the only guarantee of blessings." In applying these notions to Zionism, Walzer seems to align himself with those Israelis who want a compromise over the territories occupied by Israel since 1967, and he cites Gershom Scholem in support of the view that Zionism is not a messianic movement, but a historically—as opposed to a religiously—redemptive one.[3]

While Walzer does not explicitly justify the biblical Israelites' dispossessing the Canaanites, he ignores this aspect of the story to concentrate on the inspiring portrayal of freedom and revolution. But this is precisely Said's point: In order to draw inspiration from the story of the Israelite slaves rising up against their masters and gaining their freedom, we must ignore the second half of the story, contained mainly in Joshua and Judges, in which those same former slaves dispossess and murder another group of people. Focusing on the redemptive elements of the story, as Said argues, "elevates human beings . . . to the status of divinely inspired moral agents" and "minimizes . . . responsibility for what a people undergoing Redemption does to other less fortunate people."[4] A recent Christian interpreter is even harsher: "The story Joshua tells intersects with modern stories of conquest, dispossession, and mass killing, while the sentiments that infuse it—militant triumphalism, the construction and demonization of indigenous others, appeals to the divine to legitimize the confiscation of territory—resonate with motifs that configure the narratives of colonial empires to this very day."[5]

The text makes it very clear that God himself, through Moses, mandates genocide. In his instructions to Israelites on the eve of the conquest, Moses tells them that God will deliver the nations of Canaan into their hands, "and when the Lord thy God shall deliver them before thee; thou shalt smite them, and utterly destroy them; thou shalt make no covenant with them, nor shew mercy unto them" (Deut 7:2). If we accept the words of Moses as instructions from God—and there can be little doubt that the text of Deuteronomy presents them as exactly that—then we must also accept the judgment of the British theologian Gareth Lloyd Jones: "That which would be regarded as the most heinous crime in any civilised society is not just acceptable in ancient Israel, it is a fundamental religious obligation. . . . How does it represent Israel's God? A few adjectives spring to mind: xenophobic, militaristic, racist, exclusivist, barbaric."[6]

Both liberation and conquest are embedded deep in the heart of the Exodus typology, and there is no way to separate them from each other. The use of Exodus as a figural model for political liberation traces at least back to the work of the fourth-century Christian scholar Eusebius of Caesarea, who frequently cast the Christian emperor Constantine as a new Moses leading Roman Christians out of obscurity and persecution and into the promised land of political prominence.[7] The inspiring story of Moses setting his people free has always resonated with oppressed people in Christian lands. In the United States, it permeated the spirituals of American slaves and the speeches of abolitionists and came to a crescendo in the soaring rhetoric of Martin Luther King and the civil rights movement.[8] The story emphasizes God's love for oppressed people and his willingness to lead slaves to freedom. But the story cannot sustain these noble sentiments all the way to the end. The same God who tells Moses to liberate the children of Israel and lead them to the promised land also authorizes the genocidal conquest and colonization of the people already inhabiting said promised land. "The conquest of Canaan," explains David Brion Davis, "provided an example of divinely sanctioned colonization and violent displacement that was not lost on the English colonizers of Ireland and then North America."[9]

The nature of the Exodus typology was very much on the minds of the first English settlers in North America. The English had long considered themselves to be God's chosen people, and the Puritans who immigrated to America saw themselves as fleeing the fleshpots of London for a new Canaan.[10] The typological role of the Native Americans was less clear. Alfred Cave explains that "while some were serenely confident that the English would be the instruments of Indian redemption, others found in the scriptural accounts of the Almighty's use of the Israelites to exterminate the idolaters of Canaan a probable key to God's plan for those Indians whom the Devil would no doubt impel to resist the coming of the New Elect." Not all Puritans equated the American Indians with the Canaanites, but many of them did, and this typological connection "provided a rationale for righteous violence which would later color inter-racial interaction on the North American frontier."[11]

If we bracket the Book of Mormon's paratextual assumptions about race and Indian origins, the First Book of Nephi becomes a straightforward invocation of the Exodus type: A group of people are led by a prophet of God out of a great city where they face the imminent threat of captivity. They wander in the wilderness for a time, during which they frequently complain about their hardships, but the Lord guides them and sustains them through supernatural means. Finally, God brings them miraculously through a great body of water and to a promised land that has been prepared for them to inherit. But then the story changes. When the Lehites arrive in the promised land, it is empty.[12] There are no conquests, no military campaigns, no marching around the city walls playing trumpets. And there is no genocide. The thirty or so people in Lehi's extended family don't have to soak themselves in divinely mandated gore to receive their inheritance. They just land on the shores of a land full of everything they need and start living there.

The second major iteration of the Exodus type in the Book of Mormon occurs in the book of Omni—a very short transitional section of the scripture that contains the records of five Nephite authors, most of whom do little more than register their names and establish a chain of custody for the Nephite records.[13] Yet the final narrator of Omni, Amaleki, tells one of the most significant stories in the Book of Mormon. After extended conflicts between the Nephites and the Lamanites, the Lord warned a righteous man named Mosiah that "he should flee out of the land of Nephi—and as many as would hearken unto the voice of the Lord should also depart out of the land with him into the wilderness" (Omni 1:12). The Nephites eventually discover an inhabited city that welcomes them with open arms:

> And they discovered a people which was called the people of Zarahemla. Now there was great rejoicing among the people of Zarahemla, and also Zarahemla did rejoice exceedingly because that the Lord had sent the people of Mosiah with the plates of brass, which contained the record of the Jews.
>
> Behold, it came to pass that Mosiah discovered that the people of Zarahemla came out from Jerusalem at the time that Zedekiah, king of Judah, was carried away captive into Babylon; and they journeyed in the wilderness and was brought by the hand of the Lord across the great waters into the land where Mosiah discovered them; and they had dwelt there from that time forth. And at the time that Mosiah discovered them, they had become exceedingly numerous. Nevertheless they had had many wars and serious contentions and had fallen by the sword from time to time. And their language had become corrupted; and they had brought no records with them. And they denied the being of their Creator. And Mosiah—nor the people of Mosiah—could not understand them.

But it came to pass that Mosiah caused that they should be taught in his language. And it came to pass that after they were taught in the language of Mosiah, Zarahemla gave a genealogy of his fathers according to his memory; and they are written, but not in these plates. And it came to pass that the people of Zarahemla and of Mosiah did unite together, and Mosiah was appointed to be their king. (Omni 14–19)

The story of the Nephites discovering Zarahemla inverts the moral logic of the Israelite conquest of Canaan. Both stories begin with an exodus in which a group of people are miraculously delivered from an enemy and led to an inhabited region. In the Bible, though, the protagonists violently displace the inhabitants of their promised land—with God's support and approval. In the Book of Mormon, the inhabitants of Zarahemla cheerfully embrace the Nephites, recognize their kinship with them, and invite Mosiah to become their king and the other Nephites to become an elite ruling class. The text records no acts of violence, no armed resistance, and no divinely sanctioned acts of genocide. The Book of Mormon offers all of the good things about this exodus—divine intervention, prophetic leadership, redemption, and liberty—with none of the problems.

Or does it?

As the Zarahemla story unfolds, the colonization-without-conquest narrative becomes unstable, and we can see the ugly face of genocide peeking out from the corners of the text. The books of Alma and Helaman contain shocking acts of violence in three separate conflicts that break into open warfare between the Nephites of Zarahemla and various groups of political and religious dissidents—the Amlicites, the Zoramites, the people of Ammonihah, the Amalakites, the King-Men, and the Amalickiahites. The text does not explicitly connect any of these groups to the native Zarahemlans, but some details in each case suggest such a connection. The Exodus type is one of the clearest, most obvious narrative connections between the Bible and the Book of Mormon, and the narrators of the latter work diligently to launder the type-scene. The fact that they try so hard to decouple stories of miraculous exodus from stories of subsequent violence demonstrates just how problematic the Exodus type-scene is as a story of God's love and mercy. The fact that they fail demonstrates that the problem may not be in the framing of the typological narrative but in the underlying reality that the typology represents. This reality was playing itself out on the American stage in 1830, when the Book of Mormon was first published, as colonial settlers were actively displacing indigenous people while aggressively portraying the land they were colonizing as empty.

The Exodus Type in the Book of Mormon

One need look no further than the text of the Book of Mormon to find evidence that it intentionally connects its own Exodus narrative to the one in the Bible. Nephi knows that he is writing his family into the sacred history by reenacting the founding event of their faith. He specifically invokes the typology of Exodus when he tells his brothers, who have just been cast out of Laban's presence while trying to obtain the brass plates, that they should "be strong like unto Moses, for he truly spake unto the waters of the Red Sea and they divided hither and thither, and our fathers came through out of captivity on dry ground, and the armies of Pharaoh did follow and were drowned in the waters of the Red Sea" (1 Ne 4:2). "Nephi is keenly aware of his distinct moment in history," explains BYU professor of comparative literature George S. Tate in one of the first articles to discuss the Exodus typology in the Book of Mormon. He realizes that "he and his family are reenacting a sacred and symbolic pattern that looks back to Israel and forward to Christ," and he organizes his narrative accordingly—a strategy that Mormon picks up and uses for the remainder of the Book of Mormon.[14]

Later in the narrative, Nephi argues with his brothers about the precise significance of the Exodus story in their own lives. The discussion occurs in the land of Bountiful, immediately after God instructs Nephi to build a ship. Laman and Lemuel respond, "Our brother is a fool, for he thinketh that he can build a ship" (1 Ne 17:17). They also argue that both the ship and the journey are unnecessary because Jerusalem is under God's protection and its people have obeyed the Law of Moses. "We know that the people which were in the land of Jerusalem were a righteous people, for they kept the statutes and judgments of the Lord and all his commandments according to the law of Moses," the brothers claim. "Wherefore, we know that they are a righteous people" (1 Ne 17:22). Nephi takes the opportunity to reinterpret the meaning of the Exodus. It is not a story about God saving a righteous people, he tells them, but of God chastising complaining children who are upset that they had to leave their comfortable captivity in Egypt:

> And it came to pass that I Nephi spake unto them, saying: Do ye believe that our fathers, which were the children of Israel, would have been led away out of the hands of the Egyptians if they had not hearkened unto the words of the Lord? Yea, do ye suppose that they would have been led out of bondage if the Lord had not commanded Moses that he should lead them out of bondage? Now ye know that the children of Israel were in bondage, and ye know that they were laden with tasks which were grievous to be borne. Wherefore ye know that it must needs be a good thing for them

that they should be brought out of bondage. Now ye know that Moses was commanded of the Lord to do that great work. And ye know that by his word the waters of the Red Sea [were] divided hither and thither, and they passed through on dry ground.

. . .

And now, do ye suppose that the children of this land, which were in the land of promise, which were driven out by our fathers, do ye suppose that they were righteous? Behold, I say unto you: Nay. Do ye suppose that our fathers would have been more choice than they if they had been righteous? I say unto you: Nay. Behold, the Lord esteemeth all flesh in one; he that is righteous is favored of God. But behold, this people had rejected every word of God, and they were ripe in iniquity, and the fulness of the wrath of God was upon them. And the Lord did curse the land against them and bless it unto our fathers. Yea, he did curse it against them unto their destruction, and he did bless it unto our fathers unto their obtaining power over it. (1 Ne 17:23–26, 33–35)

Nephi's rejoinder contains a revision of the Exodus type with significant theological consequences. The assumption that Laman and Lemuel make— that the Exodus demonstrates God's unique love for the nation of Israel as long as they follow the law of Moses—corresponds closely to the assumption of the Deuteronomists who crafted large portions of the Hebrew Bible during the Babylonian captivity. This does not mean that the Deuteronomists came to the same conclusions. Laman and Lemuel, working before the Babylonian captivity, claimed that Jerusalem could not be destroyed because its inhabitants followed the law of Moses. The Deuteronomists, trying to understand the captivity after it happened, argued that Jerusalem was destroyed because the Jews did not follow the law of Moses. These arguments have the same initial assumption, which is that the Jews enjoyed the special favor of God and could not be destroyed as long as they observed the law. Nearly everything we know about the conquest of Canaan (including the assertion that it occurred at all) comes from the Deuteronomistic portion of the Old Testament.[15]

Nephi uses the story of Moses to refute the two principal claims of the Deuteronomists, both of which appear in the arguments that Laman and Lemuel make: (1) that the Israelites of Moses's time were more righteous than other people and (2) that God loved the Israelites more than other people (and was, therefore, willing to command genocide to give them the promised Land). Against the first assumption, Nephi argues that "this people had rejected every word of God, and they were ripe in iniquity." Against the second, he asserts, "the Lord esteemeth all flesh in one; he that is righteous is favored of God"—shifting the basis of God's favor away from Abrahamic lineage to personal righteousness. Under Nephi's interpretation of the Exodus story, there can be no warrant for the wholesale ethnic cleansing of the Canaanite population simply because they were not part of the Abrahamic covenant.

The way the Book of Mormon refigures the Exodus narrative—by replicating the escape and wilderness sections with great typological fidelity and then eliminating the colonization and conquest in act 3—corresponds exactly to the way Nephi reformulates Deuteronomistic theology. These innovations combine to create a canon that rejects "chosen people" narratives based on race or lineage. As Kimberly Matheson and Joseph Spencer point out, this rejection is made explicit by Nephi's younger brother, Jacob, in the sermon that he delivers in the third chapter of the book that bears his name. Jacob rebukes his fellow Nephites for judging the Lamanites based on the color of their skin. "Wherefore a commandment I give unto you, which is the word of God, that ye revile no more against them because of the darkness of their skin" (Jacob 3:9).[16] We should not overlook the importance that such a reinterpretation of the Bible could have had in early nineteenth-century America, a Bible-saturated society that deployed aspects of biblical history and theology to justify the enslavement of one race of humans and the forced migration of another.

Along with being a site of typological connection between the Bible and the Book of Mormon, the Exodus story is an important internal type-scene within the Book of Mormon itself. Both Mormon and Nephi use it to introduce key sections of the text. "The Exodus reverberates through the book," Tate argues, "not only as theme but as pattern; and the overall design of the book generalizes the patterning of community in history while at the same time concentrating the Exodus in individual conversion."[17] Tate and others have identified six subsequent scenes in the Book of Mormon that contain most or all of the elements of the Exodus type:

> 2 Ne 5:5–10: After the Lehites come to the promised land, they divide into two factions, one led by Nephi and the other led by Laman. As hostility between the two groups increases, the Lord warns Nephi that he "should depart from them and flee into the wilderness, and all they which would go with" him (2 Ne 5:5). The Nephites leave the first settlement and establish the land of Nephi, which (by all indications given in the text) they find empty. This scene begins the separation of the family of Lehi into Nephites and Lamanites.
>
> Omni 1:12–19: This is the second major exodus scene discussed in the chapter introduction above. Though it happens in a transitional sec-

tion of the Book of Mormon, and therefore comes with very few details, the exodus of the Nephites from the land of their original settlement is much more like the biblical narrative than any of the other instances of the Exodus typology. About three centuries after Nephi founded the first Nephite colony, prolonged conflicts with the Lamanites threatened the colony's population, and Mosiah led them into the wilderness. After an unspecified amount of time, the people of Mosiah discover a large city called Zarahemla. The Zarahemlans, having lost their original language and their religious beliefs, welcome the Nephites and make Mosiah the king of a united Nephite-Zarahemlan nation (Omni 1:19). This iteration of the Exodus type does not, like previous ones, depend on the promised land being vacant; rather, it frames the original inhabitants of the land as the willing subjects of the chosen people.

Mosiah 18:34: This is the first of three exodus type-scenes set in the Land of Nephi after a group of Nephites from Zarahemla travel back to their ancestral land to set up a colony that has no contact with the main body of Nephites. After a priest in this colony named Alma leaves the court of its corrupt king, Noah, he establishes his own church, and the king mobilizes an army to attack him and his followers. The new church is "apprised of the coming of the king's army. Therefore they [take] their tents and their families and [depart] into the wilderness." This scene creates the first Church of Christ in Book of Mormon lands.

Mosiah 22:9–12: After Limhi replaces Noah as king of the Nephites in the land of Nephi, his people experience increasing demands for tribute from the Lamanites. In response, Limhi provides a large tribute of wine to the Lamanites and, while they are in a deep sleep, the Nephites "depart by night into the wilderness . . . and they [go] round about the land of Shilom in the wilderness and ben[d] their course towards the land of Zarahemla" (Mosiah 22:11) This scene ends the parallel narrative of the Nephite settlement in the land of Nephi.

Mosiah 24:18–20: After the people of Alma flee the domain of King Noah, they settle in the Land of Helam, which is later conquered by the Lamanites. The Lamanite king makes Amulon, the former chief priest of King Noah, the governor of this area, and Amulon begins to persecute Alma and his people mercilessly. Once again, the people of the church "in the nighttime [gather] their flocks together" (Mosiah 24:18) and depart "into the wilderness" (Mosiah 18:20) to become subjects of King Mosiah, uniting the three different Nephite groups in Zarahemla.

Ether 1:39–42: As the Lord is confounding the languages at the Tower of Babel, the brother of Jared prays that he and his family will be spared. The Lord grants the petition and instructs Jared and his family to gather their flocks and seeds and depart into the wilderness. The Jaredites are led to a promised land, where they flourish for more than a thousand years before they destroy themselves. This scene begins the Jaredite narrative, which, in the text's internal chronology, occurs more than fifteen hundred years before the destruction of Jerusalem.

At the end of his article Tate appends a two-page chart showing points of similarity between the biblical Exodus, its fulfillment in the New Testament, and its corresponding similarities in the various Exodus type-scenes in the Book of Mormon.[18] But neither Tate nor the many critics who built on his work took notice of the one overwhelming difference between the biblical Exodus and every repetition of the type in the Book of Mormon: Not one of the seven Exodus type-scenes ends with the explicit violent conquest of a foreign people.[19]

In three of the Book of Mormon's Exodus scenes—the original flight from Jerusalem and the subsequent narratives in 1 Nephi and Esther—the promised land is presented as empty (or, at least, not clearly presented as inhabited or in need of conquest).[20] In the other four, they settle in occupied lands where they are welcomed by the inhabitants and often given leadership positions in both church and state. All four of these episodes occur within the context of the Nephite discovery of Zarahemla—the major Exodus scene narrated in Omni and three scenes involving the group of Nephites who return to colonize the land of Nephi and, three generations later, return to Zarahemla through a series of divinely assisted escapes from their enemies. Together, these four scenes initiate the second major stage of the Book of Mormon's narrative arc, which takes place in Zarahemla, the capital city established when the Nephites combined with an established indigenous population who also trace their ancestry back to pre-exilic Jerusalem and to a man named Mulek, the son of King Zedekiah, the king of Judah at the time Lehi and his family left the city.[21] The text does not explain how the Mulekites escaped Jerusalem or emigrated to the New World, but the brief history given in the text claims that they did so and then lived in the promised land for nearly four centuries with no mention of encounters with Nephites or Lamanites until the meeting described in Omni.

But there are good reasons to suspect that a Mulekite narrative, if such a thing existed, would tell a very different story. On its face, the Nephite story sounds like the story that colonizers have always created to justify their destruction of colonized cultures. According to these accounts, superior cultures have both a right and a duty—Kipling called it "the white man's burden"—to govern "inferior" people and give them the benefit of their science, their art, and their institutions.[22] The text of the Book of Mormon shows the Nephites doing the same things that settler colonialists invariably do when they conquer a land that has already been colonized. Over the course of the books of Mosiah, Alma, and Helaman, the Nephites create a ruling class with themselves at the top, impose a new religion on the populace, actively fight against native religious beliefs, eradicate the Zarahemlan language, and entirely erase the category of Zarahemlan, or Mulekite, as a possible identity. As they do these things, they fight three disastrous civil wars in a period of fifty years. In each case, the record presents these as wars caused by "Nephite dissenters," but the text contains abundant evidence that these dissenters are actually part of the native Zarahemlan population who refused to assimilate.

Recent scholarly treatments of the Book of Mormon highlight the value of reading the text against the grain of its Nephite narrators. "They write only to prop up Nephite cultural identity," claims Jared Hickman, and the resulting narrative "thus comes into view as an ethnocentric document, the governing cultural myth of the Nephite people."[23] If we read the story against the narrators who created the Nephite record, suggests Peter Coviello, the Book of Mormon itself becomes an anti-imperialist text:

> Read against the grain not of its narrative but of its narrators, this sacred and authorizing epic is secretly the story of a vilified people triumphing over enemies who, though they cannot conceive of themselves as anything other than the very pattern of exemplary and God-sanctioned virtue, are actually hubristic, backsliding, unself-knowing, and, finally, wicked. More than this, the Nephites, for all their self-heroization, are in fact damned, speeding toward a just and God-authored annihilation. In this way, the Book of Mormon may be less an exemplification of colonizing racism (and racist historiography) than a sustained performed critique of it, in which it is exactly the Nephites' imperiousness, their incapacity to recognize themselves as anything other than chosen and holy and their foes as anything other than benighted and racially degraded, that dooms them.[24]

Coviello is speaking mainly about the Nephites' relationship with the Lamanites, but his argument applies equally well to their relationship with the native Zarahemlans. To get to their story, we must try to make the text's silences speak. The strategies for doing this have been carefully worked out by post-colonial critics who have used them, often with spectacular results, to reassess novels, poems, histories, and other texts created by colonizer cultures. Edward Said, who provided the post-colonial reading of Exodus with which this chapter began, borrowed the musical term "contrapuntal" to describe the sort of interpretation that I am describing. "Contrapuntal reading," he explains, "must take account of both processes, that of imperialism and that of resistance to it, which can be done by extending our reading of the texts to include what was once forcibly excluded."[25]

Merger or Acquisition? A Contrapuntal Reading of Alma 1–3

If we take the Book of Mormon at its word, the distinction between the Nephites and the Zarahemlans simply vanished after the two peoples merged into one. Everyone became a Nephite. When the book of Mosiah opens, the land is at peace, the second generation of the Nephite monarchy is ending, and Mosiah's son, King Benjamin, is preparing to give his final address to the people. By this time, the text describes all of the people as Nephites. Everyone speaks the Nephite language and worships the Nephite God—and four centuries of Mulekite culture and religion have simply vanished into thin air, never to be (officially) heard from again.

Amaleki's narrative at the end of Omni becomes the official version of the merger between the two cultures, but his story contains warning signs that should alert readers to possible instabilities in his narrative. First, he attributes the mutual unintelligibility of their languages to the fact that the Zarahemlan language "had become corrupted" and tells us that Mosiah "caused that they should be taught in his language" (Omni 1:16–17). This is how colonizers often describe the language of the people they colonize, and it imbeds the incorrect assumption that some languages are inherently better than others because they sound more like another high-prestige language. "The text's designation of the Mulekite language as 'corrupted' is problematic," writes Daniel Belnap, "as it may reveal a long-standing Nephite bias of cultural superiority attested early in their history. . . . The use of the term corrupted and Mosiah's directive for the Mulekites to learn Nephite and not the other way around suggests that, at least to the Nephite community, the Nephite language had remained pure to the mother tongue."[26] Colonial powers frequently try to stamp out native languages in order to discourage nationalist movements. And when they do, they invariably begin by framing native languages as corrupt or inferior.[27]

We might also view with suspicion the remarkable coincidence that, in an oral culture with no written language or system of recordkeeping, Zarahemla could immediately trace his ancestry back to the son of the very same king that had just ascended to the throne of Judah when Lehi's family left Jerusalem. This gave the Nephites and the Zarahemlens a shared history, and it framed the Nephites as the superior branch of the family because God chose them to preserve the records and, therefore, the language and the religion of their shared ancestors (Omni 1:18).[28] This is the sort of common genealogy that colonized people often create for themselves to curry favor with their colonizers or that colonizers create to facilitate assimilation and justify the subordinate role of indigenous people. As we have already seen, the Book of Mormon itself is one of several attempts to give American Indians an Old World genealogy for similar reasons. We are given only Amaleki's third-hand account of an oral tradition as evidence of the remarkable proposition that the Zarahemlans shared the Nephites' Hebraic ancestry. Other than this tradition—which both parties had incentives to exaggerate—we have no reason to see the people of Zarahemla as anything other than a group of indigenous inhabitants of a land that the Nephites claimed as their own.

None of this proves that the Nephites colonized Zarahemla with the same combination of military and cultural force that has always allowed some people to dominate others. But the collective weight of convenient coincidences should encourage us to read the rest of the text carefully to see if we can detect traces of a conquest narrative lurking beneath the official story. In a 1980 article, John Sorenson, a BYU anthropologist and staunch defender of the Book of Mormon's historicity, strongly implies just such a narrative. "It is difficult to interpret the extremely brief and one-sided account we have in Omni 1:13–19," Sorenson writes. "The story from the Nephite side represents the event as not only peaceful but enthusiastically welcomed by the locals. From the point of view of some of the resident people, however, the transition may not have seemed so pleasant." He concludes that "it is plausible that later 'contentions' and 'dissensions' in Nephite society were in part led by unhappy descendants of Zarahemla who considered that they were not given their due when Mosiah became king."[29] Writing in 2015, Brant A. Gardner agrees: "Much of later Nephite history," he suggests, "may be attributed to the easy fissionability along former Nephite/Zarahemlite religious and political systems. The distinctions were never far from the illusory political and or religious unity."[30]

The Book of Mormon does not contain a record of the first two generations of Nephite-Mulekite coexistence. The record known as the Small Plates of Nephi ends with Omni, with the group of Nephites led by Mosiah$_1$ finding Zarahemla.[31] The next record—the Large Plates of Nephi—begins about fifty-five years later.[32] The book of Mosiah$_2$ begins with an assurance that all is well: "There was no more contention in all the land of Zarahemla among all the people which belonged to king Benjamin, so that king Benjamin had continual peace all the remainder of his days" (Mosiah 1:1). The formulation "no more contention" suggests that there had been some contention in the preceding five decades.

On the surface, the introduction seems to suggest that tensions between the Nephites and the Zarahemlans have been resolved and that, while the two groups might not have become one people in the time of King Mosiah₁, they have definitely done so by the end of Benjamin's reign. But Benjamin's own words belie such a narrative. The first words he says in the text are spoken to his son, Mosiah₂. "My son," he begins, "I would that ye should make a proclamation throughout all this land among all this people, or the people of Zarahemla and the people of Mosiah which dwell in the land, that thereby they may be gathered together" (Mosiah 1:10). In these lines, Benjamin confirms that the people of Zarahemla are still divided into "the people of Mosiah" and "the people of Zarahemla"—and that division is the first thing that the king thinks of when he wants to address his subjects. By the end of the book of Mosiah, a division still exists. When Mosiah calls the people together to read the records of the lost colony in the land of Nephi, "all the people of Nephi [are] assembled together, and also all the people of Zarahemla, and they [are] gathered together in two bodies" (Mosiah 25:1–4). "Thus," writes Belnap, "for at least two or three generations following assimilation, the two primary cultural designations in Zarahemla remained separate and distinct from one another, even after a direct attempt to unite them."[33]

Belnap, Gardner, and Sorenson all converge on an interpretation of the Nephite-Mulekite merger as more of a colonization than a merger of equals. If this is correct, then we should see evidence of it in the text. We should see signs of the suppressed Zarahemlan culture and religion resurfacing in inconvenient ways. We should see traditional native beliefs reasserting themselves to the chagrin of the dominant religion. We should see political movements that try to destabilize the government and forcibly disrupt the illusion of unity. And we should see acts of violence comparable to the violence that we did not see in the original colonization narrative. We should, in other words, see the return of the repressed—evidence of colonial violence bursting out of the text in spite of the narrator's best attempts to keep it down. If we look carefully, we can find all of these things in the book of Alma, where the elegant tapestry of Nephite unity that Mormon weaves in Mosiah begins to unravel.

Two things happen at the end of Mosiah that have significant implications for the population of Zarahemla. First, the Nephites from the colony in the land of Nephi (whose story comprises Mosiah 7–24) emigrate to Zarahemla. These new Nephites are refugees who escaped domination by providing the Lamanites with wine and slipping away under the cover of night (Mosiah

22:9–12). Even without further complications, a large refugee population that identifies strongly with one culture but not the other would threaten to undermine any balance between Nephites and native Zarahemlans that may have existed under Mosiah₁ and Benjamin. Moreover, the new Nephites come with a new church—an organized religious institution that fits perfectly into the Nephites' Christological tradition but was alien to the beliefs of the native Zarahemlans (Omni 1:17).

Shortly before he dies, King Mosiah₂ institutes the second major change in Zarahemlan society: He abolishes the monarchy and institutes a limited form of popular rule. His decision is driven by the fear of a civil war after his sons all declare that they do not want to become king (Mosiah 29:3). Mosiah realizes that, if he appoints a king while his sons are still alive, he will create a dangerous situation that could flare into a war should the rightful heir ever decide to claim his inheritance. This would lead to "wars and contentions . . . which would be the cause of shedding much blood and perverting the way of the Lord, yea, and destroy the souls of many people" (Mosiah 29:7–9). In place of the monarchy, Mosiah institutes a hierarchically organized network of judges, chosen by the "voice of the people," with a chief judge at the top (Mosiah 29:10–12, 28–29).[34] In a society like Zarahemla, in which a minority faction rules over the majority, transitions produce instability, and instability exacerbates divisions, as different groups vie for power under the new system. This happens in Zarahemla throughout the reign of the judges, but the determination of the Nephite recordkeepers to erase any distinction between Nephites and Zarahemlans often prevents us from seeing clearly that this very distinction is responsible for nearly all the conflicts recorded in the books of Alma and Helaman.

The social consequences of these two major transitions—the influx of Nephite refugees and the instability caused by a political transition—become much clearer when Alma the Younger becomes the leader of both the Nephite church and the Zarahemlan state, consolidating in a single person the power held by both Alma₁ and Mosiah₂. From the Nephite perspective, such a consolidation would have appeared natural; kings had always had authority over the state religion, and now that there was a state church, the successor to the king would naturally be its head. But from the perspective of at least some of the native Zarahemlans—who had endured three generations of Nephite kings and who likely thought that a popular election would give them more representation in the government—Alma's election represented a final confirmation of the Nephite colonization of their culture. That the Nephites controlled the state despite being a minority of the people meant either that a substantial number of Zarahemlans sympathized with the

Nephites or that the mechanisms for ascertaining "the voice of the people" favored the voice of the minority in power.

Alma's first test comes in the form of a popular religious leader named Nehor, who is accused of killing a prominent Nephite named Gideon in a dispute over religion:

> And it came to pass that in the first year of the reign of Alma in the judgment seat, there was a man brought before him to be judged, a man which was large and was noted for his much strength. And he had gone about among the people, preaching to them that which he termed to be the word of God, bearing down against the church, declaring unto the people that every priest and teacher had ought to become popular and they ought not to labor with their own hands, but that they had ought to be supported by the people.
>
> And he also testified unto the people that all mankind should be saved at the last day and that they need not fear nor tremble, but that they might lift up their heads and rejoice, for the Lord had created all men and had also redeemed all men; and in the end all men should have eternal life. And it came to pass that he did teach these things so much that many did believe on his words, even so many that they began to support him and give him money. And he began to be lifted up in the pride of his heart and to wear very costly apparel, yea, and even began to establish a church after the manner of his preaching. (Alma 1:2–6)

We must take care not to let Alma$_2$'s harsh religious judgments of Nehor's doctrines muddy the political picture. The text repeatedly assures us that people have freedom to choose their own religious beliefs with no compulsion from the state. "The law could have no power on any man for their belief" he writes (Alma 1:17), and "there was no law against a man's belief, for it was strictly contrary to the commands of God that there should be a law which should bring men onto unequal grounds" (Alma 30:7). Nehor's doctrine of universal salvation contradicts the Nephite church's emphasis on the importance of Christ's coming atonement.[35] Wide acceptance of such a doctrine would make it more difficult for the church to win converts. But in the panoply of ancient religious beliefs—which include ritual orgies, child sacrifice, and eating the hearts of one's enemies after a battle—the idea of universal salvation is not exactly the sort of belief that should test a state's commitment to religious freedom.

Nehor's second principle—that religious teachers "ought not to labor with their own hands, but that they had ought to be supported by the people" (Alma 1:3)—has never been particularly controversial anywhere in the world. Nearly every culture in the ancient world, including the Jerusalem that Lehi's family came from, supported a priestly class that officiated in the cultic rituals. The Pentateuch contains clear instructions for supporting the Levitical priests

(Num 18:18–30; Deut 18:1–5). Even the governing charter of the Nephite church included instructions that church members "should impart of their substance of their own free will and good desires towards God to those priests that stood in need" (Mosiah 18:28). It is difficult to see how believing that religious teachers should be paid, or accepting money from followers, rises to the level of an incorrect doctrine, much less a deadly heresy.[36]

But there is more at stake in this passage than a few controversial religious doctrines. Throughout the books of Alma and Helaman, nearly every dissident Nephite or breakaway political faction has ties to either Nehor's religion or to native Zarahemlan bloodlines—and often to both. Nehor's doctrines may have represented, as David Gore has suggested, "the evolution of doctrines once accepted and practiced among the Mulekites,"[37] or they could have been simply a convenient rallying point for anti-Nephite or anti-immigrant sentiments among the original inhabitants of Zarahemla. But the tense political environment created by Nehor's rise and support among the native population may be why Alma introduces religion into what looks like a straightforward murder case. Rather than simply trying Nehor for murder, Alma labels Nehor's doctrines "priestcraft" and frames them as dangers, not merely to true religion, but to the civic order. "This is the first time that priestcraft has been introduced among this people," he tells Nehor. "And behold, thou art not only guilty of priestcraft but hast endeavored to enforce it by the sword. And were priestcraft to be enforced among this people, it would prove their entire destruction" (Alma 1:12). Because murder carried an automatic death sentence in this society (Alma 1:18), the additional charge of enforcing priestcraft with the sword seems unnecessary. But if Alma were more concerned about the long-term influence of Nehorism than with punishing Nehor, he would try to make the trial more about the religion than the man.

Alma's charge of priestcraft appears to be based on Nephi's earlier statement that "priestcrafts are that men preach and set themselves up for a light unto the world, that they may get gain and praise of the world, but they seek not the welfare of Zion" (2 Ne 26:29). Contemporary readers of the Book of Mormon may over-rely on this previous definition in ways that its original readers would not have, having been more familiar with the term "priestcraft" in more political contexts. The term itself emerged from the English civil wars (1642–1651) to describe both Roman Catholicism and other state religions in which the state did not keep firm control over the clergy. In America, accusations of priestcraft became a staple of anti-Catholic rhetoric, as the accusation impugned the loyalty of all Catholics. All of the original British colonies in America had anti-Catholic ordinances, and seven of the original state constitutions prohibited Catholics from holding public office. Protestant Americans saw the Catholic clergy as agents of "priest-ridden" foreign monarchies such as France, Spain, and the Papal States. Priestcraft didn't simply mean a professional clergy. It meant a professional clergy working actively against the interests of the state.[38]

Americans believed that Catholics in public office would have more loyalty to these other nations than to the United States, and they saw priests as part of an organized foreign propaganda machine. Alma's use of the term "priestcraft" to describe Nehor exhibits similar concerns. The problem with Nehor's advocacy of paid religious teachers was not that it was wrong to pay people for religious duties. It was that, in creating professional priests who were not loyal to the state church, and whose religion contained elements fundamentally incompatible with the state church, Nehor would be building a network of potential full-time anti-government organizers. And these concerns are not unwarranted. We soon learn that both the Amlicites (Alma 2:1) and the Amalekites (Alma 21:4)—both of whom participate in rebellions against Alma and the Nephite state—follow the profession of Nehor.[39]

When we add these colonial dynamics to the story of Nehor, Alma's actions make more sense. Alma is facing an enormous crisis. He has inherited leadership of both the Nephite church that his father created in the previous generation and the new republican government that King Mosiah created before he died. Both institutions seem to have firm support from the Nephites—especially the most recent wave of immigrants from the land of Nephi—weaker support among the original Mulekite population of Zarahemla, and very little if any support from the native population in surrounding cities. Nehor appears on the scene and quickly gains support among people who feel displaced by the Nephite domination of both government and religion. He champions a theory of salvation that makes a foundational doctrine of the Nephite church irrelevant, and he creates an institution that will produce popular religious figures who, because they will be paid, can spend all of their time organizing disaffected Mulekites into a potent political or military force.

When Nehor kills Gideon, he creates a crisis that could bring down the new government. Gideon was a hero to the Nephite church. He had opposed King Noah back in the land of Nephi, when the king was persecuting members of Alma$_1$'s community (Mosiah 19:4–8). He then devised the plan that led the Nephites past the Lamanite armies when they escaped to Zarahemla (Mosiah 22:3–9). The micro conflict between Nehor and Gideon encapsulates the macro conflict in the land of Zarahemla, with tensions between the original population and the Nephite ruling class exacerbated by the second wave of Nephite immigrants and their new church. We can discern from the text that Alma did not believe it sufficient to convict Nehor of murder and execute him according to the law. Because this was a highly public case, it required an equally public refutation of Nehor's heresies, and, if at all possible, a confession from Nehor—not that he killed Gideon, the crime for which he was being tried—but that he intentionally led people astray by creating a religion that he knew to be false. Alma certainly knew that, unless he could discredit Nehor's teaching before executing him, the popular preacher would become a powerful martyr.

The end of Nehor's story contains precisely the kind of confession that Alma needed, but it comes in one of the most frustrating, yet intriguing passages in the entire Book of Mormon:

> And it came to pass that they took him—and his name was Nehor—and they carried him upon the top of the hill Manti, *and there he was caused [to] or rather did acknowledge* between the heavens and the earth that what he had taught to the people was contrary to the word of God, and there he suffered an ignominious death. (Alma 1:15, emphasis mine)

The narrative interjects a dramatic ambiguity just when we need it to be clear. It starts to say that Nehor "was caused" to acknowledge something, but the narrator immediately corrects this to "did acknowledge," removing what one might very plausibly consider evidence of some kind of coercion in this final testimony.[40] We don't know where this correction comes from: Alma or a contemporary scribe? Mormon in the final redaction? Joseph Smith in the oral translation? Oliver Cowdery in the written transcription? Under the terms of the narrative itself, any one of these would be possible. But, as Grant Shreve points out in his essay "Nephite Secularization," the "semantic gulf between 'was caused' [to] and 'did acknowledge' is not a trivial one and leaves the actual case of Nehor's repentance frustratingly indeterminate."[41]

Alma's plan to refute Nehor with his own confession did not work; the next verse informs us that Nehor's death "did not put an end to the spreading of priestcraft through the land, for there [were] many who loved the vain things of the world. And they went forth preaching false doctrines, and this they did for the sake of riches and honor" (Alma 1:16). Killing a popular religious leader is rarely a good way to destroy a religious movement. By executing Nehor, Alma creates a martyr and a powerful symbol of the Nephite dominance of church and state that will soon explode into full-scale revolt. The remainder of chapter 1 tells us two crucial things about the five-year period before the first great war begins:

1. Many people who had been converted to the church when Alma₁ first set it up leave it and "were remembered no more among the people of God. And also many withdrew themselves from among them" (Alma 1:24).
2. Significant socioeconomic inequality emerges between those who do and those who do not belong to the church. "Because of the steadiness of the church," Mormon tells us, "they began to be exceedingly rich, having abundance of all things whatsoever they stood in need: abundance of flocks and herds and fatlings of every kind, and also abundance of grain and of gold and of silver and of precious things. . . . And thus they did prosper and become far more wealthy than those who did not belong to their church" (Alma 1:29, 31).

When people feel that their culture and livelihood are being destroyed by immigrants, they invariably turn to nationalist demagogues who promise to restore their rightful place in the world. In Alma 2, which takes place five years after Alma becomes chief judge, just such a demagogue appears in the person of Amlici, an adherent of Nehor's religion. Mormon describes him, perhaps a bit defensively, as "after the order of the man that slew Gideon by the sword, who was executed according to the law" (Alma 2:1). Amlici's followers demand that the monarchy be restored with Amlici as the king, and the judges take this argument seriously enough to call all of the people together "to cast in their voices concerning the matter" (Alma 2:6). This, too, merits attention. This is the only occasion in the Book of Mormon in which the text acknowledges that a sitting judge must seek the voice of the people in order to continue ruling.[42] Since people rarely take political risks when they don't have to, this suggests that Alma had no choice because his governing mandate was on the line. Amlici's supporters represented a large enough faction that Alma had to take their demand seriously. He must have felt that, if he failed to submit the question to a popular vote, the opposition would resort to violence—which they in fact did when Amlici was rejected by the voice of the people and he commanded his supporters "that they should take up arms against their brethren" (Alma 2:10).

We should note that the followers of Amlici were not, in the strict sense, monarchists. They did not want to return to the monarchy and find a descendant of King Mosiah₂ to take the throne. If anything, they wanted to restore the Zarahemlan monarchy that Mosiah₁ supplanted. From their perspective, they gave the new government a chance, and they ended up with less power than they had under the king. The head of the Nephite church became the head of the new government, and the first thing he did (according to the record) was kill a popular religious figure who had great support among the native Zarahemlans. They gave the voice of the people another chance and tried to beat Alma$_2$ in a fair election, which they felt they should have won because of their superior numbers, but Alma$_2$ emerged from the election unscathed. The Amlicites' armed rebellion was thus neither irrational nor unpredictable. When a sizable faction of people in a democracy feel that they can never win an election—either because the faction they represent is a permanent minority or because they lack faith in the integrity of the voting process—they have no incentive to keep participating in civic affairs. And there will always be someone like Amlici telling them that they don't have to, that, if they will just follow him into battle, he can make Zarahemla great again.

In the course of the rebellion, the Amlicites are joined by an army of Lamanites (Alma 2:23–25), and they mount a joint attack on the Nephites. Soon, the Nephites discover that the Amlicites "had marked themselves with red in their foreheads after the manner of the Lamanites" (Alma 3:4). The Amlicites don't merely join forces with the Lamanites; they change their appearance to actually become Lamanites. And from this point on, everybody in the Book of Mormon is either a Nephite or a Lamanite:

> And it came to pass that whosoever would not believe in the tradition of the Lamanites, but believed those records which were brought out of the land of Jerusalem, and also in the tradition of their fathers, which were correct, which believed in the commandments of God and kept them, were called the Nephites or the people of Nephi from that time forth. And it is they which have kept the records, which are true, of their people and also of the people of the Lamanites.
>
> Now we will return again to the Amlicites, for they also had a mark set upon them; yea, they set the mark upon themselves, yea, even a mark of red upon their foreheads. Thus the word of God is fulfilled, for these are the words which he saith to Nephi: Behold, the Lamanites have I cursed; and I will set a mark upon them, that they and their seed may be separated from thee and thy seed from this time henceforth and forever except they repent of their wickedness and turn to me, that I may have mercy upon them. (Alma 3:11–14)

By the end of the Amlicite rebellion, Zarahemlan-Mulekite identity has been completely erased from the Book of Mormon. Everyone must forge an identity on one end of the Nephite-Lamanite binary that has operated in the text since the beginning of 2 Nephi. The text is explicit about this erasure. Descendants of Mulek who follow Alma, join the church, and participate in the new quasi-republican system of government become "Nephites." Those who stick to the old beliefs, who favor a restoration of the monarchy, or who take up arms to defend their non-Nephite beliefs are either "Lamanites" or "Nephite dissenters."[43] This is a textbook example of the phenomenon that post-colonial critics call "the binary logic of imperialism," or the impulse to reduce complicated situations and diverse populations to a simple binary that operates within the framework of the dominant culture. From the binary perspective, one set of terms represents everything the culture considers good (righteousness, whiteness, literacy, culture, religion = Nephites) and the other everything that it considers bad (unrighteousness, darkness, illiteracy, savagery, paganism = Lamanites). Such binary thinking tends to "suppress ambiguous or interstitial spaces between the opposed categories, so that any overlapping region . . . becomes impossible according to binary logic."[44]

And yet, for the rest of the book of Alma, and in the book of Helaman, too, the indigenous Zarahemlan identity persists in the corners of the text. The last third of Alma narrates a second civil war between the Nephites and the Amalickiahites, yet another group of "Nephite dissenters" with strong ties to the Zarahemlan population.[45] In Heleman, a third rebellion (by this point it makes sense to categorize this as a type-scene) is led by "a man whose name was Coriantumr, and he was a descendant of Zarahemla; and he was a dissenter from among the Nephites, and he was a large and mighty man" (Hel 1:15).[46] This revealing sentence tells us that 130 years after the supposedly friendly merger between the Nephites and the Zarahemlans, a descendent of the last Mulekite king is leading a rebellion against Nephite rule—a New World Bonnie Prince Charlie asserting his right to the throne. This suggests that the indigenous population of Zarahemla never assimilated fully with the Nephites—all of Mormon's assurances to the contrary—and that the religious, cultural, and socioeconomic differences between Mulekites and Nephites persisted throughout the reign of the judges and played a role in nearly all of the wars, rebellions, and dissident movements the text describes in great detail and attributes to other things.

Conclusion

In the contrapuntal reading that I propose, the books of Alma and Helaman in the Book of Mormon become the rough equivalents of the books of Joshua and Judges in the Old Testament: books that record the colonization and conquest that followed the Exodus. Alma's stories of dissident preachers, hostile cities, and major civil wars make much more sense when we see them as parts of a larger narrative of colonial resistance rather than as stand-alone stories of backsliding Nephites. Like most contrapuntal interpretations, this reading presumes a tension between the narrators and their narratives. This is always a tricky way to interpret any text, especially a text that many people consider sacred. Even more than most texts, scriptures come with a very strong presumption of narrative reliability. But unreliable narration cannot be avoided in any work that presents itself as history. Flawed and biased human beings create history and, under the Book of Mormon's own claims about itself, the original recorders of history were the people most involved in the events they describe—and therefore the least likely to have a disinterested point of view.

The names of the defeated Nephite dissenters underscore their similarity to the conquered Canaanites of the biblical Exodus. The Nephites contend with three key groups of dissenters: the Amlicites (Alma 2–3), the Amalickiahites (Alma 46–63), and the mysterious Amalekites (Alma 21–27), a previously unknown group of Nephites who lived among Lamanites and followed "the order of the Nehors" (Alma 21:4).[47] The names of all three people appear to have a common origin that links them to the Amalekites of the Bible, one of the main Canaanite tribes that the Israelites fought during the conquest and colonization of the promised land. The Israelites battled them under Joshua (Exod 17:8–13), and, hundreds of years later, under Saul, who is commanded by God to put the entire people under the ban—to "utterly destroy all that they have, and spare them not; but slay both man and woman, infant and suckling, ox and sheep, camel and ass" (1 Sam 15:3). The correspondence in their names underscores a correspondence in their typologies. In both the Bible and the Book of Mormon, the Amalekites are the people who already live in the places that the chosen people occupy after God leads them through a miraculous exodus.

In both works of scripture the Amalekites are a side effect of a miracle, a problem that needs to be solved in order to give closure to the epic narrative. The two most important iterations of the Exodus type-scene in the Book of Mormon deal with this aspect of the story in different ways. The Exodus of Lehi and his family, which opens the Book of Mormon, ends in an empty land—or, at least, a land that the text presents as uninhabited; therefore, there is no description of conquest. The exodus that happens right before the opening of the book of Mosiah, on the other hand, does involve native inhabitants in the land prepared for the faithful Nephites. And this narrative presents the Nephite colonization of Zarahemla as something that the city's inhabitants endorsed enthusiastically, thus demonstrating the Book of Mormon's superiority to the Bible and attempting to use typological connections to write conquest and genocide out of the typology that underlies the Exodus event.

As the story of Zarahemla progresses, the Book of Mormon's kinder, gentler colonialism starts to look more and more like the Israelite conquest of Canaan. The Nephites immediately become kings over the more numerous Zarahemlans, and when they abolish the monarchy, they ensure that the governing class consists primarily of fellow Nephites. They import a church and give it official sanction and favored status. And nearly every time the native Zarahemlans try to effect religious or political changes, the whole city ends up in a massive civil war in which the Mulekites and the Lamanites join forces to oppose the Nephites. As they are presented in the text, these wars are no less bloody than and every bit as destructive as the wars of conquest that the Israelites fight as they secure Israel from the Canaanites. The Book of Mormon presents both exodus and colonization more optimistically than the Bible does by challenging the idea that one people's miraculous victories always come at another people' divinely mandated defeats. But the alternative narrative that the Book of Mormon creates cannot withstand the facts that the narrative itself places in evidence. Against its best intentions, the Book of Mormon's Exodus narrative constantly undermines and disrupts its own narrators to show that stories of miraculous colonization invariably try to erase the impact that settler colonialism has on the colonized. And just as invariably, they fail to root out the traces of the people they erase.

CHAPTER FIVE

Divided Kingdoms

> Thus saith the Lord God; Behold, I will take the stick
> of Joseph, which is in the hand of Ephraim, and the
> tribes of Israel his fellows, and will put them with
> him, even with the stick of Judah, and make them
> one stick, and they shall be one in mine hand.
>
> —Ezekiel 37:16–19

Since the start of the Restoration movement, this passage from Ezekiel 37 has been presented as a biblical prophecy of the Book of Mormon.[1] According to the standard LDS interpretation, "sticks" in this passage refers to scrolls, or ancient books. The stick of Judah, then, represents the Bible, and the stick of Joseph represents the Book of Mormon, as Lehi claims descent from the biblical Joseph (2 Ne 3:4). The coming forth of the Book of Mormon to join the Bible as part of a new canon, according to this interpretation, represents the fulfillment of Ezekiel's prophecy that the two sticks shall become "one stick, and they shall be one in [God's] hand." This interpretation is canonized in section 27 of the Doctrine and Covenants, in which the Lord tells Joseph Smith that the Book of Mormon contains "the fulness of my everlasting gospel, to whom I have committed the keys of the record of the stick of Ephraim" (D&C 27:5).

The Mormon interpretation of Ezekiel 37 is starkly at odds with other Christian interpretations and Jewish ones, as well.[2] No other interpretive tradition holds that Ezekiel's sticks are books or scrolls or anything else that could be considered a scriptural text. The Hebrew word עֵץ can mean "tree," "timber," or "wood." It is the word used to describe the trees in the Garden of Eden in the opening chapters of Genesis—but there are no instances in the Hebrew Bible of it being used to describe a scroll or a book.[3] Most contemporary interpreters see this passage as a description of a "sign act," or a sort of prophetic visual aid that Ezekiel uses to describe the eventual reunification of Israel and the united monarchy.[4] In a recent article on Mormon interpretations, Joseph Spencer acknowledges that "the overall thrust of Ezekiel 37:15–19 is . . . entirely noncontroversial within the field of biblical scholarship. The point of the prophecy is to predict the reunification of divided Israel."[5] Despite a long tradition of interpreting Ezekiel's sticks as the Bible and the Book of Mormon, Spencer insists, this is not official doctrine, and "Latter-day Saints have no obvious reason to defend the idea that the word stick . . . actually refers to books or records or writing implements."[6]

However one interprets the passage in Ezekiel, there can be little doubt that the Book of Mormon presents itself as the inaugural event in a sequence that will culminate in the gathering of Israel, the Second Coming of Jesus Christ, and some version of the end of the world as we know it.[7] The apocalyptic vision that Nephi has in 1 Nephi 11–14 makes it clear that "the remnant of the seed of [Nephi's] brethren" were the "saving remnant" described by Isaiah that would inaugurate the restoration of Israel in the last days (Isa 11:11–16/2 Ne 21:11–16). At the end of 2 Nephi, after Nephi prophesies the coming forth of a book written by his descendants, he explains exactly how the Book of Mormon will usher in the millennial age. It will, he argues, convert the American Indians, who are a remnant of the line of Joseph, and then sweep over the earth, eventually converting the Jews to Jesus Christ. At that point, Joseph and Judah will be reunited, and both will accept both the Christian Bible and the Book of Mormon as records of God's dealings with their ancestors:

> For after the book of which I have spoken shall come forth and be written unto the Gentiles and sealed up again unto the Lord, there shall be many which shall believe the words which are written, and they shall carry them forth unto the remnant of our seed. . . . And the gospel of Jesus Christ shall be declared among them; wherefore they shall be restored unto the knowledge of their fathers and also to the knowledge of Jesus Christ, which was had among their fathers. . . . And it shall come to pass that the Jews which are scattered also shall begin to believe in Christ, and they shall begin to gather in upon the face of the land. And as many as shall believe in Christ shall also become a delightsome people. And it shall come to pass that the Lord God shall commence his work among all nations, kindreds, tongues, and people, to bring about the restoration of his people upon the earth. (2 Ne 30:3–8)

We should note that the first readers of the Book of Mormon would have seen nothing new in the idea that the Jews would convert en masse to Christianity before the Second Coming. This had been standard Puritan orthodoxy since the mid-seventeenth century. In England, it motivated Oliver Cromwell to partly rescind England's 366-year-old ban on Jewish settlement in 1656.[8] In New England, it led to a fascination with all things Jewish and a steady stream of books by well-known public figures such as Increase Mather's *The Mystery of Israel's Salvation* (1669) and Samuel Willard's *The Fountain Opened: or, The Admirable Blessings Plentifully to Be Dispensed at the National Conversion of the Jews* (1700).[9] The conversion of the Jews was a well-established part of the eschatological script that Joseph Smith and the early Mormons were working from. The Book of Mormon adds only the primary mechanism by which the conversion will occur, which is the Book of Mormon itself.

This scripture, then, presents its own publication as the event that will lead to the fulfillment of Old Testaments prophecies about the unification of Israel. And it presents the American Indians as the remnant of the tribes of Joseph that Isaiah and other Old Testament prophets referred to in their prophecies.[10] The Book of Mormon also presents the division and reunification of Joseph and Judah typologically, with the Nephites and the Lamanites acting as antitypes of the Kingdoms of Judah and Israel. Throughout the course of the Book of Mormon, the family of Lehi, like the family of Jacob, divides into tribes that assemble themselves into two deeply interconnected nations that recombine and split apart again in a different combination before one of them is destroyed and the other lives on as a remnant.

The Original Tribes

The closing chapters of Genesis constitute one of the clearest examples we have of a type-scene that repeats, in very similar circumstances, in the Book of Mormon. This occurs in the opening chapters of 2 Nephi, when the dying patriarch Lehi gathers his children and grandchildren for a series of blessings that have both a prophetic and a constitutional function. Most of Lehi's blessings are much longer than those in Genesis, and the two longest and most complex are reserved for the two sons born after the escape from Jerusalem: Jacob and Joseph, who, not at all coincidentally, have been named after the biblical patriarch and his most favored son. Lehi ties his blessings back to Genesis in his blessing of his own Joseph. As we saw in Chapter 1, Lehi identifies himself not only as a descendant of the biblical Joseph but as the "righteous branch" that fulfills Jacob's description of Joseph as "a fruitful bough by a well; whose branches run over the wall" (Gen 49:22/2 Ne 3:5).

The constitutional functions of Lehi's blessings are more difficult to see than, but just as important as, their prophetic functions. John W. Welch first identified this function in his essay "Lehi's Last Will and Testament: A Legal Approach," which briefly glosses ancient Near Eastern inheritance customs and argues that Lehi's blessings of his sons in 2 Nephi 1 functions exactly like

Jacob's blessings in 48–49 in creating a social structure that would govern the rest of the Book of Mormon. Lehi addresses his blessings, Welch notes, to exactly seven groups of descendants:

> Lehi spoke (1) to Zoram in 2 Nephi 1:30–32, (2) to Jacob in 2 Nephi 2, (3) to Joseph in 2 Nephi 3, (4) to the children of Laman in 2 Nephi 4:3–7, (5) to the children of Lemuel in 2 Nephi 4:8–9, (6) to the sons of Ishmael in 2 Nephi 4:10, and (7) to Sam together with Nephi in 2 Nephi 4:11. The seven groups recognizable here are exactly the same as the seven tribes mentioned three other times in the Book of Mormon, each time in the rigid order of "Nephites, Jacobites, Josephites, Zoramites, Lamanites, Lemuelites, and Ishmaelites" (Jacob 1:13; 4 Ne 1:37–38; Morm 1:8; see also D&C 3:17–18).[11]

If this analysis is correct, then Lehi does more than just give blessings to seven different groups. He explicitly follows the model of Jacob and organizes his posterity into exactly seven tribes. Much as Jacob adopted Ephraim and Manasseh, Lehi adopts Zoram, the servant of Laban who joined the Lehites after Nephi killed his master, into his own lineage.[12] He also very likely incorporates two unnamed daughters into the tribal structure by making a single tribe of the two sons of Ishmael who had become his sons-in-law.[13] And, for reasons not mentioned in the text, he combines the posterities of Nephi and Sam into a single tribe called simply "Nephites."

As Welch reports, these same tribal names occur in multiple places in the Book of Mormon, which correspond exactly to the seven groups, in order, that Lehi blessed. They first appear in the Book of Jacob, toward the beginning of the Book of Mormon, when Jacob announces Nephi's death and groups the people of the land into these seven groups (Jacob 1:13). They occur seven centuries later, in 4 Nephi, when, after two hundred years of living in a tribeless society, the people once again divide into the same seven groups (4 Ne 1:36–38). And then they appear in Mormon 1:8–9, at the very end of Nephite civilization—always the same tribes in the same order.[14] "The fact that this exact organization persisted so long," Welch writes, "is evidence that Lehi's last words to his sons in this regard were taken as constitutionally definitive—just as the organization of Israel into twelve tribes in the earlier age had been essential to the political, social, religious and legal structure there."[15]

The timing of Lehi's blessings is extremely important to our understanding of the Book of Mormon. They occur immediately before the curse in 2 Nephi 5 that divides the Lehites into Nephites and Lamanites. This means that the seven-tribe structure that Lehi created predates the two-tribe structure that the people fall in and out of for the rest of the Book of Mormon. "Nephite" and "Lamanite" are categories of convenience, and they mean different things

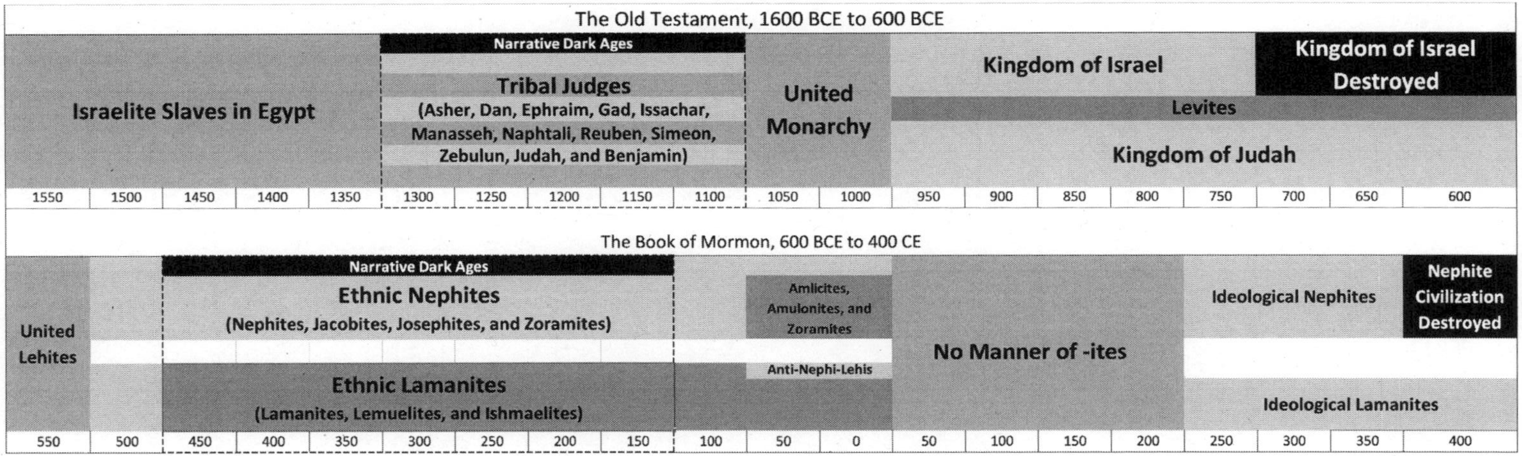

Figure 1. Unity and division among Bible and Book of Mormon peoples over one thousand years of civilization.

at different times in the story, but "Nephite, Jacobite, Josephite, Zoramite, Lamanite, Lemuelite, and Ishmaelite" appear to be divinely sanctioned divisions of people within a single united community to which they all belong. This makes them exactly parallel to the twelve tribes of Israel in the Hebrew Bible, while the Nephite-Lamanite division is—like the division between the northern and southern Kingdoms—a random and tragic split among people whom God intended to be together.

Figure 1 shows, in very broad strokes, the thousand-year trajectory of the main bodies of people in the Bible and the Book of Mormon. The Israelite narrative begins with the period of slavery and the exodus from Egypt, and the Lehite narrative begins with the exodus from Jerusalem before the Babylonian captivity.

From this figure we can see the similarities in the way both narratives have been shaped. In both cases, the people begin as a single group whose exodus from a great historical population center—Egypt in the Old Testament and Jerusalem in the Book of Mormon—is recorded in great detail. This burst of narrative activity is followed by periods of narrative silence lasting several hundred years, during which very little information is recorded.[16] In the Hebrew Bible this period is represented by the Book of Judges, while in the Book of Mormon it is represented by the very short books of Enos, Jerom, Omni, and the Words of Mormon, each of which consists of only a single chapter.[17] Both cultures emerge from the narrative dark ages, and, for a brief time, the people are unified in a single group that both texts present as the high point of their civilizations. Then the original divisions reassert themselves, and the people break into two superordinate groups that oppose each other until one group is destroyed and erased from the narrative. Through all of this, however, the idea of original unity remains a powerful cultural memory that eventually overwhelms the texts—both of which, in their final canonical forms, attempt to heal the divisions they describe.

The Divided Kingdoms of Israel

According to the biblical record, the united monarchy of Israel lasted for less than a hundred years, but it became the standard by which future writers of the Bible measured any future incarnation of Israel, mainly because it was supposed to last forever. The record is quite clear regarding this point. Soon after Saul's son Ishbosheth was murdered (2 Sam 4:6–7), ending the brief period of divided rule that followed Saul's death, David was anointed king over all of Israel (2 Sam 5:1–3). Soon thereafter, the prophet Nathan confirmed that the new dynasty would rule Israel forever:

Also the Lord telleth thee that he will make thee an house. And when thy days be fulfilled, and thou shalt sleep with thy fathers, I will set up thy seed after thee, which shall proceed out of thy bowels, and I will establish his kingdom. He shall build an house for my name, and I will stablish the throne of his kingdom for ever.... And thine house and thy kingdom shall be established for ever before thee: thy throne shall be established for ever. (2 Sam 7:11–13, 16)

Despite Nathan's multiple assurances, however, the house of David did not rule forever, and it did not rule over all of Israel for more than one generation after David's death. When his son Solomon died, the tribes of Israel gathered in Shechem to make his son Rehoboam the new king.[18] Solomon's temple and other building projects had increased taxation and labor requirements throughout Israel, however, and the northern tribes formally demanded that Rehoboam reduce these burdens (1 Kgs 12:4). Politically tone deaf and probably not very bright, Rehoboam announced that he had no intention of decreasing the tax burden on the people and that, in fact, that he planned to make it worse (ibid.). All of the tribes except Judah and Benjamin rejected Rehoboam and made Jeroboam, an Ephraimite, their king, dividing the monarchy that had only been united for three generations (1 Kgs 12:14–15). In both Kings and Chronicles, the story closes with the same words: "So Israel rebelled against the House of David unto this day" (1 Kgs 12:19; 2 Chr 10:19).

The new Ephraimite king faced a serious problem before his reign began. The only Yahwhist temple in the world was in Jerusalem, and sacrifices could not be performed anywhere else. The official cultic center of the Israelite religion was in a hostile foreign nation, which meant that Jeroboam's people would always have a reason to be loyal to the king of Judah. "If this people go up to do sacrifice in the house of the Lord at Jerusalem," Jeroboam says in his heart, "then shall the heart of this people turn again to their lord ... and they shall kill me and go again to Rehoboam king of Judah" (1 Kgs 12:16–27). To avoid this, Jeroboam makes two golden calves and sets them up at opposite ends of the kingdom and tells the people, "Behold thy gods, O Israel, which brought thee up out of the land of Egypt" (1 Kgs 12:28). In addition to replacing the temple with his own shrines, he replaced the Levites in the northern kingdom with his own priests—an impious action whose consequences reverberate throughout the Hebrew Bible.

The members of the tribe of Levi, alone among Israelites, did not receive a land inheritance; they were consecrated to God to be priests to all the tribes and ended up part of both kingdoms (Deut 18:1–5). Their livelihood depended on their ability to perform religious services, but Jeroboam "made priests of the lowest of the people, which were not of the sons of Levi" (1 Kgs 12:31). According to the book of Chronicles, the Levites of the northern kingdom revolted en masse against Jeroboam's rule and "left their suburbs and their possession, and came to Judah and Jerusalem, for Jeroboam and his sons had cast them off from executing the priest's office unto the Lord," writes the Chronicler (2 Chr 11:14). But the revolt included more than just the Levites, because "after them out of all the tribes of Israel such as set their hearts to seek the Lord God of Israel came to Jerusalem, to sacrifice unto the Lord God of their fathers. So they strengthened the kingdom of Judah, and made Rehoboam the son of Solomon strong" (1 Chr 11:16–17).

The apostasy of the northern kingdom set off a migration that began with the Levites but came to include people from "all the tribes of Israel." This is important to the narrative in at least two ways. First, it is an ironic comeuppance for Jeroboam, whose entire purpose in setting up altars in Dan and Bethel was to prevent people from doing what they in fact did, precisely because he set up those altars. More important, it gives us the first indication that we have in the text of ordinary Israelites placing religious identity above national loyalty. They became part of the kingdom of Judah because they could not practice their religion as part of the northern kingdom, and their opposition to Jeroboam took the form of political loyalty—not to Rehoboam, who very quickly departed from the ways of God (2 Chr 12:1), but to the idea of a restored Davidic monarchy in which all the tribes unite together the way that God meant them to.

Most scholars believe that the migration of the Levites and other tribes to the southern kingdom described in Chronicles had profound consequences for the creation of the Hebrew Bible. In *Levites and the Boundaries of Jewish Identity*, Mark Leuchter argues that the disaffected northern Levites eventually coalesced into the Deuteronomist school, which heavily influenced the development of the Pentateuch and produced the books of Deuteronomy, Joshua, Judges, 1 and 2 Samuel, and 1 and 2 Kings.[19] Leuchter joins a significant number of Old Testament scholars who see Levite immigrants as wholly or partly responsible for the parts of the Old Testament attributed to the Deuteronomist school.[20] The migration most likely came later than described in Chronicles—not in the tenth century BCE, when the united monarchy collapsed, but in the late eighth century BCE, after the northern kingdom fell to Assyria. With regard to the archeological evidence of dramatic population growth, Israel Finkelstein and Neil Asher Silberman conclude, that "up to half of the Judahite population in the late eighth/early seventh century BCE was of North Israelite origin cannot be too far from reality."[21] And these refugees brought with them a pan-Israelite ideology that shaped the historical parts of the Hebrew Bible. The Deuteronomistic history was hyperfocused on the relatively few times when the twelve tribes were united in the service of Yahweh: during the Exodus under Moses, the conquest of Canaan under Joshua, and the united monarchy under Saul, David, and Solomon. The division of the kingdom was a tragedy, and its eventual restoration became an article of faith.

Finkelstein and Silberman further see the early parts of the Deuteronomistic history as "an instrument for reconciliation between South and North *within* Judah, and a vehicle for the rise of pan-Israelite ideology."[22] The Kingdom of Judah had become a cosmopolitan center where the northern and southern tribes mingled freely. And the priestly castes from both kingdoms would likely have had what Mary Douglas referred to as an "ultramontane loyalty" to their shared heritage and faith. "They grieved over the ancient split between Judah and the Northern Kingdom of Israel; they dreaded another rift between the two great communities, both descended from Abraham, Isaac, and Jacob, both worshipping the same, unique, omnipotent God, both heirs to the great promises of Genesis."[23] And all of this eventually found its way into the Bible.

The restoration of Israel was a major theme of Jewish and Israelite prophecy even before the fall of the northern kingdom. But when the southern kingdom was destroyed and its inhabitants taken captive in Babylon, the prophets saw the redemption of the Jews as an inherently pan-Israelite affair. All of Israel would be restored together. Jeremiah, for example, wrote, "publish ye, praise ye, and say, O Lord, save thy people, the remnant of Israel. Behold, I will bring them from the north country, and gather them from the coasts of the earth" (Jer 31:7–8). And Ezekiel prophesied, "Thus saith the Lord God; Behold, I will take the children of Israel from among the heathen, whither they be gone, and will gather them on every side, and bring them into their own land: And I will make them one nation in the land upon the mountains of Israel; and one king shall be king to them all: and they shall be no more two nations, neither shall they be divided into two kingdoms any more at all" (Ezek 37: 21–22). The threatened destruction of Judah, as horrible as it was to those who lived through it, seemed to provide God with a good opportunity to restore everything at once, and this became an essential part of the prophets' message.

When Cyrus the Great conquered Babylon and permitted the Jews to return to Palestine and rebuild the temple, most pious Jews saw this as a fulfillment of the many prophecies of the restoration of Zion. Many of them expected that the lost tribes of Israel would be restored at the same time. But, as Zvi Ben-Dor Benite explains in his fascinating book *The Lost Ten Tribes:*

A World History, they stayed lost. "To understand the hole created when the tribes did not return" Benite writes, "one must recognize the promise of return as the main legacy of the Babylonian captivity."[24] By continuing to be lost, the ten tribes challenged the ideas of restoration and return that the Jews had worked out so carefully during their captivity. And, as the lostness of the tribes continued, Jewish prophets began to speak of a figure who would reunite Israel and usher in the final restoration of the throne of David. The word they used to refer to this figure was *messiah*, and finding the lost tribes was a major part of the Messiah's job description.[25]

Second Temple Judaism developed a considerable body of prophecy and literature concerning the lost tribes, much of which passed directly to the early Christian church through works now considered apocryphal such as 2 Esdras, a series of apocalyptic visions written shortly after the fall of Jerusalem in 70 CE that claimed to know where the lost tribes went and how they would return.[26] Belief in the literal return of the lost tribes has persisted among Jews and Christians for twenty-five hundred years, primarily because the biblical prophecies about the restoration of David's kingdom are so clear. The scribes who put the Hebrew Bible into its final form came to their task with a strong pan-Israelite ideology forged by both the natives of the southern kingdom and refugees from the north who came with a passionate commitment to the restoration of the united monarchy. And they wrote these beliefs in the Bible in the form of a longing for Israelite unity that still resonates today.

Israelite Typology in the Book of Mormon

Like the family of Israel, the family of Nephi begins with stories about a favored younger son and his resentful older brothers.[27] "Like his biblical counterpart," notes Grant Hardy, "Nephi is a teenager with older brothers who resent his apparent self-righteousness and favored status with their father. He receives a revelation promising that someday he will rule over them, and they respond by trying to kill him."[28] The typological connection between Nephi and Joseph continues throughout the first part of the Book of Mormon. Nephi uses the power of God to interpret his father's dream of the tree of life (1 Ne 11) much as Joseph interprets the dreams of the Pharaoh (Gen 41). And both end up saving their families, including their older brothers, and leading them to a land where they can flourish.

One part of the biblical story of Joseph is conspicuously missing in the Book of Mormon, however. Nothing in the story of Nephi parallels the reconciliation scene between Joseph and his brothers in Genesis 45. The author of the Joseph story ends on a high note: Joseph tests his brothers and gives them a chance to show that they have changed, and then he forgives them forthrightly and unconditionally. This is part of a much larger pattern of reconciliation in the Hebrew Bible. Joseph's father, Jacob, reconciles with his brother, Esau, immediately after his angel-wrestling adventure (Gen 33). Aaron and Miriam have a powerful reconciliation scene with Moses after they criticize his Ethiopian wife (Num 12). In the New Testament, the failure of the older brother to reconcile with the prodigal son is portrayed as a grave moral failing (Luke 15:11–32). And since the earliest days of Christianity, Joseph has been read as a type of Christ and his reconciliation with his brothers a type of the Atonement.[29] For readers who recognize this type, the lack of a final reconciliation between Nephi and his brothers leaves an unmet expectation in the text.

In the remainder of this chapter, I argue that Nephi's failure to reconcile with his brothers leaves a gap—a healing moment between brothers that, while part of the underlying typology, does not appear anywhere in the text. And the rest of the Book of Mormon responds to this hole by making reconciliation between Nephites and Lamanites one of the most important themes in the entire extended narrative. As it does so, it specifically invokes, and inserts itself directly into, the typology of a united Israel. The Book of Mormon is both an extension of this typology (because the Nephites and the Lamanites are both a lost remnant of the House of Israel) and another iteration of the type (because the Nephite-Lamanite division duplicates many of the elements of the northern kingdom–southern kingdom division). And we will badly misread both narratives if we do not acknowledge the deep longing of their authors and narrators for reconciliation.

Exposing Narrative Bias:
Jacob's Sermon and Jesus's Reproof

The first two books of the Book of Mormon introduce an anti-Lamanite bias that the rest of the book struggles to reject. This is a straightforward function of the unfiltered first-person narrative that these books employ. Not every narrator is Humbert Humbert, but every human being has a limited perspective, which a first-person narrative immediately foregrounds and exposes. Nearly all of the Old Testament uses an omniscient third-person narrative that resists attempts to interrogate the limitations of any one perspective. To do otherwise, Meir Sternberg insists, would be to "forfeit its claim to truth by catching at [a] straw of realism." Rather than encouraging us to attribute textual problems to a narrator's limitations, biblical prose directs us to "make sense of the violence done to the constraints on access by appeal to inspirational convention: the narrator speaks with the authority of omniscience."[30]

Much of the Book of Mormon, on the other hand, does come from first-person narrators, and it acknowledges the possibility of narrative limitation on the title page, which concludes, "And now, if there are faults they are the mistakes of men; wherefore, condemn not the things of God, that ye may be found spotless at the judgment-seat of Christ."[31] And the record of Nephi—the largest portion of the text not filtered through Mormon's redaction—is especially susceptible to narrator bias. The Book of Mormon itself seems to recognize the possibility that Nephi's narrator bias could unfairly anchor readers' perceptions of the Lamanites. Almost immediately after announcing Nephi's death, his brother, Jacob, begins trying to loosen the anchor. In the first sermon that Jacob preaches as the spiritual leader of the people, Jacob harshly criticizes his fellow Nephites concerning two topics: sexual immorality and anti-Lamanite prejudice. The two topics come together when he forcefully tells his audience that the Lamanites are more righteous than they are because they are faithful to their families:

> Behold, the Lamanites your brethren, whom ye hate because of their filthiness and the cursing which hath come upon their skins, are more righteous than you. For they have not forgotten the commandment of the Lord which was given unto our father, that they should have save it were one wife, and concubines they should have none, and there should not be whoredoms committed among them. . . .
>
> Behold, their husbands love their wives and their wives love their husbands, and their husbands and their wives love their children. And their unbelief and their hatred towards you is because of the iniquity of their fathers; wherefore how much better are you than they in the sight of your great Creator? O my brethren, I fear that unless ye shall repent of your sins that their skins will be whiter than yours when ye shall be brought with them before the throne of God.
>
> Wherefore a commandment I give unto you, which is the word of God, that ye revile no more against them because of the darkness of their skin. Neither shall ye revile against them because of their filthiness, but ye shall remember your own filthiness and remember that their filthiness came because of their fathers. (Jacob 3:5–9)[32]

The two themes that Jacob introduces in this sermon—the superior righteousness of the Lamanites and the unwarranted pride of the Nephites—run throughout the Book of Mormon's narrative. The crucial difference that he draws here is that the sins of the Lamanites come from a lack of understanding, whereas the sins of the Nephites come from the desire to be sinful, which places them in an entirely different category of wrongdoers. Within their understanding of God's will, the Lamanites show honor and integrity, especially in their relationships with their families. As Deidre Green has written, the Lamanites of Jacob's day "live aspects of the covenant life in a way that excels the Nephites; the Nephites, therefore, are to be their students rather than their judges."[33]

Even with Jacob's warning against unrighteous judgment and mistaking lack of understanding for natural depravity, various narrators in the Book of Mormon persist in describing the Lamanites as a "wild and ferocious and a bloodthirsty people" (Enos 1:20) who "loved murder" (Jarom 1:6) and had "an eternal hatred towards the children of Nephi" (Mosiah 10:17). The tendency to reduce scripture to chapter-and-verse proof texts often encourages readers to see these assessments as accurate representations of reality, rather than evaluations saturated with cultural biases. The text of the Book of Mormon itself simply does not support the harsh judgments that some of its Nephite narrators make about their Lamanite cousins. Just as many narrators present the Lamanites as more righteous than the Nephites.[34] And many of the passages in which Nephite narrators criticize the Lamanites are starkly at odds with the facts that these same narrators relate.

For an example, consider the narrative of Zeniff, who, in the beginning of the Book of Mosiah, leads an expedition from Zarahemla to the ancestral land of Nephi in search of a previous expedition that had left many years earlier. Zeniff describes the Lamanites as

> a wild, and ferocious, and a blood-thirsty people, believing in the tradition of their fathers, which is this: believing that they were driven out of the land of Jerusalem because of the iniquities of their fathers, and that they were wronged in the wilderness by their brethren, and they were also wronged while crossing the sea. (Mosiah 10:12)

Zeniff clearly has nothing good to say about the Lamanites.[35] But the story he tells is actually full of wild, ferocious, and blood-thirsty Nephites like King Noah, who taxes his own people into penury to sustain his dissolute lifestyle (Mosiah 11:13–14) and burns Abinadi to death for daring to call him to repentance (Mosiah 17:20). The Lamanites in the story are relatively peaceful, showing compassion to the Nephites and permitting them to stay in their land in exchange for a tribute payment (Mosiah 19:14–15). The Lamanites honor their agreement and live peacefully with the Nephites until a group of Nephite priests kidnap and rape the daughters of the Lamanites (Mosiah 20:1–6). Zeniff's opening evaluation of the Lamanites stands in ironic contrast to the parade of horrible actions by Nephites that he describes.

Moving on to the narrative of Samuel the Lamanite, we see a glaring example of Nephite bias rebuked by Jesus Christ. Samuel appears in the book of Helaman, just a few years before Christ's birth in the Old World. At this point in the narrative, "the Nephites did still remain in wickedness—yea, in great wickedness—while the Lamanites did observe strictly to keep the commandments of God" (Hel 13:1). Much as the Lord sent Amos from Judah to prophesy in the northern kingdom (Amos 1:1), he sent Samuel from the righteous Lamanites to warn the wicked Nephites of their impending destruction (Hel 13:2). The Nephites expel him from the city and refuse to let him back in, so he stands on the city wall and preaches a standard Old Testament sermon, saying that God is angry with this people, they seek riches and ignore the poor, they commit grievous sins, and, unless they repent, God will destroy them from the face of the earth. When Christ comes a few years later, he reads their record and specifically asks the people whether Samuel ever spoke to them. When they say that he had, Christ chastises them for leaving his words out of their record:

> Verily I say unto you: I commanded my servant Samuel the Lamanite that he should testify unto this people that at the day that the Father should glorify his name in me that there were many saints which should arise from the dead and should appear unto many and should minister unto them. And he said unto them: Were it not so? And his disciples answered him and said: Yea, Lord, Samuel did prophesy according to thy words, and they were all fulfilled.
>
> And Jesus saith unto them: How be it that ye have not written this thing?—that many saints did arise and appear unto many and did minister unto them. And it came to pass that Nephi remembered that this thing had not been written. And it came to pass that Jesus commanded that it should be written. Therefore it was written according as he commanded. (3 Ne 23:9–13)

Once we read Christ's criticisms back into the Samuel narrative, argues Max Perry Mueller, "Samuel's ascent atop the walls of Zarahemla signifies the inversion of the Book of Mormon's normal racial hierarchies."[36] Although the speakers in the narrative continue to link skin color to righteousness, what the narrative actually shows is that "in the half century before Christ comes to the New World, conversion among many Lamanites makes them 'righteous,' while the Nephites become wicked" and that "the signifying link between whiteness and righteousness . . . proves to be far from fixed."[37] Jared Hickman goes even further in his influential article "The Book of Mormon as Amerindian Apocalypse," which sees the divine shade that Jesus throws at

the Nephites as part of the text's destabilization of its entire editorial apparatus. Until now, the Nephites have had the privilege of telling the story—and
portraying the Lamanites—as they saw fit. But here, "the literal voice of God
in the text singles out for distinction precisely the voice that the Nephite
narrative does *not*, at least willingly, include." This does more than simply
highlight the importance of Samuel's words. It calls into question the entire
narrative structure of the Book of Mormon up to this point.[38] When God
speaks without human filters, he roundly criticizes the Nephite-centrism
of the record in which his words appear. Jesus himself agrees with Armand
Mauss's assessment that the Nephites, as the authors of the record, "were
free to characterize their antagonists as they wished, and demonizing of the
'other' has been a recurrent process in all of human history."[39]

Destabilizing Categories: The Anti-Nephi-Lehis

Understanding the ways in which the Book of Mormon invokes the typology
of a united Israel may help shed light on the much-debated origins of the term
"Anti-Nephi-Lehis"—the name of the Lamanites who convert to Christianity and bury their swords to atone for their violent pasts. When the Nephites
and the Lamanites oppose each other in a great war, the Anti-Nephi-Lehis
stick to their pacifist oaths. But their children, who did not take the oath,
form an elite army unit under Helaman's command that somehow survives
a major battle without a single fatality. The "2,000 Stripling Warriors" or the
"Army of Helaman" is one of the most iconic passages in the entire Book of
Mormon—a feel-good story about courage, valor, mothers, and unshakable
righteousness coming together to produce a miraculous martial victory.

But what does the term "Anti-Nephi-Lehi" mean? Generations of Book
of Mormon scholars have failed to arrive at a consensus about the term, but
there is no shortage of theories. Hugh Nibley looked at the Latin, Greek,
Arabic, and Old Norse variants of the prefix "anti-" and concluded that it
meant "a face-to-face meeting, a joining together with somebody."[40] The official LDS Institute Manual quotes Stephen D. Ricks, who suggests that "the
name 'Anti' of 'Anti-Nephi-Lehi' may be a reflex of the Egyptian *nty* 'he of,
the one of.' Thus, rather than having the sense 'against,' it has the meaning 'the
one of Nephi and Lehi.'"[41] And Royal Skousen, the editor of the definitive *The
Book of Mormon: The Earliest Text* and other critical editions argues—citing
Book of Mormon names such as Antionah (Alma 12:20), Antionum (Alma
31:3), and Antiparah (Alma 56:14)—that "Anti-" seems "to be a proper noun
in the Nephite-Lamanite language" and that Anti-Nephi-Lehi is the name

of a place or a person that "has something to do either with that part of their territory or with the righteous heritage of Nephi and Lehi."[42]

I believe that a close examination of the textual variants, combined with an understanding of the Book of Mormon's structure and its incorporation of biblical typology, suggests a different origin for the term, one that Skousen considers briefly before rejecting. The term "Anti-Nephi-Lehi" occurs twelve times in the Book of Mormon. All twelve citations occur in the surviving portion of the original manuscript that Joseph Smith dictated to a succession of scribes including David Whitmer, Martin Harris, Oliver Cowdery, and Emma Smith. All are also in the complete printer's manuscript that Oliver Cowdery copied from the original manuscript to give to E. B. Grandin, who printed the 1830 edition of the book. Four of the twelve instances of "Anti-Nephi-Lehi" in the original manuscript and three in the printer's manuscript are spelled "Ante-Nephi-Lehi." One of the instances is spelled "Ante-" in both manuscripts, so, in six of the twelve instances when the term appears, it is spelled "Ante-Nephi-Lehi" in at least one of the original handwritten manuscripts. This tells us, at the very least, that Smith pronounced the term *ant-ee* and not *ant-eye*, because "anti-" can be pronounced both ways, but "ante-" cannot. In the final text, the printer standardized them all as Anti-Nephi-Lehi.[43]

But what if he standardized it the wrong way? The Latin root *ante-* means "before," as in antebellum (before the war), antediluvian (before the flood) and antecedent (thing that comes before). But spelling was much less standardized in the early nineteenth century, and *anti-* was a variant spelling of many such words.[44] And there remain words in English that use the *anti-* prefix to mean "before," such as *antique, anticipate*, and *antipasto*. Given the variant spellings in the manuscript, it is very likely that the term that fell from Joseph Smith's mouth was *ANTEE-Nephi-Lehi*, with the prefix sometimes rendered *ante-* and sometimes *anti-* by his scribes.

If this is the case, then the meaning of Anti-Nephi-Lehi becomes an important part of the Book of Mormon's reconciliation narrative because it is a term that can apply to everybody in Book of Mormon society. The names "Nephite" and "Lamanite" prioritize the split between Lehi's descendants. When we read "Anti-Nephi-Lehi" as something like "Lehites before the split between Nephi and Laman," the term formally and intentionally erases the division and asserts the importance of common descent. In this sense, it is analogous to the term "Israelite," which establishes the common ancestry of all people descended from Jacob/Israel and asserts that this unity overrides the divisions created by terms such as "Jew" (or "Judahite") and "Ephraimite." Contemporary ecumenicists do much the same when they name Christianity, Judaism, and Islam as "Abrahamic faiths" and therefore related to each other through the covenant that Abraham made with God.

If this is the correct etymology of Anti-Nephi-Lehi—and I believe very strongly that it is—then we can infer that at least some people on both sides of the Nephite-Lamanite divide understood the concept of pan-Lehite unity. The Lamanites who converted to Christianity included two prominent kings: Lamoni, who was converted by Ammon, was the king of a land called Ishmael that was named for one of the seven original tribes (Alma 17:21). Lamoni's father, whose name is not given, was "king over all the land" (Alma 20:8). The missionaries who converted these kings—Ammon and Aaron—were sons of King Mosiah and close friends of Alma the Younger, who headed both the church and the state in Zarahemla. When the king of the Lamanites wanted to change the name of his people, he "consulted with Aaron and many of their priests" (Alma 23:16) and together they created a name that emphasized the identity that they all shared. This strongly suggests something like a cross-border pan-Lehite movement committed to erasing the distinctions introduced into society at the time of Nephi, something directly comparable to the coalition of Levites and other northerners in the southern kingdom who sought to restore the Davidic monarchy and promote an ideal of pan-Israelite unity across all the tribes.

Redefining the Remnant

The society of the middle portion of the Book of Mormon—the books of Mosiah, Alma, and Helaman—does not survive until the end of the narrative. This society is irrevocably changed by two events. First, after Christ is crucified in the Old World, a series of cataclysmic natural disasters kills a large number of people as whole cities, including Zarahemla, are burned to the ground, sunk into the ocean, and buried in the earth (3 Ne 8:3–12). After listing the cities that he destroyed, Christ tells the remaining people that he spared them "because ye were more righteous than they" (3 Ne 8:13). And, for the rest of 3 Nephi, he ministers to the people in ways reminiscent of his New Testament ministry: He preaches the Sermon on the Mount (3 Ne 12–14), calls twelve apostles (3 Ne 12:1), and sets up a church to minister to the people after he is gone (3 Ne 27:1–9). Christ's ministry is the second major event that changes society, and he converts nearly all of the people he teaches. But we must keep in mind that Jesus begins with only the most righteous people in the society, culled from the Nephite and Lamanite populations with no regard for skin color or lineage.

Through destruction and conversion, Nephite-Lamanite society changes dramatically, and the two ethnic categories cease to exist, along with all of the other categories that had divided the people into different groups. For nearly two hundred years the descendants of the people who survive the cataclysms of 3 Nephi 8 live in a society without distinctions:

> And it came to pass in the thirty and sixth year the people were all converted unto the Lord upon all the face of the land, both Nephites and Lamanites. And there was no contentions and disputations among them. And every man did deal justly one with another. And they had all things common among them; therefore there were not rich and poor, bond and free, but they were all made free and partakers of the heavenly gift.
> . . .
> And there were no envyings nor strifes nor tumults nor whoredoms nor lyings nor murders nor no manner of lasciviousness. And surely there could not be a happier people among all the people who had been created by the hand of God. There were no robbers nor murderers, neither were there Lamanites, nor any manner of -ites, but they were in one, the Children of Christ and heirs to the kingdom of God. And how blessed were they! For the Lord did bless them in all their doings; yea, even they were blessed and prospered until an hundred and ten years had passed away. And the first generation from Christ had passed away, and there was no contention in all the land. (4 Ne 1:2–3, 16–18)

The events of Three and 4 Nephi bring an end to phenotypical and genealogical distinctions in the Book of Mormon, and the people live in an -iteless wonderland until 210 years after the birth of Christ (about 176 years after Christ's New World ministry).[45] When categories re-emerge, they are clearly presented as ideological choices rather than ethnicities:

> And now it came to pass in this year—yea, in the two hundred and thirty and first year—there [was] a great division among the people. And it came to pass that in this year there arose a people which was called the Nephites, and they were true believers in Christ. And among them there were they which was called by the Lamanites Jacobites, and Josephites, and Zoramites.
> Therefore the true believers in Christ and the true worshipers of Christ . . . were called Nephites and Jacobites and Josephites and Zoramites. And it came to pass that they which rejected the gospel were called Lamanites and Lemuelites and Ishmaelites. And they did not dwindle in unbelief, but they did willfully rebel against the gospel of Christ. And they did teach their children that they should not believe, even as their fathers from the beginning did dwindle. (4 Ne 1:35–38)

We need to be very clear about what happens in this passage. The text does not say, though it is often read as saying, that "Lehi's progeny return to their original roles."[46] It does not say that the Nephite and Lamanite bloodlines were rigidly segregated over the course of the seven generations in which all such distinctions were considered too unimportant to mention, or that the descendants of Nephi became righteous again and the descendants of Laman and Lemuel became wicked. It says, rather, as Armand Mauss correctly concludes, "the Nephite and Lamanite antagonists were distinguished only by their differential spiritual condition rather than by skin color or other 'racial' characteristics."[47] Both categories became labels that people can adopt or apply to others based on religious belief or lifestyle choices—much as a contemporary teenager might be called, and may even self-identify as, a goth (or maybe described by others as a vandal) without any genealogical or phenotypical connections to the Germanic nomads of late Antiquity who caused so many problems for the Roman Empire.

The great transformation that occurs in 4 Nephi has to be read back into the text—and into the prophecies about the future that come from the Nephite prophets and scribes. For example, it changes the way we should read the prophetic vision in which Nephi reports seeing "the people of the seed of my brethren that they had overcome my seed. And they went forth in multitudes upon the face of the land" (1 Ne 12:20). This prophecy simply cannot mean that people who are ethnically Lamanite will defeat people who are ethnically Nephite, since, when the Lamanites destroy the Nephites, neither category retains any trace of its original meaning. The remnant that survived the civilizational collapse at the end of the Book of Mormon did not consist of Lamanites under the definition that operates in the text from 1 through 3 Nephi. It was, rather, a population of Lehite/Mulekites whose recent ancestors either chose to identify as Lamanites or made religious and political choices that caused other people to label them as such.

The controlling narrative arc in the Bible and in the Book of Mormon tells the story of a people who belong together and are separated into arbitrary categories (northern kingdom/southern kingdom, Nephite/Lamanite) that discount the original tribal designations and frustrate the unity that God expects from his people. Both books present these divisions as tragedies that are healed briefly during each culture's highest point—the united monarchy in the Bible and the period following Christ's visit in the Book of Mormon. These periods of unity become the models for restoration. The Hebrew prophets of the sixth century BCE lamented the split and prophesied of a reunion that would correspond to the coming of the Messiah and the restoration of the Davidic throne. In the Book of Mormon, the two-hundred-year period of peace following Christ's visit is announced as a model of the Kingdom of God, in which there are "no manner of -ites," or no divisions in the Body of Christ. In both instances, though, the categories dividing the people have already been emptied of genealogical meaning by the time the people understand the importance of overcoming the divisions. During the Babylonian captivity, the people called "Jews" were well represented by people from all twelve tribes. And by the final battle in the Book of Mormon, "Nephite" and "Lamanite" had become arbitrary and tragic categories whose only purpose was to fuel division and bloodshed. One of the most urgent messages of both scriptures is that all human divisions are ultimately arbitrary and tragic and that we can only have the Kingdom of God when we give them up.

CHAPTER SIX

Prophets and Prophecy

The personal call is the decisive element distinguishing the
prophet from the priest. The latter lays claim to authority by
virtue of his service in a sacred tradition, while the prophet's
claim is based on personal revelation and charisma. . . . The
priest . . . dispenses salvation by virtue of his office. Even in
cases in which personal charisma may be involved, it is the
hierarchical office that confers legitimate authority upon the
priest as a member of a corporate enterprise of salvation.

—Max Weber, *The Sociology of Religion*

Nowhere in the Hebrew Bible do we find a clear definition of the word
"prophet," nor do its authors apply the term consistently. Sometimes it applies
to such great founders and patriarchs of the Israelite religion as Abraham and
Moses; at other times it describes such court religious advisors as Nathan or
Ahijah or Yahwist champions such as Elijah and Elisha.[1] By the time of the
Babylonian captivity, though, the writers of the Hebrew Bible had settled on
a consistent prophet-type. The figures most often called prophets—Isaiah,
Jeremiah, Ezekiel, and the twelve so-called minor prophets—stood on the
margins of society. They called the Israelites to repentance before the Assyr-
ian invasion of Israel and again before the Babylonian conquest of Judah.
And the term "prophet" even has a feminine counterpart, "prophetess," that
the Bible applies to women such as Miriam (Exod 15:20), Deborah (Judg
4:4), and Huldah (2 Kgs 22:14–20). The Talmudic tradition recognizes
forty-eight men and seven women as prophets and prophetesses,[2] and these
fifty-five people have very few characteristics in common—which, Joseph
Blenkinsopp writes, "greatly complicates the task of coming up with an ad-
equate definition of the phenomenon."[3]

By the time of the Babylonian captivity, though, the writers of the Hebrew
Bible had a concrete type of the prophet to work with when they assembled
the *Nevi'im*, or the middle section of the *Tanakh* containing the writings of
the prophets. The "later prophets," or "literary prophets," including Isaiah,

Jeremiah, Ezekiel, and the twelve minor prophets that conclude the *Nevi'im*, all conform to this type.[4] These prophets, Blenkinsopp explains, played a very different role in Israelite society than priests did. Priests exercised religious authority by "occupying an office." They were part of an institution, and their role was defined and constrained by their role in that institution. Prophets, on the other hand, were "called to a mission." Their calling came directly from God, and only they had authority to speak in God's name.[5] Prophets came from the margins of society or from outside of it altogether, and they aimed their righteous outrage at peasants, priests, and kings, with no thought for the consequences.

Like many other contemporary scholars, Blenkinsopp begins his discussion of prophecy with the German sociologist Max Weber's definition of a prophet as "a purely individual bearer of charisma, who by virtue of his mission proclaims a religious doctrine or divine commandment."[6] This definition, Blenkinsopp suggests, creates three functional criteria for calling someone a prophet: "the possession of charisma, a distinctive mission, and a specifically religious message."[7] The first criterion sets the prophet apart from priests and other institutional religious officers. Charisma, for Weber, is not merely a characteristic of individual attractiveness or magnetism; it is one of the main ways in which authority is legitimated within social groups.

Throughout his writings Weber identified three broad categories of authority, each of which depends on different factors for its legitimation: traditional authority, legal authority, and charismatic authority. Traditional authority—such as that exercised by kings, chiefs, and heads of households—comes from custom and from the social structure of a society. People obey traditional authority because it feels natural to them. They accept the legitimacy of leaders and governing structures "on the basis of the sanctity of the order and the attendant powers of control as they have been handed down from the past."[8] Legal authority, sometimes called legal-rational authority, comes from laws and social contracts and resides in an office, rather than an individual. Presidents and prime ministers exercise legal authority during their term of office, police officers exercise authority while they are on duty, and bureaucrats of every stripe have power over certain things at certain times because of the positions they hold. People obey legal authority because they have accepted the legal and political structures that underlie it—and because they benefit from living in a society governed by rules and laws.[9]

Weber's third category of authority concerns us the most. Charismatic authority derives entirely from the personal characteristics of an individual. In *The Theory of Social and Economic Organization*, Weber defines "charisma" as "a certain quality of an individual personality by virtue of which he is set apart from ordinary men and treated as endowed with supernatural, super-human, or at least specifically exceptional powers or qualities." People see charismatic leaders as possessing traits "not accessible to the ordinary person." They regard these traits as being "of divine origin or as exemplary, and on the basis of them the individual concerned is treated as a leader."[10] As "individual bearers of charisma," prophets do not depend on institutional positions for their authority. They do not need to come from any specific bloodline or be ordained to any ecclesiastical office. They are not appointed or elected, and they cannot pass their prophetic nature down to their children. Their authority is neither traditional nor legal; it attaches to their persons and comes directly from their perceived relationship with a divine being or power.

Weber's understanding of prophecy works well with the Old Testament prophets, from Moses through Malachi. In nearly every case, those described as prophets exercise their authority outside of the established traditional and legal networks. They were called by God directly, not by the church or the state, and the few who did come from the priestly class, such as Samuel and Jeremiah, separated their prophetic authority from their priestly duties. Most of the prophets of the eighth and sixth centuries BCE operated entirely outside the political and ecclesiastical structures that existed in their societ-ies. These ecclesiastical structures were often targets of prophetic warnings; the prophets condemned priests and temple bureaucrats for their hypocrisy and their inattention to the poor.

Charismatic leadership has always been a powerful legitimizing force in human societies, but it is also the most unstable. Charismatic leaders are unpredictable and revolutionary, which means that most charismatic move-ments fail when they lose their leader. In order to survive as institutions, they must find a way to, in Weber's terms, "routinize" the charismatic author-ity—to take the revolutionary and unstable authority of the leader and turn it into something predictable and rule-governed—something that retains the rhetorical authority of the original charismatic leadership while containing its disruptive forces and allowing for mundane administrative tasks. Perhaps the most important step in routinizing charismatic authority is to regular-ize the institution's financial affairs. "For charisma to be transformed into a permanent routine structure," Weber explains, "it is necessary that its anti-economic character should be altered. It must be adapted to some form of fiscal organization to provide for the needs of the group and hence to the economic conditions necessary for raising taxes and contributions."[11]

Contemporary sociologists of religion often use Mormonism as a starting place for discussing Weber's concept of charisma. Joseph Smith is one of the two historical figures whom Weber names as examples of charisma in

Theory of Social and Economic Organization,[12] and subsequent scholarship has used the transition from Joseph Smith to Brigham Young as a textbook example of routinization. In this model Smith represents the classical charismatic prophet, whereas Young represents the hard-minded organizational genius necessary to shape the prophetic charisma into lasting institutions.[13] The transition from Smith to Young (the argument goes) set in motion the routinization of charisma that resulted in the modern church being led by prophets who derive their authority entirely from their position in a religious hierarchy.

This simple narrative breaks down quickly on both sides of the equation. Brigham Young did not simply reflect Smith's charismatic light. He exercised significant charismatic authority in his own right, and he used that authority to require much greater sacrifices from his followers than his predecessor ever did. And Joseph Smith was not devoid of organizational skill. As Thomas O'Dea explains, Smith's status as a prophet was itself the result of Mormonism's need to contain its early revelatory enthusiasm by "restricting revelation and prophecy to one man, and develop[ing] a centrally directed organization about that one leader."[14] Throughout his time as church leader, Smith created multiple institutions and bureaucracies designed to transform his prophetic authority into an enduring institution.[15] The routinization of charisma in Mormonism began when Smith organized six people into a church in Fayette, New York, in 1830. It was during Smith's lifetime, not after his death, that the role of a prophet came to be seen and understood as an office within an institutional bureaucracy.

In his study *Paul and Power*, Bengt Holmberg proposes a revision to Weber's terminology to explain the rise of Christianity after Jesus—a revision that might also help us understand the evolution of charismatic authority within Mormonism. Weber's concept of routinization, Holmberg suggests, has generally been used to describe an event rather than a process. "Often," he writes, it is the death of the leader and the problem of succession that gives impulse to the routinization process."[16] Charismatic leaders, for Weber, exercises authority by the force their personalities. Absent that force, their disciples and their followers must transfer the original leader's charisma into traditional or rational frameworks that allow others to exercise the same authority by virtue of their position. Holmberg believes that this formulation underestimates both the pervasiveness and the complexity of social institutions. Rather than trying to revise Weber's terminology, Holmberg proposes the term "institutionalization" to describe a process of which routinization is only a small part. "Institutionalization is not a process that may arise after a time," he insists, "but is a process that inevitably starts almost as soon as human interaction begins and continues for as long as the group, association, or society exists."[17] Holmberg proposes "making a distinction between the terms institutionalization and routinization. Institutionalization is the whole process of consensus generalization, structural solidification, legitimation, etc., whereas routinization is part of a secondary phase in this general process, viz. a change in the set of personal motives of the actors."[18]

In order to succeed as a religious movement, Mormonism had to find ways to institutionalize Joseph Smith's charismatic authority. The current Church of Jesus Christ of Latter-day Saints has a plethora of prophets. Fifteen men—the three members of the First Presidency and the twelve members of the Quorum of the Twelve Apostles—carry the titles "prophet, seer, and revelator," with the president of the church also commonly referred to as "the prophet." For Latter-day Saints, however, the title "prophet" is an institutional category—a designation that conveys to whoever occupies it a certain position on an organizational chart. Prophetic authority can only be exercised by those who have risen through the ranks of the hierarchy and been formally ordained. There are few precedents in either the Old or the New Testament for a prophet who holds a formal institutional position, but there are multiple precedents in the Book of Mormon, where men described as prophets hold both ecclesiastical and political positions and pass those positions down to their sons.

In this chapter I adopt Holmberg's terminology to argue that the Book of Mormon anticipates the modern institutionalization of prophetic charisma by first mimicking, and then revising, the Old Testament models of prophets and prophecy. I focus on the section of the Book of Mormon that begins with the founding of the Nephite church and ends with the visit of Jesus Christ to Zarahemla—consisting of the books of Mosiah, Alma, Helaman, and 3 Nephi. This is the only portion of the text in which both the church and the state are well-defined, hierarchical institutions.[19] The civilization that precedes Mosiah consists of a single extended family, whereas the civilization of Mormon and Moroni is in the midst of a collapse that has decimated its political and ecclesiastical institutions.

This middle portion of the text identifies only a handful of people with the term "prophet."[20] The first of these, Abinadi, conforms closely to the biblical model: He is an apparent outsider who seems to come from nowhere to warn both religious and political authorities in harsh and shocking terms that they have incurred God's displeasure. Soon after Abinadi is killed, Alma leads the Nephite church to become the official state religion under King Mosiah. Alma is succeeded by his son, Alma the Younger, a prophet who becomes both the high priest of the church and the ruler of the state—combining religious, political, and prophetic power in the hands of a single individual and paving the way for the expansive, fully institutionalized definition of "prophet" that now characterizes Latter-day Saint religion.

But the Book of Mormon also sounds a cautionary note about the institutionalization of prophetic authority. Alma's tenure as head of both church and state ends in a disastrous war, and after he resigns his political office to focus on his ministry, his prophetic leadership is severely damaged by the memory of his political failures. Three of Alma's descendants—Helaman$_1$, Helaman$_2$, and Nephi—lead the Nephite church and maintain the sacred records; the latter two also serve as the political head of the government. Though the Book of Mormon portrays these leaders as righteous, it does not always depict them as effective, nor does it portray the comingling of prophecy and politics as a beneficial arrangement for either the church or the state. Toward the end of the reign of the judges, when the Church of Christ was well established and after two successive prophets had held the chief judgeship for twenty years, God sent another outsider-prophet to continue Abinadi's work. With no formal political or ecclesiastical sanction, Samuel the Lamanite stands on Zarahemla's city wall and warns the people to repent or face the wrath of God.

Abinadi: A Voice from the Wilderness

During the reign of the original King Mosiah—two generations before the Book of Mosiah opens with King Benjamin's final speech (Mosiah 2–5) and the coronation of his son Mosiah$_2$ (Mosiah 6)—two groups of settlers left Zarahemla to return to and reclaim the original settlement of their ancestors. The first of these groups failed to find the land of Nephi and began to fight among themselves, resulting in the death of all but fifty members of the party (Omni 1:27–28). The second group left about seventy years before Mosiah begins and never made contact with Zarahemla (Omni 1:29–30). As the book of Mosiah begins, the people of Zarahemla are both curious and concerned about the fate of these settlers, and the new king sends a search party to try to find them.

The bulk of Mosiah (7–24) consists of the story of this colony, where the Nephite church is born—a Christian organization formed 150 years before the birth of Christ. In the most narratively complex section of the Book of Mormon, the story of the colony and the birth of the church is told through four separate layers of narration: (1) the writings of Ammon, the leader of the expedition dispatched to find the settlers, (2) the official records of the colony itself, kept by its first and third kings, (3) Alma's records of Abinadi's visit, and (4) the editorial perspective of Mormon, who redacted these records nearly six hundred years later. The central event of the story, which changes the course of Nephite history and the entire Book of Mormon, is the conflict between the wicked King Noah and the mysterious prophet Abinadi.

Abinadi is the closest thing in the Book of Mormon to an Old Testament prophet.[21] The text gives him no history until the moment that he shows up and starts prophesying.[22] He comes as a messenger from God to the people of Nephi, and he inveighs against both the king and the priests, showing no deference to either the political or the ecclesiastical structures. With words that could have come from any prophetic book of the Old Testament, he begins, "Behold, thus saith the Lord, and thus hath he commanded me, saying, Go forth, and say unto this people, thus saith the Lord—Woe be unto this people, for I have seen their abominations, and their wickedness, and their whoredoms; and except they repent I will visit them in mine anger" (Mosiah 11:20). He continues in this vein:

> And it shall come to pass that they shall know that I am the Lord their God and am a jealous God, visiting the iniquities of my people. And it shall come to pass that except this people repent and turn to the Lord their God, they shall be brought into bondage; and none shall deliver them except it be the Lord the Almighty God. Yea, and it shall come to pass that when they shall cry unto me, I will be slow to hear their cries. Yea, and I will suffer them that they be smitten by their enemies. And except they repent in sackcloth and ashes and cry mightily to the Lord their God, I will not hear their prayers, neither will I deliver them out of their afflictions. And thus saith the Lord, and thus hath he commanded me. (Mosiah 11:22–25)

Abinadi speaks here in fairly generic prophetspeak probably designed to do no more than establish that he is indeed an Old-Testament-style prophet. He mixes words and phrases found throughout the King James Bible into a warning that could fit, intact, into almost any of its prophetic books. Nothing in the speech ties Abinadi's words to any place, time, or people. We know from the narration that Noah and his people "did commit whoredoms and all manner of wickedness" (Mosiah 11:2), that the king taxed the people heavily for building projects (Mosiah 11:3), and that he installed and supported priests who would not object to his behavior (Mosiah 11:5). The underlying misdeeds—sexual immorality, economic oppression, and a corrupt priesthood—line up reasonably well with the traditional concerns of Old Testament prophets. The last item, creating a professional clergy supported by taxation, will become a pillar of Nehor's religion and will be condemned vigorously as "priestcraft" in Alma (Alma 1:12). But Abinadi does not mention any of these sins explicitly. He assumes that the people know what they are guilty of. Abinadi has no interest in educating his audience, only in calling out their behavior.

Predictably, the audience responds with anger. "They were wroth with him and sought to take away his life" (Mosiah 11:26). King Noah demands that Abinadi be arrested and brought before him to be killed. But the prophet disappears as suddenly as he appeared and goes into hiding for two years, after which he comes among them "in disguise" (Mosiah 12:1). On his second visit, he begins with a similarly generic prophetic warning that soon becomes a personal diatribe against the king. "And it shall come to pass that the life of king Noah shall be valued even as a garment in a hot furnace," he pronounces, "for he shall know that I am the Lord" (Mosiah 12:3). He also predicts that the people of Nephi will be smitten "with famine and with pestilence" and that "they shall howl all the day long" and "be driven . . . like a dumb ass" (Mosiah 12:4–5). This time, the people bind him and take him before King Noah to be judged and condemned (Mosiah 12:9). And then things get interesting.

The narrator frames the confrontation between Abinadi and Noah as a courtroom drama in which each side gets to ask questions of the other. The first salvo concerns the proper interpretation of a passage from Isaiah—specifically, Isaiah 52:7–10:

> And it came to pass that one of them saith unto him: What meaneth the words which are written and which have been taught by our fathers, saying: How beautiful upon the mountains are the feet of him that bringeth good tidings, that publisheth peace, that bringeth good tidings of good, that publisheth salvation, that saith unto Zion: Thy God reigneth! Thy watchmen shall lift up the voice; with the voice together shall they sing. For they shall see eye to eye when the Lord shall bring again Zion. Break forth into joy! Sing together, ye waste places of Jerusalem! For the Lord hath comforted his people; he hath redeemed Jerusalem. The Lord hath made bare his holy arm in the eyes of all the nations, and all the ends of the earth shall see the salvation of our God. (Mosiah 12:20–24)

Joseph Spencer, who analyzed this part of the Abinadi story at length in *An Other Testament*, points out that the priests of Noah appear to believe that this passage had "a single, obvious, incontrovertible meaning . . . that everyone in the land of Nephi would immediately see." This interpretation, he continues, "would have to be well-known and rooted in a culture-wide ideology."[23] This might include, but must go beyond, a general understanding that prophets are supposed to bring "messages of joy," as opposed to the judgmental diatribes that Abinadi levels against the people of Nephi.[24] Isaiah himself, in passages that were already part of the Book of Mormon, issued plenty of warnings and calls to repent. This passage comes from the part of the book usually attributed to Second, or Deutero-Isaiah, a prophet who ministered to the Jews after the destruction of Jerusalem and during the Babylonian captivity. Unlike most other Old Testament prophets, including First Isaiah, Deutero-Isaiah does not need to warn his people of an impending catastrophe. The catastrophe has already happened; his job is to point the way forward, to give comfort, and to prophesy about the redemption of Jerusalem as the new and beautiful city of Zion. Isaiah's rapturous prophecies speak to a time when Jerusalem has been redeemed and Zion has been established.

The true dispute between Abinadi and the priests concerns the proper fulfillment of Isaiah's prophecies of redemption. Spencer puts it well: Noah's father, Zeniff, "seems to have seen himself as the major player in a remarkable restoration—the refounding of the original Nephite monarchy in the land of Nephi." There is, therefore, "reason to suggest that Zeniff took his own refounding to fulfill the likened writings of Second Isaiah."[25] The ruling elite of the land of Nephi, in other words, saw themselves as the fulfillment of Isaiah's prophetic references to Zion. And the fulfillment of the prophecy obviated the need for Abinadi's dire warnings. The priests, at least, saw themselves as the very people who redeemed Israel—those whose feet were beautiful upon the mountain because of the good tidings they bore. Abinadi's warnings do not apply to them because they are the end to which Isaiah's prophecies ultimately pointed.

When the priests invoke the law of Moses to justify their doctrines (Mosiah 12:18), Abinadi harshly accuses them of not obeying or even understanding it, and he proceeds to discourse on the preparatory nature of the law. He specifically brings up the concept of typology to explain the practices and ordinances of Mosaic law as "types of things to come" (Mosiah 13:31), and he insists that Christ is the proper subject of Isaiah's prophecies. To support this argument, Abinadi quotes from the chapter that follows the passage that the priests quote: Isaiah 53, one of the most typologically significant chapters in the Old Testament.[26] In this chapter Isaiah describes a suffering servant who was "despised and rejected of men" (53:3), "wounded for our transgressions," "bruised for our iniquities" (53:5), and then "brought as a lamb to the slaughter" (53:7)—images that have become central to the Christian story. Abinadi argues that any spiritually sensitive reader of these and other passages in the Old Testament should be able to understand that the prophets were talking about the promised Messiah:

For behold, did not Moses prophesy unto them concerning the coming of the Messiah and that God should redeem his people? Yea, and even all the prophets which have prophesied ever since the world began, have they not spoken more or less concerning these things? Have they not said that God himself should come down among the children of men and take upon him the form of man and go forth in mighty power upon the face of the earth? Yea, and have they not said also that he should bring to pass the resurrection of the dead and that he himself should be oppressed and afflicted? (Mosiah 13:33–35)

With this speech, Abinadi provides the priests and King Noah with the evidence they need to execute him. Noah condemns Abinadi for saying that "God himself should come down among the children of men"—a charge of blasphemy, which warranted death under the law of Moses (Lev 24:16).[27] Noah gives Abinadi the choice of recalling his words or suffering death. When Abinadi refuses to recant and declares that his blood will "stand as a testimony against you in the last day," Noah becomes fearful and plans to release him. But when he waivers, the priests take Abinadi "and [bind] him and scourg[e] his skin . . . even unto death" (Mosiah 17:13). Like many charismatic leaders, Abinadi frightens those who wield traditional authority, and he becomes a martyr for his beliefs.

Before he dies, though, Abinadi makes one convert among the priests of King Noah's court, and that convert, Alma, changes the trajectory of the Book of Mormon by establishing a church. Before Alma, the Nephites had a national religion, much as the Kingdom of Judah had in the Old Testament, with leaders establishing the basic tenets of belief and priests officiating in certain cultic rituals. But they did not have a church in any sense that most of us would recognize: a group of people who affirmatively choose to affiliate with a congregation that is connected to other congregations by some sort of superordinate institutional structure. This is exactly what Alma sets up, first on the outskirts of the settlement in the land of Nephi and later in Zarahemla and the other Nephite cities. When Alma defends Abinadi, Noah casts him out and dispatches servants to kill him (Mosiah 17:3). But Alma evades the king and goes into hiding, where he records the words of Abinadi and begins preaching Abinadi's doctrine to the people of Nephi. Soon, the group becomes a movement that meets outside the city in a place called the Waters of Mormon, where Alma baptizes his followers and establishes a church. When they are baptized, Alma's followers pledge to "bear one another's burdens," "mourn with those that mourn," and "comfort those that stand in need of comfort" (Mosiah 18:8–9).

In the baptismal scene, Alma takes the religion that he learned from Abinadi and turns it into a church. The people originally baptized "were in number about two hundred and four souls" (Mosiah 18:16), or about the size of a modern church congregation. The congregational nature of this religious community is what makes it a church. There are hard cognitive limits to the number of people that human beings can mourn with, comfort, and share the burdens of.[28] And the close relationship among congregants is as important to Alma's church as the doctrines they believe. As the congregation grows larger, Alma divides it into smaller groups, with "one priest to every fifty of their number" (Mosiah 18:18). Alma creates a new kind of kinship network—one that people must affirmatively choose to join by accepting baptism. Once in place, the new kinship network becomes both a site for shared belief and a mechanism for mutual support.

When the group of believers grows to "about four hundred and fifty souls" (Mosiah 18:35), they can no longer hide from Noah and his priests. Alma leads them all into the wilderness permanently. For a brief time Alma and his followers separate from the main narrative of the land of Nephi (which is itself a diversion from the main narrative of the Nephites in Zarahemla). By the end of Mosiah, both groups of people—Alma and his followers and the remaining population of the land of Nephi—end up with the main body of the Nephites in Zarahemla, where King Mosiah fully embraces Alma's new church. Mosiah allows Alma to preach to the people of the city (Mosiah 25:14–15) and to appoint priests and create churches. Once again, the narrative emphasizes the importance of individual congregations.

> Now this was done because there were so many people that they could not all be governed by one teacher, neither could they all hear the word of God in one assembly. Therefore they did assemble themselves together in different bodies, being called churches, every church having their priests and their teachers, and every priest preaching the word according as it was delivered to him by the mouth of Alma. And thus notwithstanding there being many churches, they were all one church, yea, even the church of God; for there was nothing preached in all the churches except it were repentance and faith in God. (Mosiah 25:20–22)

Thus Alma creates churches in both senses of the word—a superordinate organization and a group of specific congregations. This also means that Alma creates a religious hierarchy—a bureaucracy that requires rules, policies, and careful oversight so that the congregations remain connected to, and doctrinally consistent with, the larger body. Perhaps more consequential, by defining a category of people who affirmatively elect to affiliate with an organization as "the church," Alma also defines a clear space for "not the church," or people who choose not to join the state-sanctioned religion or to end their affiliation after they have joined. The existence of "members" only makes sense if there are also "non-members." And, as Grant Shreve demonstrates, this leads to a secularization of Nephite culture in which the right to choose one's religious affiliation is enshrined in both custom and law.[29]

Alma presents as clear a case as we might want to illustrate the institutionalization of Abinadi's charismatic authority. Like most Old Testament prophets, Abinadi comes from the margins of his society. He derives his prophetic authority directly from God, unmediated by human institutions. He excoriates both the king and the priests, who fiercely oppose him with all of the institutional force available. Almost everything we read about Alma, on the other hand, has to do with creating policies and institutions. While he is at the Waters of Mormon he creates a formal baptism ritual, gives the church a name, ordains priests, sets a curriculum, clarifies expectations for Sabbath observance, and establishes rules for those ordained to the priesthood (Mosiah 18:17–26). When he arrives in Zarahemla he obtains permission from King Mosiah to "establish churches throughout all the land of Zarahemla" and "to ordain priests and teachers over every church" (Mosiah 25:19). He pays close attention to congregational sizes because "there were so many people that they could not all be governed by one teacher, neither could they all hear the word of God in one assembly" (Alma 25:20). He personally supervises the teachers and priests in every congregation to ensure that they taught only "the word according as it was delivered to [them] by the mouth of Alma" (Alma 25:21).

Alma the Younger: Prophet, Priest, and Politician

In Chapter 4 we saw how the record of Alma the Younger's interactions with Nehor and Amlici conceal a colonial narrative. But it conceals another narrative, too. When Alma becomes the head the Nephite church and the chief judge of the Nephite state, he steps into institutional roles that at times prevent him from functioning as a prophet. Prophets must be free to criticize both church and state when they fall short of God's expectations, and they can't do that when they control churches and states. Even without the burden of prophecy, Alma's two institutional roles are difficult to reconcile. The government of Zarahemla officially guarantees the freedom of belief. "The law could have no power on any man for their belief" Mormon tells us (Alma 1:17), and "there was no law against a man's belief, for it was strictly contrary to the commands of God that there should be a law which should bring men onto unequal grounds" (Alma 30:7). As the head of a state that guarantees religious freedom, Alma must act in ways that are incompatible with his role as the head of a church that feels compelled to chastise and dispute with members of other religions.

These conflicts become Alma's first major test as chief judge, which occurs when he tries a theological heretic named Nehor who is accused of a civil crime, murder, that arose from a religious dispute with a prominent member of Alma's church. The nature of the case makes it almost impossible for Alma to fulfill his conflicting institutional responsibilities—protecting the church from heresy and protecting citizens from violence—while upholding the laws that protect freedom of belief. Even if he can separate Nehor's belief from his corrupt practices and his religious practices from his violent actions, Alma can never escape the perception that he uses his chief judgeship to favor the interests of his own faction. When Nehor kills a popular Nephite hero in a religious dispute, he sets up a confrontation between the opposing sides of a culture war that could engulf the entire society in a civil war. He puts Alma in a no-win situation precisely because of his dual responsibilities. Anything Alma does against Nehor, no matter how justified, risks being perceived as an abuse of his office: the chief judge, who is also the high priest of the Church of Christ, using the coercive mechanisms of the state to persecute non-Christians.

Alma condemns Nehor to death and extracts a half-hearted retraction of his heretical views, but Nehor becomes a martyr, and his church continues to grow (Alma 1:16). The rise of Nehor's religion parallels the rise of the Nephite church, although the narrative's religious perspective conceals the similarities between the two movements. If the story of Nehor's encounter with Alma were told from the Nehorite perspective, it would sound very much like the story of Abinadi's encounter with King Noah. A brave religious leader goes throughout the land preaching the true gospel in spite of opposition from the established religion. He is arrested and accused of a crime against the state, but he cannot receive a fair trial because the ruler of the state is closely aligned with the corrupt religious orthodoxy that he opposes. After a trial in which his accusers spend more time arguing against his religious beliefs than presenting evidence of an actual crime, he is found guilty and executed. Yet the execution does not put an end to his religious influence. He becomes a martyr for his cause, and the religious movement he started makes new converts and spreads throughout the land.

Conflicts between the two religious movements escalate in Zarahemla (Alma 1:20), and resentments build (Alma 1:23–25) until, in the fifth year of Alma's reign, an open civil war breaks out, with the Nephites who support Alma and the reign of the judges on one side and the followers of Amlici, who professes the religion of Nehor, demanding that the judges be abolished and the monarchy restored with Amlici as the king. However violent and disruptive the Amlicites may be, their demands are not irrational. Democracy, even in the limited sense in which it was practiced in Zarahemla, only works when everybody believes that the system is fair. The society of Zarahemla is sharply divided along cultural lines that manifest themselves in two competing religious factions. The most powerful political officer in the land—the very person responsible for enforcing the laws protecting religious freedom—is also the leader of a religious faction that condemns the other faction as insincere heretics who merely "pretended to preach according to their belief" (Alma 1:17). This sends a powerful signal to the Nehorites that the voice of the people does not represent or protect their interests.

The war between the Christian and Nehorite factions takes up the second and third chapters of Alma, with the Lamanites joining the Amlicites against the Christian Nephites. When the war ends, the followers of Nehor have abandoned Zarahemla and become Lamanites (Alma 3:4–18), leaving the city largely in the hands of the Christians. The Christian Church experiences prosperity and large-scale conversions for a time (Alma 4:4–5) but begins to experience apostasy and internal divisions, including "envyings and strifes and malice and persecutions and pride, even to exceed the pride of those who did not belong to the church of God" (Alma 4:9). Alma concludes that these problems in the church require his full attention, so he "select[s] a wise man who was among the elders of the church and [gives] him power according to the voice of the people" (Alma 4:16). Nephihah becomes the new chief judge, while Alma retains the position of high priest. As the ninth year of the reign of the judges begins, Alma embarks on an extended mission trip to repair the damage done to the church through war and inattention.

Alma first goes to the land of Gideon, where he replicates his dual roles of prophet and church administrator. He preaches a sermon on Christ and repentance and "establishe[s] the order of the church according as he had done before in Zarahemla" (Alma 8:1). He then returns to Zarahemla briefly before traveling to the land of Melek, where he experiences similar success (Alma 8:3–5). Then he goes to the land of Ammonihah, whose people recognize and reject Alma as soon as he enters the city:

> Behold, we know that thou art Alma; and we know that thou art high priest over the church which thou hast established in many parts of the land according to your tradition. And we are not of thy church, and we do

not believe in such foolish traditions. And now we know that because we are not of thy church, we know that thou hast no power over us. And thou hast delivered up the judgment seat unto Nephihah; therefore thou art not the chief judge over us. (Alma 8:11–12)

The mission to Ammonihah ends almost as soon as it begins. The people "reviled him and spit upon him and caused that he should be cast out of their city" (Alma 8:13).

But an angel commands Alma to tell the people of Ammonihah that "except they repent the Lord God will destroy them" (Alma 8:16). When he returns, he finds that the Lord has prepared a man named Amulek to receive him and become his missionary companion (Alma 8:18–21). Alma and Amulek go throughout the land preaching repentance and warning the people of their impending destruction. They dispute in the marketplace with a lawyer named Zeezrom, who ends up converting, as do a number of women and children, people from the margins of society (Alma 14:6–7). In perhaps the most disturbing scene in the entire Book of Mormon, the men of Ammonihah burn the new converts alive, and Alma and Amulek are forced to watch (Alma 14:8–9).[30] Afterward, the chief judge of Ammonihah makes it clear that the punishment given to the Christian converts was based on Alma's and Amulek's words. He "smote them with his hand upon their cheeks and saith unto them: After what ye have seen, will ye preach again unto this people that they shall be cast into a lake of fire and brimstone[?]" (Alma 14:14). The two missionaries are then imprisoned and tortured before being freed by a divine intervention (Alma 14:27). They leave Ammonihah, and their prophecies are fulfilled almost immediately when the entire city is destroyed by the Lamanites (Alma 16:3).

The hostility that Alma experiences in Ammonihah, a city that used to fall within his jurisdiction as the chief judge, goes well beyond anything that we might expect from a religious dispute in a supposedly pluralistic society. The people of the city treat Alma as a mortal enemy and those who take his side as irredeemable traitors. Mormon attributes their actions to the usual influences of Satan (Alma 8:9) and a perverse attraction to wickedness (Alma 8:14)—but he downplays a crucial part of the story. The people of Ammonihah were followers of Nehor and, therefore, part of the faction that opposed Alma during the Amlicite war. Mormon does not mention this identity up front, but he gradually establishes it in the latter part of the story. First, he tells us that the judge who sends Alma and Amulek to prison was "after the order and faith of Nehor" (Alma 14:16). While in prison, "there came many lawyers and judges and priests and teachers, who were of the profession of Nehor" (Alma 14:18). After Alma and Amulek leave the city and experience success elsewhere, Mormon lets us know that the people of Ammonihah were generally "of the profession of Nehor" (Alma 15:15), and after the city is destroyed, the ruins become known as the "'Desolation of Nehors' for they were of the profession of Nehor which were slain; and their lands remained desolate" (Alma 16:11).

From the Nehorite perspective, it makes sense to treat Alma as an enemy. He was the chief judge who killed the founder of their religion, and he was the military commander who led an army against their co-religionists. Alma walking into Ammonihah five years after the war would have been something like Abraham Lincoln (assume that he was not assassinated in 1865) strolling all alone into Alabama in 1869—if Lincoln, in addition to being the former president of the United States, had also been the pope, and everyone in Alabama had been Protestant. Alma had opposed the followers of Nehor in his ecclesiastical and his civil roles. In the former capacity, he denounced them as heretics; in the latter, he attacked them as secessionists. However justified his actions may have been, they made it very difficult for him to approach them as a prophet and convince them to repent. Alma's mission ended the only way that it could end: with the people of Ammonihah rejecting Alma, who was unable to prevent their total destruction at the hands of the Lamanites (Alma 16:2–3).

The rise of the Nephite church—the narrative arc that begins when Abinadi appears in the land of Nephi (Mosiah 11:20) and ends when $Alma_2$ leaves Zarahemla and is "never heard of more" (Alma 45:18)—functions, narratively and theologically, like the book of Acts. The typological connections support this comparison as well. The most important character in Acts is the Apostle Paul, who takes Christ's message throughout the Roman Empire setting up Christian churches, a function that is split between $Alma_1$ and $Alma_2$ in the Mosiah-Alma arc. And in both narratives the Christian message does not go directly from Christ to the church-builders. In each case, a charismatic intermediary—Stephen in the Bible and Abinadi in the Book of Mormon—sets the action in motion before dying a martyr's death and leaving the building of the church to the second figure.[31]

The parallels between Abinadi and Stephen are legion. Both begin preaching to a community that considers itself religious but that overemphasizes the law of Moses and has no understanding of Christ (Acts 6:8–9/Mosiah 11:20–25). Both are brought before a council of religious authorities, where they are accused of blasphemy (Acts 6:12/Mosiah 7:8) and where they deliver lengthy sermons disputing their captors' understanding of both doctrine and

Israelite history (Acts 7:1–51/Mosiah 13:7–16:15). During their sermons, Stephen and Abinadi undergo similar physiological changes. The priests who conducted Stephen's council "saw his face as it had been the face of an angel" (Acts 6:15), and while Abinadi spoke to Noah's court, "his face shone with exceeding luster even as Moses' did while in the mount of Sinai while speaking with the Lord" (Mosiah 13:5). When they conclude their final sermons, both Stephen and Abinadi are condemned to death (Acts 7:59/ Mosiah 17:6–8).

If we combine the Alma who witnessed Abinadi's death with his son Alma the Younger into a single type, we get a composite figure that serves almost the same narrative and ecclesiastical functions in the Book of Mormon that Paul does in the New Testament. Over two generations, Alma and Alma the Younger build the Christian church in the land of Zarahemla in much the same way that Paul builds the church in the Roman Empire. The similarities begin when each man, as a priest in the Mosaic tradition, witnesses the execution of a charismatic prophet figure (Acts 8:1/Mosiah 17:2). Abinadi's final message directly causes Alma to convert to Christianity and start the Nephite church. The New Testament does not present Paul's conversion as a direct consequence of his role in Stephen's death, but it does indicate that the event moved Paul deeply and set in motion the events that led to his conversion (Acts 22:17–21), which becomes a type of Alma the Younger's conversion in the Book of Mormon. The two stories share a narrative arc, and they frequently use the same words and phrases to describe events. After his conversion, Alma$_2$ becomes both a civic and a religious leader. But after a terrible civil war he gives up his office and, like Paul, travels from city to city preaching and setting up churches throughout Zarahemla. If Abinadi and Stephen represent a prophet-type that proclaims the gospel and becomes a martyr, then the Alma$_{1/2}$ figure fits nicely into the second type: the charismatic organizer and builder who takes the first figure's message and turns it into an organization.

Nephi on the Tower, Samuel on the Wall

When Alma dies, his son and grandson, both named Helaman, succeed him as keepers of the plates. Both also hold important civic and ecclesiastical positions in the church and the state: Helaman$_2$ was a high priest in the church (Alma 46:6) and was a noted military commander in the war with Amalickiah (Alma 53:22).[32] Helaman$_3$ served as the chief judge for eleven years before passing the office on to his son Nephi$_2$, the first of Alma$_2$'s descendants to be described as a prophet in the text. Like Alma$_2$, Nephi$_2$ serves as the chief judge for nine years and leads the people through a ruinous war against an army of Lamanites and Nephite dissenters (Hel 4:1–26). Nephi$_2$ also follows Alma$_2$ in stepping down from the chief judgeship to focus on his ecclesiastical responsibilities:

> And it came to pass that in this same year, behold, Nephi delivered up the judgment seat to a man whose name was Cezoram. For as their laws and their governments were established by the voice of the people and they who chose evil were more numerous than they who chose good, therefore they were ripening for destruction, for the laws had become corrupted. Yea, and this was not all. They were a stiffnecked people, insomuch that they could not be governed by the law nor justice save it were to their destruction. And it came to pass that Nephi had become weary because of their iniquity; and he yielded up the judgment seat, and took it upon him to preach the word of God all the remainder of his days. (Hel 5:1–4)

There are several strong indications in the text that Nephi$_2$ did not surrender the judgment seat voluntarily, the way Alma did when he selected Nephihah to replace him. In the latter case, Mormon gives no indication that Nephi$_2$ either resigned voluntarily or had any say in the choice of his successor. The phrase "delivered up the judgment seat" could mean that he resigned his position. But it could just as easily mean that he conceded electoral defeat, which would explain why, after announcing Cezoram as the new chief judge, Mormon explains that "their governments were established by the voice of the people," that "they which chose evil were more numerous than they which chose good," and that "they were a stiffnecked people" who "could not be governed by the law nor justice save it were to their destruction" (Hel 5:1–3). These phrases make much more sense as excuses for losing an election than they do as reasons to abdicate voluntarily. And Mormon's concluding statement that Nephi$_2$ "yielded up the judgment seat" employs a verb, "yield," that normally carries the connotation of conceding or giving in to something or someone. The balance of the evidence suggests that Cezoram mounted a successful campaign to become the chief judge, and Nephi$_2$ yielded to the voice of the people.

Nephi$_2$ and his brother Lehi embark on a mission of about ten years of preaching and baptizing in Nephite and Lamanite lands. While they are gone, Cezoram is assassinated by the Gadianton Robbers, a secret society that sought to infiltrate all levels of Nephite and Lamanite societies by means of treachery and murder. Cezoram is succeeded by his son, also named Cezoram, who is assassinated by the same group within a year. When Nephi$_2$ returns from his missionary journeys, a Gadianton Robber named

Seezoram (who should not be confused with either of the Cezorams) has become chief judge, and the society itself has "overspread all the land of the Nephites and . . . seduced the more part of the righteous until they [came] down to believe in their works and partake of their spoils and to join with them in their secret murders and combinations" (Hel 6:38). The pervasive influence of these secret combinations compels Nephi$_2$ to stand atop a tower in his garden and call the Nephites to repentance (Hel 7). In this sermon he sounds very much like an Old Testament prophet lamenting the sinfulness of his people and predicting great catastrophes unless they repent (Hel 7:13–29). But Nephi$_2$ goes off message when some current judges, who belong to Gadianton's band, object to his words and shout out: "Why do ye suffer this man to revile against us? For behold, he doth condemn all this people, even unto destruction—yea, and also that these our great cities shall be taken from us, that we shall have no place in them" (Hel 8:5).

With this line of questioning, the corrupt judges in the crowd successfully change the focus of Nephi$_2$'s speech. Some people in the crowd become angry with him and others defend him, saying, "Let this man alone, for he is a good man; and those things which he saith will surely come to pass except we repent" (Hel 8:7). The crowd divides into factions and argues about whether Nephi$_2$ is a legitimate prophet, forcing him to abandon his primary objective of commanding the people to repent and focus on the secondary question of whether he had the authority to command the people to repent or the ability to foresee the future:

> Therefore he was constrained to speak more unto them, saying: Behold, my brethren, have ye not read that God gave power unto one man, even Moses, to smite upon the waters of the Red Sea and they departed hither and thither, insomuch that the Israelites, which were our fathers, came through upon dry ground; and the waters closed upon the armies of the Egyptians and swallowed them up. And now behold, if God gave unto this man such power, then why should ye dispute among yourselves and say that he hath given unto me no power whereby I may know concerning the judgments that shall come upon you except ye repent? But behold, ye not only deny my words, but ye also deny all the words which hath been spoken by our fathers, and also the words which [were] spoken by this man Moses, which had such great power given unto him—yea, the words which he hath spoken concerning the coming of the Messiah. (Hel 8:11–13)

Nephi$_2$ invokes other prophets such as Abraham (Hel 8:17), Isaiah, Jeremiah (Hel 8:20), and Lehi (Hel 8:22) and to say that, if they reject his prophetic statements, they must reject all of the other prophets as well. He closes with a dramatic finish designed to prove his prophetic calling conclusively: He announces that the chief judge has just been murdered by his own brother and challenges the crowd to go and see it for themselves (Hel 8:27–28).

Rather than continuing to warn the people, Nephi₂ quickly becomes embroiled in political intrigue. He, rather than his prophetic message, becomes the crowd's primary focus, and his warnings are absorbed into a partisan division that likely traces back to his own chief judgeship. I suggest that this result was inevitable—not because of what Nephi₂ said but because of who he was. There is no way someone like Nephi₂ could stand before a deeply divided audience without being considered a partisan. He is a former chief judge, son of a chief judge, grandson of a military hero, great-grandson of the founding chief judge of the republic, and the great-great grandson of the founder of the church. He and his family have long held civil and ecclesiastical authority in a society that has always had sharp divisions. Everybody knows where he stands politically, which, as Alma also discovered, makes it difficult to function prophetically with regard to his political opponents.

After Nephi₂ unmasks the conspiracy to assassinate the chief judge, God grants him what Latter-day Saints call "the sealing power," or the ability to use God's power directly for any reason.[33] "If ye shall say unto this temple: It shall be rent in twain," God tells Nephi₂, "it shall be done. And if ye shall say unto this mountain: Be thou cast down and become smooth!—and it shall be done. And behold, if ye shall say that God shall smite this people, it shall come to pass" (Hel 10:7–10). When the Gadianton Robbers work in secrecy to plunge the nation into yet another civil war, Nephi₂ uses the sealing power to call down a famine instead, hoping that it will compel the people to repent (Hel 11:4). The plan works for a while. After the famine kills thousands of people, the Nephites humble themselves and beg Nephi₂ to end the famine, and, at his request, the Lord "did turn away his anger from the people and caused that the rain should fall upon the earth" (Hel 11:17). The people repent for a season and begin to prosper. But even the power to call God's wrath down on the entire city is not enough to bring about lasting repentance. Within two years the divisions resurface, and the Gadianton Robbers become strong enough to wage war against the Nephites and the Lamanites simultaneously. The culture continues its downward march to collapse.

Before Nephi₂ disappears from the historical record, the people of Zarahemla experience a very different kind of prophet in Samuel the Lamanite, who comes from nowhere and begins prophesying—first in the city and then from atop the outer wall—in the eighty-sixth year of the reign of the judges. The parallel prophecies of Nephi₂ and Samuel present a unique dynamic and an interesting interpretive challenge. This is the first time since the creation of the church that we have seen two prophets with no apparent connection to each other prophesying to the same people at roughly the same time. And the location of each prophet's major public address has enormous symbolic and practical importance. Nephi₂ speaks from a tower in his own garden, which is "by the highway which led to the chief market which was in the city of Zarahemla" (Hel 7:10). He speaks both symbolically and geographically from the center of his culture. Samuel, on the other hand, speaks entirely from the margins. He is a Lamanite, a member of a culture that the Nephites have historically despised. He holds no formal position of authority in his own government and no office (that we know of) in the church. After he is ejected the first time, Samuel cannot enter the city of Zarahemla. By prophesying from the city's outer wall, he underscores the marginal nature of his social position.[34]

Samuel's appearance in Zarahemla repeats the narrative pattern established when Abinadi begins preaching in the land of Nephi. Both prophets begin preaching in the city, are cast out by angry residents, are instructed by God to return, and complete their prophetic missions before disappearing from the text. Samuel's message, too, is very similar to Abinadi's. They both decry the people's wickedness and declare that they must repent or be destroyed. Not surprisingly, it is the same message we see in most of the works of Old Testament prophecy as well. We read it in the works of, among others, Isaiah, Amos, Hosea, Ezekiel, and Micah. It is the message that Jonah preached, however half-heartedly, to the people of Nineveh. And it is the message that Jeremiah preached so often and so passionately that we now use the term "jeremiad" to describe the broad condemnation of an entire people or society.

As an outsider, Samuel cannot be distracted by Zarahemlan politics. Rather than demonstrating his prophetic abilities by solving local crimes, Samuel sticks to the more common topic of the people's wickedness and the utter destruction of civilization. As Kimberly Matheson frames it, "Nephi₂ gave us something like a fine zoom on Nephite life, Samuel provides readers with a wide-angle lens."[35] And yet, when talking about the coming of the Messiah, Samuel gets very specific about times. After warning the people that they have offended God with their wickedness and abominations, Samuel makes it clear that, if they do not repent immediately, God will destroy them in four hundred years. Both the specificity and the time frame of this prophecy seem strange. Prophets generally predict that doom and destruction will happen immediately if people don't repent. Few people will be motivated by destruction four centuries in the future. It probably would not have been effective to tell the pilgrims who landed at Plymouth Rock in 1620 that they needed to get their lives in order or their descendants in 2020 would be sorry. Nor would a prophetic warning of God's wrath being unleashed on the world of 2420 convince most of us to mend our evil ways. But the future that Samuel speaks of corresponds exactly to the time of Mormon's redaction. Mormon also knew exactly when the Nephites would be destroyed because he witnessed their destruction at first hand. It would have been strange for him not to gravitate toward prophecies that spoke clearly to his day and interpret them in light of the events that he was experiencing.

But something else is going on here. As we have already seen, the Book of Mormon claims to restore the "plain and precious truths" of the Bible. One of the ways it claims to do this is by stating clearly that the Christian tradition has only been able to read itself into the Old Testament by appealing to the complicated interpretive system of typology. The most important way in which the Book of Mormon distinguishes itself from the Bible is in its clear descriptions of Jesus Christ's birth, death, and mission centuries before the Christian Era. But in order to make these predictions, the Book of Mormon developed a much more direct form of prophetic discourse than we see in the Hebrew Bible. The eventual destruction of the Nephites at the hand of the Lamanites was established by a vision that Nephi had before reaching the promised land and before the children of Lehi split into factions (1 Ne 12:19–20). Similarly, in another vision, Nephi established that the Messiah would be born six hundred years after his family left Jerusalem (1 Ne 10:4). Samuel's dates for these events are in line with the prophetic tradition of which he is a part.

Samuel's prophecies about Christ's birth, however, become extremely important to the plot of the Book of Mormon because he makes very specific predictions with a very clear timeline:

> And behold, he saith unto them: Behold, I give unto you a sign. For five years more cometh, and behold, then cometh the Son of God to redeem all those who shall believe on his name. And behold, this will I give unto you for a sign at the time of his coming. For behold, there shall be great lights in heaven, insomuch that in the night before he cometh there shall be no darkness, insomuch that it shall appear unto man as if it was day. Therefore there shall be one day and a night and a day, as if it were one day and there were no night. And this shall be unto you for a sign.... And behold, there shall a new star arise, such an one as ye never have beheld; and this also shall be a sign unto you. And behold, this is not all. There shall be many signs and wonders in heaven. (Hel 14:2–6)

Samuel's prophecy about an imminent event created a testable claim of fact for his audience. And although Samuel had no formal institutional affiliation, it is his prophecy, rather than Nephi₂'s, that became the standard by which the Nephites judged the claims of the church. In the first chapter of 3 Nephi, we discover that the unbelievers of Zarahemla set a date by which Christians would be executed if the signs that Samuel predicted failed to appear (3 Ne 1:9). The signs came, however, and the church survived to greet Christ when he visited them thirty-three years later, after a massive societal collapse (3 Ne 7:1–6) and a series of large-scale natural disasters (3 Ne 8:5–25). Nephi₂'s son, Nephi₃, becomes one of Christ's disciples (3 Ne 13:25). And, as if to provide a final clarification of Samuel's marginal status, when Christ asks to see the records and notices that Samuel's words were not recorded, it is Nephi₃ who must tell him that the recordkeeper at the time—his father—failed to record them (3 Ne 13:8–13).

Conclusion

The four prophets discussed in this chapter—Abinadi, Alma₂, Nephi₂, and Samuel—represent two distinct prophet-types. The first, let's call it prophet-type A, describes both Abinadi and Samuel. This type is entirely consistent with the main prophet-type in the Bible: a figure from the margins of society who holds no institutional authority and who preaches repentance and issues dire predictions in the name of God. Prophet-type B describes a figure who comes from the center of society and holds ecclesiastical and often political authority. Some aspects of prophet-type B occur in the Old Testament. Patriarchs such as Abraham and Isaac are described as prophets and exercise near-absolute power as the heads of their households in a tribal society, and Joseph exercises prophetic power in Egypt, where he also holds a high civic office. And Moses, more than any other Old Testament figure, is a prophet, a priest, and the undisputed leader of his people as they wander through the wilderness before inheriting the promised land. Once the Israelites have stable political and religious institutions, however, prophets invariably operate outside of them, on the margins of the community. We find no figures like Alma₂ or Nephi₂—prophets who serve at the head of both the government and an established church—in any of the Hebrew states described in the Old Testament.

Prophet-type B in the Book of Mormon comes much closer to the way the term is used in the contemporary Church of Jesus Christ of Latter-day Saints. Like many of the prophets named there, they act primarily within an institutional context, which means that their prophetic authority is entirely mediated through the regulations and conventions of the institutional church. Laura Thiemann Scales locates the origins of this difference in the way the Book of Mormon frames prophet-figures within its narrative. "Unlike biblical prophets, who tend to present themselves as vessels for God's words," she writes, "Latter-day Saint (LDS) prophets are distinctive in their often-simultaneous embodiment of multiple narrative identities." By investing its prophet-characters with multiple narrative roles, the Book of Mormon "fundamentally changed the narrative practice of scripture."[36] As a consequence of this narrative change, many of these prophets have non-prophetic roles to play. They are kings and politicians and military leaders and other things that are incompatible with the Old Testament's understanding of a prophet as an empty vessel to be filled by the word of God. By presenting prophets as political and military leaders, the Book of Mormon supports the routinization of prophetic charisma that has characterized the modern LDS Church.

Yet the Book of Mormon also cautions against the complete institutionalization of prophetic authority. Alma's tenure as head of both church and state ends in a disastrous war, and after he resigns his political office to focus on his ministry, his prophetic leadership is severely damaged by the memory of his political failures. Alma's primogenital descendants—Helaman$_2$, Helaman$_3$, and Nephi$_2$—hold leadership roles in the Nephite church, and the latter two also serve as chief judge for a combined total of 20 years. Though the Book of Mormon portrays these leaders as righteous, it does not always portray them as effective, nor does it portray the comingling of prophecy and politics as a beneficial arrangement for either the church or the state. Toward the end of the Reign of the Judges—when the Church of Christ was well-established and after two successive prophets had held the chief judgeship for 20 years—God sent another outsider-prophet to continue Abinadi's work. With no formal political or ecclesiastical sanction, Samuel the Lamanite stands on Zarahemla's city wall and warns the people to repent or face the wrath of God. In the process, he re-injects the Bible's more limited view of prophetic charisma into a highly routinized and unfortunately politicized religious bureaucracy prevented by its own institutional constraints from ministering effectively to the people of Zarahemla.

CHAPTER SEVEN

"We Talk of Christ, We Rejoice in Christ"

> And we talk of Christ, we rejoice in Christ, we preach of Christ, we prophesy of Christ; and we write according to our prophecies that our children may know to what source they may look for a remission of their sins.
>
> —2 Ne 25:26

> Smith makes Nephi express every truth found in the writings of the Apostles concerning the calling and blessing of the Gentiles, and even quotes the 11th chapter of Romans, and many other passages before he had a son grown in the wilderness able to aim an arrow at a deer. Paul says these things were secrets and unknown until his time; but Smith makes Nephi say the same things 600 years before Paul was converted! One of the two is a false prophet. Mormonites, take your choice!
>
> —Alexander Campbell, *Delusions: An Analysis of the Book of Mormon*

The detailed knowledge of the New Testament Christ in a narrative set nearly six hundred years before the New Testament has always put some pressure on the Book of Mormon's historical claims.[1] Without original, verifiably ancient records to examine, the Nephite's detailed Christology seems best explained by, or at least most parsimoniously attributed to, a more recent provenance. And the fact that the Book of Mormon contains no information about Christ's earthly life that cannot be found in the New Testament makes it even more likely that its creator had access to the modern New Testament.[2] Alexander Campbell, who, like Smith, led a movement to restore primitive Christianity, based much of his criticism of the Book of Mormon on its extensive foreknowledge of Jesus Christ in parts of the text set hundreds of years before Christ's birth.[3] In his 1832 pamphlet *Delusions*, Campbell complained that Joseph Smith "represents the christian institution as practised among his Israelites before Jesus was born. And his Jews are called Christians." Campbell mocks the idea that the Nephites "were good christians, believers in the doctrines of the Calvinists and Methodists, and preaching baptism and other christian usages hundreds of years before Jesus Christ was born!"[4]

Campbell goes on to detail specific places in the text where the Book of Mormon's characters displayed knowledge that they weren't supposed to have about Christ's life and ministry:

> "For it behoveth the Great Creator that he die for all men." "It must needs be an infinite atonement." "This flesh must go to its mother earth." "And this death must deliver up its dead" (70), were common phrases 2300 years ago—"for the atonement satisfieth the demands of his justice upon all those who have not the law given them" (81). The Calvinists were in America before Nephi. . . . "The atonement is infinite for all mankind" (104). The Americans knew this on the Columbo 2400 years ago. "His name shall be called Jesus Christ the Son of God." An angel told this to Nephi 515 years before it was told to Mary (105). . . . "Wherein did the Lamb of God fill all righteousness in being baptised by water" (118). This question was discussed 2300 years ago. . . "The baptism by fire and the Holy Ghost was preached in the days of Cyrus" (119). "The only true doctrine of the Father and of the Son and of the Holy Ghost which is one God without end. Amen" (120). This was decided in the time of Daniel the Prophet. . . . "Christ will show you that these are his words the last day" (122). Too late to prove your mission, Mr. Nephi!
>
> "After that ye have obtained a hope in Christ, ye shall obtain riches if you seek them." So spoke Jacob in the days of Ezekiel the Prophet. "They believed in Christ and worshipped the Father in his name" (129). This was said by Jacob in the time of Daniel. . . "And his mother shall be called Mary" (160). "The Son of God and Father of heaven and earth." "The infant perisheth not, that dieth in his infancy." "For the natural man is an enemy of God and was from the fall of Adam, and will be forever and ever" (161). . . . "They were baptised in the waters of Mormon, and were called the church of Christ" (192). This happened 100 years before Christ was born. "Alma, why persecuteth thou the church of God" (122). "Ye must be born again; yea, born of God—changed from their carnal and fallen state to a state of righteousness" (214). This was preached also 100 years before Christ was born.[5]

Campbell's reading of the Book of Mormon was much more substantial than those of almost any of its other early critics. Though it contains, as Frederik Kleiner demonstrates, "only contempt for the text and Joseph Smith,"[6] his sixteen-page pamphlet displays a basic understanding of the text, its narrators, and its internal timeline.[7] His arguments about the anachronistic nature of the text's Christology, though, are problematic when considered in light of his own theology. Like most Protestants, Campbell believed that the Bible was a coherent volume whose most important purpose was to testify about Christ. And he believed that the Old Testament testified by means of types and symbols. "The Jewish religion was divine," he said in a published 1839 debate with social reformer Robert Owen, and "all its rites were in their nature symbolical and prophetic . . . the sacrifice of a lamb, the building of an altar, the consecration of the priesthood, and the whole ritual of Moses were symbolical and prophetic of christianity."[8]

Orthodox Christian believers such as Campbell walk a thin line when they criticize the Book of Mormon for speaking clearly about Christ in 600 BCE while, at the same time, insisting that nearly everything in the Old Testament speaks unclearly about precisely the same things. According to the New Testament, the ancient Hebrew prophets knew many of the same things about Christ that the people of the Book of Mormon knew: that he would be announced by a "voice crying in the wilderness," that he would be born of a virgin, that he would work great miracles, that he would be crucified for the sins of the world, that he would be miraculously resurrected, and that he would be a literal son of God. The Book of Mormon says all of these things directly, which often strikes readers as strange. According to the New Testament, however, the Old Testament said all of these things in a typological code that can only be interpreted by referring to the New Testament. This should strike us as a much stranger claim about Christ than the Book of Mormon makes. But Christians have been making this claim for two thousand years—and the Christian Bible cannot exist as a coherent canon without it—so much of the world has been conditioned to see it as normal.

In terms of logic, the various phrases and plot elements that Christians interpret as prefigurations make a weak case for Jesus Christ as the primary figure of the Hebrew Bible. These passages usually refer to contexts shared by the writer and the original audience and can only be understood retroactively once the antitype has occurred and the pattern reveals itself. It is difficult to imagine why God would choose to reveal the most important things in the Bible—the life, mission, and godhood of Jesus Christ—in ways that nobody would be able to understand until hundreds of years later when the interpretive key came along. Why bother communicating information about future events in obscure ways? Why not just prophesy in plain terms?

This is exactly the kind of problem that the Book of Mormon perceives itself as solving. As Samuel Brown has argued in *Joseph Smith's Translations*, the Book of Mormon sees the Bible as irredeemably inadequate—both because centuries of redaction and translation errors left the text unreliable and because the Bible was a "limited, regional document" that did not reflect the temporal or geographical expansiveness of God's love as manifest in textual records. The Book of Mormon addresses this not through correction or emendation but by "retranslating the Bible in a new key" and transforming it "into the texts that it always should have been."[9] I argue in this chapter that a key part of this effort consists of taking the typological Christ in the Old Testament and replacing him with the Christ of prophecy, whose coming is foretold in plain, direct language. And the plain discussion of Christ in the early books of the Book of Mormon dramatically recontextualizes his appearance in its later books in such a way that exactly the same words have radically different meanings. This, I believe, is what Brown means when he says that the Book of Mormon retranslates the Bible in a new key.

Plainness and Preciousness in Nephi's Visions

The great prophetic theme of Nephi's vision of the tree of life (1 Ne 11–14) is that God will one day be incarnated as Jesus Christ and will, in that form, redeem humanity from sin and death by his own death and resurrection. As we saw in Chapter 2, these concepts would have been extremely difficult for any Judean of the sixth century BCE to understand. In order to overcome Nephi's deep cultural resistance to these ideas, the angel who guides him through most of the vision uses concrete images and straightforward language to convey unfamiliar ideas such as the virgin birth, the preparatory role of John the Baptist, the New Testament's miracles, and the Crucifixion. Unlike other texts in the apocryphal tradition, Nephi's apocalypse does not rely on obscure symbols to make its prophecies. There are no seven-headed beasts or polymetallic statues.[10] When the angel wants to explain the virgin birth, he shows Nephi an image of "a virgin most beautiful and fair above all other virgins" (1 Ne 11:15) and says, "behold, the virgin whom thou seest is the mother of God after the manner of the flesh" (1 Ne 11:18). Nephi records his vision in the same plain language that the angel uses.

The clarity of Nephi's vision contrasts sharply with the obscurity of his father's dream. Someone who already understands the nature of the Atonement might be able to understand the connection between the tree of life and "the condescension of God" from the symbolism that Lehi supplies. But Lehi's family, living six centuries before Christ's birth, lacks the conceptual framework to invest such symbolism with meaning. Even Nephi, Lehi's most spiritually sensitive child, needs a detailed, specific explanation before he can process the magnitude of God's incarnation as Jesus Christ. The differences between the dream and the vision parallel the differences between the Bible and the Book of Mormon. The Old Testament of the Christian Bible—when interpreted through the Christological claims of the New Testament—speaks of the Messiah only obliquely and in code. The encoded information includes some of the concepts that would have seemed the strangest to any Judahite living in the Kingdom of Judah before the Babylonian exile—things like the incarnation of God as a human infant, the virgin birth, the political execution of a deity, and an infinite atonement in which a divine being sacrifices himself to secure forgiveness for all of humanity.

Table 2 illustrates the ways in which the New Testament interprets passages in the Old Testament as prophecies of Christ and the way the Book of Mormon prophesies much more directly of the same elements of Christ's life and ministry. The point is not that the Book of Mormon predicts the future more accurately than the Old Testament does; given the late publication date of the Book of Mormon, such a comparison would not prove anything worth proving. What it does show, though, is that the Book of Mormon does not claim any greater foreknowledge of Christ among its pre-Christian inhabitants than the New Testament claims for the Old. In each instance, the Book of Mormon alone says clearly the same things that the Old Testament says when interpreted through the New Testament.

Consider, for example, the passage from Acts 2:29–35, which argues that David knew of and prophesied about Christ's resurrection. The author of Acts sets this speech at the feast of Pentecost, just fifty days after Christ's death and resurrection, with an audience consisting of Jews whom Peter wants to convince to see Jesus as the Messiah. In order to do this, he ingeniously weaves together snippets from three different psalms to create a single argument:

> Men and brethren, let me freely speak unto you of the patriarch David, that he is both dead and buried, and his sepulchre is with us unto this day. Therefore being a prophet, and knowing that *God had sworn with an oath to him, that of the fruit of his loins, according to the flesh, he would raise up Christ to sit on his throne* (Psalms 132:11). He seeing this before spake of the resurrection of Christ, that *his soul was not left in hell, neither his flesh did see corruption* (Pss 16:10). This Jesus hath God raised up, whereof we all are witnesses. Therefore being by the right hand of God exalted, and having received of the Father the promise of the Holy Ghost, he hath shed forth this, which ye now see and hear. For David is not ascended into the heavens: but he saith himself, the Lord said unto my Lord, *sit thou on my right hand, Until I make thy foes thy footstool.* (Pss 110:1)

Table 2. Fulfillment of Messianic prophecies in the New Testament and the Book of Mormon

	Old Testament	New Testament	Book of Mormon (1 & 2 Nephi)
Virgin Birth	**Isaiah 7:14:** Behold, a virgin shall conceive, and bear a son, and shall call his name Immanuel.	**Matthew 1:20–23:** But while he thought on these things, behold, the angel of the Lord appeared unto him in a dream, saying, Joseph, thou son of David, fear not to take unto thee Mary thy wife: for that which is conceived in her is of the Holy Ghost. And she shall bring forth a son, and thou shalt call his name Jesus: for he shall save his people from their sins. Now all this was done, *that it might be fulfilled which was spoken of the Lord by the prophet, saying, Behold, a virgin shall be with child, and shall bring forth a son, and they shall call his name Emmanuel, which being interpreted is, God with us.*	**1 Nephi 11:18:** And he said unto me: Behold, the virgin which thou seest is the mother of God after the manner of the flesh.
John the Baptist	**Isaiah 40:3–5:** The voice of him that crieth in the wilderness, Prepare ye the way of the Lord, make straight in the desert a highway for our God. Every valley shall be exalted, and every mountain and hill shall be made low: and the crooked shall be made straight, and the rough places plain: And the glory of the Lord shall be revealed, and all flesh shall see [it] together: for the mouth of the Lord hath spoken it.	**Luke 3:4–6:** *As it is written in the book of the words of Esaias the prophet, saying, The voice of one crying in the wilderness, Prepare ye the way of the Lord, make his paths straight.* Every valley shall be filled, and every mountain and hill shall be brought low; and the crooked shall be made straight, and the rough ways [shall be] made smooth; and all flesh shall see the salvation of God. (See also Matt 3:3, Mark 1:3, and John 1:23.)	**1 Nephi 11:27:** And I looked and beheld the Redeemer of the world, of which my father had spoken. And I also beheld the prophet which should prepare the way before him. And the Lamb of God went forth and was baptized of him. And after that he was baptized, I beheld the heavens open and the Holy Ghost came down out of heaven and abode upon him in the form of a dove.

Table 2. continued

	Old Testament	New Testament	Book of Mormon (1 & 2 Nephi)
Miracles of Jesus	**Isaiah 53:4–5**: Surely he hath borne our griefs, and carried our sorrows: yet we did esteem him stricken, smitten of God, and afflicted. But he was wounded for our transgressions, he was bruised for our iniquities: the chastisement of our peace was upon him; and with his stripes we are healed.	**Matthew 8:16–17**: When the even was come, they brought unto him many that were possessed with devils: and he cast out the spirits with his word, and healed all that were sick. *That it might be fulfilled which was spoken by Esaias the prophet, saying, Himself took our infirmities, and bare our sicknesses.*	**1 Nephi 11:31**: And he spake unto me again saying: Look! And I looked and I beheld the Lamb of God going forth among the children of men. And I beheld multitudes of people which were sick and which were afflicted of all manner of diseases and with devils and unclean spirits — and the angel spake and shewed all these things unto me — and they were healed by the power of the Lamb of God, and the devils and the unclean spirits were cast out.
Crucifixion	**Psalms 22:15**: My strength is dried up like a potsherd; and my tongue cleaveth to my jaws; and thou hast brought me into the dust of death.	**John 19:28**: After this, Jesus knowing that all things were now accomplished, *that the scripture might be fulfilled,* saith, I thirst.	**1 Nephi 11:33**: And I Nephi saw that he was lifted up upon the cross and slain for the sins of the world.
	Psalms 22:18: They part my garments among them, and cast lots upon my vesture.	**Matthew 27:35**: And they crucified him, and parted his garments, casting lots: *that it might be fulfilled* which was spoken by the prophet, They parted my garments among them, and upon my vesture did they cast lots.	
	Exodus 12:46: In one house shall it be eaten; thou shalt not carry forth aught of the flesh abroad out of the house; neither shall ye break a bone thereof.	**John 19:33, 36**: But when they came to Jesus, and saw that he was dead already, they brake not his legs. . . . For these things were done, *that the scripture should be fulfilled,* a bone of him shall not be broken.	

Table 2. continued

	Old Testament	New Testament	Book of Mormon (1 & 2 Nephi)
Entombment (3 Days)	**Jonah 1:17:** Now the Lord had prepared a great fish to swallow up Jonah. And Jonah was in the belly of the fish three days and three nights.	**Matthew 12:38–40:** Then some of the scribes and Pharisees told Jesus, "Teacher, we want to see a sign from you." But he replied to them, "An evil and adulterous generation craves a sign. Yet no sign will be given to it except the sign of the prophet Jonah, because just as Jonah was in the stomach of the sea creature for three days and three nights, so the Son of Man will be in the heart of the earth for three days and three nights."	**2 Nephi 25:13a:** Behold, they will crucify him. And after he is laid in a sepulcher for the space of three days. . . .
Resurrection	**Psalms 16:10–11:** *For thou wilt not leave my soul in hell; neither wilt thou suffer thine Holy One to see corruption. Thou wilt shew me the path of life: in thy presence is fulness of joy; at thy right hand there are pleasures for evermore.*	**Acts 2:29–35:** Men and brethren, let me freely speak unto you of the patriarch David, that he is both dead and buried, and his sepulcher is with us unto this day. Therefore being a prophet, and knowing that *God had sworn with an oath to him, that of the fruit of his loins, according to the flesh, he would raise up Christ to sit on his throne.* He seeing this before spake of the resurrection of Christ, that *his soul was not left in hell, neither his flesh did see corruption.* This Jesus hath God raised up, whereof we all are witnesses. Therefore being by the right hand of God exalted, and having received of the Father the promise of the Holy Ghost, he hath shed forth this, which ye now see and hear. For David is not ascended into the heavens: but he saith himself, *the Lord said unto my Lord, Sit thou on my right hand, Until I make thy foes thy footstool.*	**2 Nephi 25:13b:** . . . he shall rise from the dead with healing in his wings, and all they that shall believe on his name shall be saved in the kingdom of God. Wherefore my soul delighteth to prophesy concerning him, for I have seen his day, and my heart doth magnify his holy name.
	Psalms 110:1–2: *The Lord said unto my Lord, sit thou at my right hand, until I make thine enemies thy footstool. The Lord shall send the rod of thy strength out of Zion: rule thou in the midst of thine enemies.*		
	Psalms 132:11: The Lord hath sworn in truth unto David; he will not turn from it; *of the fruit of thy body will I set upon thy throne.*		

Peter begins by citing Psalm 132, which recalls God's promise that he would set one of David's descendants on the throne. The verse immediately after the one that Peter cites reads, "If thy children will keep my covenant and my testimony that I shall teach them, their children shall also sit upon thy throne for evermore" (Pss 132:12). This is one of several passages in the *Tanakh* that promise that the Kingdom of David—by which most Jews understood the united Kingdom of Israel—would last forever. After the destruction of the northern kingdom in 722 BCE and the destruction of Judah in 586 BCE, the surviving Israelites began to search their scriptures for evidence that the Kingdom of David would be restored and that, soon thereafter, the world in its present form would come to an end. Though it does not occur at all in the Hebrew scriptures per se, the idea of a messiah as a "concrete eschatological figure" who would usher in the world's final epoch became common among the Jews of the Second Temple period.[11] Psalm 132 was frequently cited as a prophecy of new king, who was simply called "King" or "Anointed One" (מָשִׁיחַ or *ma·ší·ak*)—a form of which (בִמְשִׁיחֶ֑ךָ) does appear in Psalm 132:10—making this one of the texts that Peter's contemporaries would have understood as a messianic prophecy.[12]

After citing this passage, Peter immediately connects it to a passage that had never been part of the messianic tradition: Pss 16:10, in which David rhapsodizes, "For thou wilt not leave my soul in hell; neither wilt thou suffer thine Holy One to see corruption." The word translated here as "in hell" is actually "in Sheol" (לִשְׁאוֹל), which refers to a generic underworld where all souls go after death, rather than to a moral judgment against the unrighteous. Thus, the psalmist is expressing his love of God and his hope that the Lord will reciprocate that love and grant him some kind of immortality. The text gives us no reason to think that the poem describes a Davidic descendant—Messiah or otherwise—because the text is entirely in the first person and deals explicitly with the hopes and desires of the speaker. The Jewish tradition did not see Psalm 16 as a messianic prophecy before Peter made this argument,[13] and many contemporary Christian scholars today consider it an interpretive error or, at best, a prophetic reading that the original text does not support.[14]

Peter concludes his argument with the opening words of Psalm 110: "The Lord said unto my Lord, sit thou at my right hand, until I make thine enemies thy footstool" (Pss 110:1). This sentence is quoted or alluded to eleven times in the New Testament, more than any other passage from the Hebrew Bible. This includes seven passages in which Christ applies the text to himself to demonstrate that he is the Messiah, and five times when Paul or another writer describes the resurrected Christ as being on "the right hand of God."[15]

Though there is no evidence that Psalm 110 was read as a messianic psalm in the Hebrew tradition,[16] it has become a cornerstone of Christian interpretation.[17] The New Testament's use of this passage makes it abundantly clear that, from a very early date, followers of Jesus saw this as a messianic prophecy that establishes the rise of a new kingdom, albeit a spiritual one, where Jesus Christ rules at God's side.

By weaving these three citations together, Peter successfully pre-empts the most obvious objection that his audience would have had to his argument, which is: If Jesus was indeed the Messiah, then why is he dead? Why didn't he restore the Davidic monarchy and reunite the tribes of Israel? Why are we still under Rome's thumb?[18] Peter had to shift his audience's expectations from temporal restoration to eschatological salvation, which he did by tying commonplace arguments about the Messiah (that he would sit on the restored throne of King David) with novel and even radical reinterpretations of scripture (that the psalmist's hope for eternal life was really a prophecy that the Messiah would be resurrected from the dead). And he speaks the entire argument in David's words using carefully arranged selections from the Psalms. The overall argument is something like, "You all know that, a thousand years ago, David knew that God would one day install one of his descendants on an everlasting throne. But he did not mean an earthly throne, since no earthly kingdom can be everlasting. He foresaw that this descendant would defeat death itself and sit on an eternal throne on the right hand of God."

Peter's original audience seems to have been persuaded by the speech; three thousand people were baptized in the name of Jesus Christ at the end of the Pentecost festival (Acts 2:38, 41). But Peter did have some help. The manifestations of the spirit that accompanied Peter's words—and the fact that people heard the speech in their own languages—gave a powerful divine endorsement to the arguments he used. But even without rushing winds and flaming tongues, Christians have always seen the Hebrew Bible's messianic prophecies as evidence that Christ's birth, earthly ministry, death, and resurrection were known and understood by the prophets of ancient Israel. These prophecies, however, only made sense after the events that they prophesied had already happened. Nobody in the first century BCE read the Psalms and the Book of Isaiah and concluded that the Messiah would be God incarnate, born to a virgin, crucified by the Romans, or resurrected to glory on a spiritual plane. The messianic prophecies of the Old Testament became useful descriptors of the New Testament's Messiah only after he had come and gone.

But that is not how the early Christian church saw the matter. By the early fourth century it was an article of faith among Christians that the messianic prophecies in the Hebrew scriptures gave the Jews all the information they needed to recognize Christ as the Messiah. Early church fathers such as Justin Martyr and Eusebius wrote broad polemics condemning the Jews for misreading their own scriptures and missing the clear and obvious fact of Jesus's Messiahship. In these works, writes Rosemary Ruether, "the Jews are said to be incapable of understanding or interpreting their own Scriptures or even finding God in them. The Jews are 'blind,' 'hard of heart,' and a 'veil lies over their eyes.' All this prevents them from seeing the inner meaning of the text, i.e., its Christological meaning."[19] This, then, led to the belief that the Jews were punished by God primarily for failing to recognize the Messiah that they were sent—which the Hebrew prophets also foretold. "The divine oracles foretold that the Advent of Christ and the call of the Gentiles would be accompanied by the total collapse and ruin of the whole Jewish race," writes Eusebius in *Proof of the Gospel*. "The Hebrew oracles foretell distinctly the fall and ruin of the Jewish race through their disbelief in Christ."[20]

The Book of Mormon rejects the mode of prophecy that the New Testament writers attributed to the Hebrew Bible. It does not, however, reject the conclusion of that reading, namely, that Jesus was the Messiah, or the Christ. Like the New Testament, the Book of Mormon teaches that Christ is at the center of the ancient records and that the law of Moses and "all things which have been given of God from the beginning of the world unto man are the typifying of him" (2 Ne 11:4). But the Book of Mormon rejects the notion that the Jews, or anybody else, could have understood the Messiah's nature from typological references alone.[21] Nephi's vision clearly states that the version of the Hebrew scriptures that he has—the records on the plates of brass that he and his brothers liberated from Laban (1 Ne 3–4)—contains clear descriptions of Christ that we do not find in our modern Bibles:

> And the God of our fathers, which were led out of Egypt out of bondage, and also were preserved in the wilderness by him, yea, the God of Abraham and of Isaac and the God of Jacob yieldeth himself according to the words of the angel as a man into the hands of wicked men, to be lifted up, according to the words of Zenoch,[22] and to be crucified, according to the words of Neum, and to be buried in a sepulcher according to the words of Zenos, which he spake concerning the three days of darkness which should be a sign given of his death unto them who should inhabit the isles of the sea, more especially given unto those who are of the house of Israel. (1 Ne 19:10)

Zenoch, Neum, and Zenos, of course, do not appear in the canonical Christian Old Testament, but Zenoch and Zenos appear in other places in the Book of Mormon. Nephi's brother, Jacob, quotes an extended passage from the prophet Zenos expanding on Paul's use of an olive tree as a symbol of Gentiles being grafted into the Abrahamic covenant (Rom 11:13–16).[23] Alma, when preaching to the Zoramites, invokes both Zenos and Zenoch to establish that the Messiah will be the Son of God (Alma 33:12–15), and Amulek follows up with the statement, "My brother hath called upon the words of Zenos, that redemption cometh through the Son of God, and also upon the words of Zenoch. And also he has appealed unto Moses to prove that these things are true" (Alma 34:7). And Nephi$_2$, in the years immediately preceding Christ's visit, insisted the prophet Zenos "did testify boldly" of the coming of the Son of God, "for the which he was slain" (Hel 8:19).

By pointing to quoting in part prophetic texts that give Christological details not found in the Old Testament, the Book of Mormon gestures to an original version of the Christian Bible that no longer exists. Samuel Brown calls this the "primordial Bible" and argues that "the Book of Mormon saw one of its central roles as saving the primordial Bible by killing the corrupt Protestant one."[24] In this primordial Bible prophets speak as clearly and directly about Christ as Nephi and Jacob do. And Nephi's vision prophetically details the way the Bible of the future will be corrupted:

> And the angel of the Lord said unto me: Thou hast beheld that the book pro-
> ceeded forth from the mouth of a Jew. And when it proceeded forth from
> the mouth of a Jew, it contained the fulness of the gospel of the Lamb,[25] of
> whom the twelve apostles bear record. And they bear record according to the
> truth which is in the Lamb of God. Wherefore these things go forth from
> the Jews in purity unto the Gentiles, according to the truth which is in God.
> And after that they go forth by the hand of the twelve apostles of the Lamb
> from the Jews unto the Gentiles, behold, after this thou seest the formation
> of that great and abominable church, which is the most abominable above
> all other churches.[26] For behold, they have taken away from the gospel of
> the Lamb many parts which are plain and most precious; and also many
> covenants of the Lord have they taken away. And all this have they done
> that they might pervert the right ways of the Lord, that they might blind
> the eyes and harden the hearts of the children of men. (1 Ne 13:24–27)

The phrase "plain and precious" becomes a recurring theme of the vision. Later, the angel tells Nephi that the Gentiles of the latter day "do stumble exceedingly because of the most plain and precious parts of the gospel of the Lamb which hath been kept back by that abominable church" (1 Ne 13:34). And when describing the future coming forth of the Book of Mormon, the angel tells Nephi that the last records he sees "shall make known the plain and precious things which have been taken away from them" (1 Ne 13:40).[27] Much of the analysis of this phrase by Latter-day Saint scholars focuses on the loss of truths or doctrines that were removed from the Bible and restored in the Book of Mormon.[28] But this is not quite what the Book of Mormon says. It never follows the phrase "plain and precious" with "truths" or "doctrines"—only with such curiously generic terms as "things" and "parts."[29] Furthermore, unlike most set-phrase doublets ("aid and abet," "cease and desist," and so on), "plain" and "precious" mean two very different things. Plainness describes the nature of the something, while preciousness judges its value. This sets up a cause-and-effect relation between the terms: The plainness of some things increases their value. Such things are precious because they are plain. If they are made less plain, they become less precious.

According to the Book of Mormon, then, the enemies of God removed plainness from the teachings of the original, uncorrupted Bible. And the most important thing that the Bible is supposed to teach plainly is the nature of the Messiah, Jesus Christ—the doctrine that both the Old Testament and the New are supposed to be testaments of. Throughout his writings Nephi constructs a version of the Christian Old Testament that teaches the key doctrines of Christ—the Incarnation, the Atonement, and the Resurrection—clearly and in plain language. As we have already seen, the New Testament and the subsequent Christian tradition maintain that these doctrines were taught in the Old Testament but were concealed in an extraordinarily complex typological code. The fact that they are no longer clear shows why the world needs a plainer and, therefore, more precious record. The Book of Mormon makes a case for its own existence when Nephi reports, "Because of the many plain and precious things which have been taken out of the book, which were plain unto the understanding of the children of men according to the plainness which is in the Lamb of God . . . an exceedingly great many do stumble, yea, insomuch that Satan hath great power over them" (1 Ne 13:29).[30]

This emphasis on plainness and clarity becomes one of the strongest themes of Nephi's writing, and it is thrown into sharp relief by Nephi's copious borrowing from the book of Isaiah in his record. The first two books of Nephi contain eighteen full chapters from the book of Isaiah, consisting of more than four hundred verses and nearly twelve thousand words.[31] About 40 percent of this text comes verbatim from the King James Bible, with the rest containing primarily inconsequential variations.[32] These passages are dense, difficult, tied to a specific context, and (according to the New Testament) full of intensely Christological types and symbols—everything that Nephi objects to in the name of "plainness." And immediately after hand-engraving the largest block of Isaiah text in the Book of Mormon, Nephi states that he will not teach his people how to interpret the words of Isaiah (2 Ne 25:1–6) and that he will follow a completely different model for his own prophetic discourse. Why did Nephi engrave twelve thousand words of a text that all of his readers, ancient and modern, already had access to—and then immediately invalidate his efforts by declaring that he would never teach his people to interpret them? This is one of the most puzzling and important interpretive questions in the entire Book of Mormon.

Isaiah and Nephi on the Promised Messiah

A story often told by Latter-day Saint speakers has it that a Mormon soldier once survived being shot in the chest because a pocket Book of Mormon stopped the bullet. When asked how this could be, the soldier pulled it out of his pocket and showed that the bullet hole went to about halfway through 2 Nephi, where it simply stopped. "The bullet couldn't get through the Isaiah chapters either," said the soldier. At this point, audiences laugh loudly, if nervously, knowing that they, too, have struggled to make it through the lengthy blocks of text from Isaiah that make up a large portion of Nephi's later writings.[33]

The "Isaiah chapters" have always presented a formidable barrier to readers of the Book of Mormon.[34] They would be dense and opaque in any translation, but in the King James prose that the Book of Mormon employs, they are almost impenetrably archaic. When readers do manage to decode the words on the page, much of the text deals with political and social issues from the eighth century BCE that few nonspecialist readers today know anything about. After reading Nephi's relatively straightforward account of his people's flight from Jerusalem and journey to the promised land, the Isaiah chapters seem to come from a completely different world. In a well-known and frequently cited 1986 talk, LDS apostle Boyd K. Packer urged first-time readers of the Book of Mormon to "move forward through those difficult-to-understand chapters of Old Testament prophecy, even if you understand very little of it. Move on, if all you do is skim and merely glean an impression here and there. Move on, if all you do is look at the words."[35]

The largest continuous quotation from Isaiah in the Book of Mormon occurs in chapters 12 through 24 of 2 Nephi—thirteen chapters copied into his record directly from the writings of Isaiah.[36] In chapter 25, immediately after this 7,500-word block quote, Nephi begins his analysis of Isaiah by telling us that he really doesn't want his people reading it:

Now I Nephi do speak somewhat concerning the words which I have written, which have been spoken by the mouth of Isaiah. For behold, Isaiah spake many things which were hard for many of my people to understand, for they know not concerning the manner of prophesying among the Jews. For I Nephi have not taught them many things concerning the manner of the Jews, for their works were works of darkness and their doings were doings of abomination. . . .

Yea, and my soul delighteth in the words of Isaiah, for I came out from Jerusalem and mine eyes hath beheld the things of the Jews. And I know that the Jews do understand the things of the prophets. And there is none other people that understand the things which were spoken unto the Jews like unto them, save it be that they are taught after the manner of the things of the Jews. But behold, I Nephi have not taught my children after the manner of the Jews. . . . But behold, I proceed with mine own prophecy, according to my plainness, in the which I know that no man can err. (2 Ne 25:1–2, 5–7)

Nephi gives Isaiah a mixed review at best. He says that his soul "delighteth in the words of Isaiah," but he admits that his delight depends on the interpretive skills that he learned in Jerusalem. And he also acknowledges that nobody who has not studied these methods can understand Jewish prophecy, so the fact that Nephi's people find Isaiah difficult should not be surprising. In order to understand how the Isaiah passages function in the Book of Mormon, then, we must try to understand why Nephi refuses to teach his people the exegetical methodologies that would allow them to understand the things he spent his life studying and transcribing. Nephi answers this question himself: "For I Nephi have not taught them many things concerning the manner of the Jews, for their works were works of darkness and their doings were doings of abomination." What does he mean by this? What about a particular set of interpretive tools does Nephi consider so dangerous that even learning about them could set a person on a perilous spiritual path? What would cause Nephi to deprive his descendants of the spiritual value and the aesthetic pleasure that he feels when he reads and understands Isaiah?

Grant Hardy suggests that Nephi may be "still bitter about the way that he and his father were treated in Jerusalem, but he is not hostile to Jewish scholarship." He sees the Jews as "excellent stewards of their sacred writings," and he resists teaching Jewish interpretive techniques to his people because he realizes that he will never be part of the culture that produced them. "Being completely cut off from his homeland means that Hebrew literature is no longer a living tradition for him or his descendants."[37] Joseph Spencer concurs. "These words," he suggests, "should probably be read as the words of someone still upset at how things went for his family in Jerusalem."[38] Bradley Kramer, in a book designed to show how the Book of Mormon rejects the anti-Semitism often seen in the New Testament, attributes Nephi's sentiments in this passage to his righteous anger at pre-captivity Jews—an anger that he shares with prophets like Jeremiah—which cannot be transferred to the Second Temple Judaism of the New Testament.[39]

These explanations don't quite account for the danger that Nephi perceives in the interpretive tradition that allows readers to understand Isaiah. Nor can they explain Jacob's subsequent statement that the Jews "were a stiffnecked people, and they despised the words of plainness and . . . *sought for things that they could not understand*" (Jacob 4:14, emphasis mine). Jacob states explicitly what Nephi only hints at: that the Jews of Nephi's day actively rejected plain words and clear meaning, and sought out confusing and complicated texts, because they liked difficult interpretive problems that could be solved only with the great learning that they had acquired. Anyone who learned the art of textual interpretation in a modern graduate program should have no trouble understanding how this might have worked. Highly skilled textual interpreters don't like clear and straightforward texts; we either see them as simpleminded and not worthy of our efforts or we mistrust their simplicity and look for deeper meanings. Unnecessary complexity and impenetrable prose frequently occur in cultures that value and reward intellectual achievement. This is not a Jewish problem; it is a scholarship problem. Complex interpretive methodologies require complex interpretive problems.

None of this will make much sense if we look at the actual interpretive practices common in Palestine in the sixth century BCE. The scholarly traditions most closely associated with Judaism would not develop until after the fall of Jerusalem and the period of captivity in Babylon. By setting the text in a canonical context, though, we can make better sense of the apparent contradiction between Nephi's admiration for Isaiah and his distrust of the interpretive tradition that makes his own understanding possible. The scriptural canon to which the Book of Mormon attaches itself operates from the fundamental assumption that the writers of the Old Testament concealed references to Jesus Christ in their text that could only be decoded by using the New Testament as a key. This assumption allowed Christians to transform the Hebrew *Tanakh* into the "Old Testament," which then combined with the New Testament to become the Christian Bible—and the writings of Isaiah played an oversized role in the transformation. Early Christians saw the book of Isaiah as a "fifth gospel." Saint Jerome wrote that Isaiah "should be called an evangelist rather than a prophet because he describes all the mysteries of Christ and the church so clearly that you would think he is composing a history of what has already happened rather than prophesying about what is to come."[40]

Nephi makes it very clear that he values Isaiah for the same reasons that the early Christian fathers did. "My soul delighteth in his words," he exclaims; "he verily saw my Redeemer, even as I have seen him" (2 Ne 11:2). The chapters that Nephi incorporates into his own record immediately before his analysis of Isaiah contain some of the passages most frequently cited in the New Testament as prophecies of the Messiah:

- "Therefore the Lord himself shall give you a sign; Behold, a virgin shall conceive, and bear a son, and shall call his name Immanuel" (Isa 7:14/2 Ne 17:14; quoted in Matt 1:23).[41]
- "And he shall be for a sanctuary; but for a stone of stumbling and for a rock of offence to both the houses of Israel, for a gin and for a snare to the inhabitants of Jerusalem" (Isa 8:14/2 Ne 18:14; quoted in 1 Pet 2:8).
- "And I will wait upon the Lord, that hideth his face from the house of Jacob, and I will look for him. Behold, I and the children whom the Lord hath given me [are] for signs and for wonders in Israel from the Lord of hosts, which dwelleth in Mount Zion" (Isa 8:17/2 Ne 18:17; quoted in Heb 2:13).
- "Nevertheless the dimness shall not be such as was in her vexation, when at the first he lightly afflicted the land of Zebulun and the land of Naphtali, and afterward did more grievously afflict her by the way of the sea, beyond Jordan, in Galilee of the nations. The people that walked in darkness have seen a great light: they that dwell in the land of the shadow of death, upon them hath the light shined" (Isa 9:1–2/2 Ne 19:1–2; quoted in Matt 4:12–16).
- "And in that day there shall be a root of Jesse, which shall stand for an ensign of the people; to it shall the Gentiles seek: and his rest shall be glorious" (Isa 11:10.2/Ne 21:10; quoted in Rom 15:12).

Also included in the chapters that Nephi quotes is perhaps the most famous Christian prophecy in all of the Old Testament, set to music and made famous by Handel in *Messiah*: "For unto us a child is born, unto us a son is given: and the government shall be upon his shoulder: and his name shall be called Wonderful, Counsellor, The mighty God, The everlasting Father, The Prince of Peace" (Isa 9:6/2 Ne 19:6).

Though Nephi initially says that he reads his people passages from Isaiah "that I might more fully persuade them to believe in the Lord their Redeemer" (1 Ne 19:23), when he concludes, he realizes that "Isaiah spake many things which were hard for many of my people to understand, for they know not concerning the manner of prophesying among the Jews" (2 Ne 25:1). He acknowledges that the words of Isaiah "are plain unto all those that are filled with the spirit of prophecy" (2 Ne 25:4), but this does not appear to be a large enough subset of Nephi's readers to obviate the need for clear language. So, Nephi does not ultimately depend on Isaiah to teach the truth of the Messiah to his people. As we have already seen, Nephi states plainly nearly everything about Christ that the New Testament and later Christian writers wrung from Isaiah through typological readings and complex interpretive strategies.

At some point in his record Nephi tells readers that Christ's ministry would be preceded by a prophet who would baptize followers in "Bethabara beyond Jordan" (1 Ne 10:9), that he would be from a place called Nazareth, that his mother would be a virgin (1 Ne 11:14–18), that Jesus would have twelve special disciples (1 Ne 12:7–10), and that he would work "mighty miracles, signs, and wonders among the children of men" (2 Ne 26:13). Nephi also prophesied that Christ would be crucified and buried in a sepulcher (1 Ne 19:10), where he would lie for three days and then "rise from the dead with healing in his wings" (2 Ne 25:13). And he clarified that "the Messiah cometh in six hundred years from the time that my father left Jerusalem. And according to the words of the prophets and also the word of the angel of God, his name should be Jesus Christ, the Son of God" (2 Ne 25:19). Nephi wraps up his discussion of Jewish learning and Isaiah with a decidedly un-Isaianic encomium to plainness:

> And we talk of Christ, we rejoice in Christ, we preach of Christ, we prophesy of Christ; and we write according to our prophecies that our children may know to what source they may look for a remission of their sins. . . . And now behold, my people, ye are a stiffnecked people. Wherefore I have spoken plain unto you, that ye cannot misunderstand. And the words which I have spoken shall stand as a testimony against you, for they are sufficient to teach any man the right way. For the right way is to believe in Christ and deny him not, for by denying him ye also deny the prophets and the law. (2 Ne 25:26, 28)

So, why did Nephi hammer about a third of the book of Isaiah onto metal plates when he knew that his readers—both ancient and modern—would have access to the original material? This only makes sense if he intended for readers to engage in a comparison of some kind. This might mean comparing Nephi's version of Isaiah to the version in the King James Bible that it most resembles. Both critics and defenders of the Book of Mormon have put substantial effort into doing precisely this and have generated side-by-side comparisons and red-line versions of every quotation from Isaiah in the Book of Mormon.[42] These comparisons show hundreds of minor changes and a few differences that affect the meaning of a passage in nontrivial ways. But they do not reveal any important doctrinal or historical differences that would justify the laborious insertion of thousands of duplicative words into the Book of Mormon's text. And even if there were such differences, Nephi could have corrected them with much less effort by simply explaining the doctrinal point clearly the way he does with many of the other doctrines that the Book of Mormon refines or clarifies.

Nephi's extensive citations from Isaiah are difficult to explain either theologically or Christologically. They simply do not provide enough new information to justify their repetition in a canon that already includes them in a nearly identical form. But what if Nephi includes them not for their positive doctrinal value but for their value as a negative example—how not to write prophecy if you really want people to understand it? The long, difficult quotations make sense if Nephi wants us to experience the difficulty of trying to make sense of the Isaiah chapters before he tells us why he is going to do things differently. "Isaiah is an amazing and important prophet," Nephi seems to suggest, "but the way his writings were preserved and transmitted to Jewish scholars made them too hard to understand. The references to Jesus Christ are all buried in types and riddles, and this is why the Jews failed (or, from Nephi's perspective, will fail) to recognize the Messiah. As subtle and aesthetically pleasing as I find Isaiah's prophecies, I am going to write in a much plainer style because understanding the nature of Christ is so important that I don't want people misinterpreting what I say."

In this reading of the text, the difficulty that readers have with Nephi's Isaiah chapters becomes the point. Nephi shows us what he tells us: that the words of Isaiah in their canonical form require too much exegetical training for nonprophets to understand them easily. For Nephi, Isaiah becomes a stand-in for the dominant mode of messianic prophecy in the Old Testament, as interpreted by the New Testament, which finds oblique and complex figurations of Christ in nearly every corner of the text but cannot point to a single unambiguous reference to New Testament Christianity in the Hebrew Bible. Nephi rewrites the prophecies of Isaiah as they should have been written in the primordial Bible that should have been, restating the Christian message of the Old Testament clearly and directly "with mine own prophecy according to my plainness, in the which I know that no man can err" (2 Ne 25:7).

When Jesus Christ visits the people of the Book of Mormon, he says many of the same words, and does many of the same things that are recorded in the Gospels. But even when the texts are identical, the contexts could not be more different. In the New Testament, Jesus is born as a child, raised in a small village, lives in relative obscurity, and is ultimately executed by the Roman state. In the Book of Mormon, his coming is a bona fide eschatological event. He starts by triggering cataclysmic disasters that lay waste to the major cities and destroy the institutions of the old society.[43] He then descends from the sky in a pillar of light and ushers in an era of peace and prosperity that lasts for two hundred years. The Jesus Christ who appears in the Book of Mormon behaves the way the Messiah was supposed to behave: He comes in power and glory and fundamentally reshapes the world.[44] The Book of Mormon, then, rewrites Christ's earthly ministry the way it should have happened—and it reimagines the New Testament ministry of Christ as what it might have been if the Old Testament prophets had been more forthcoming and the Jewish tradition less concerned with creating complex puzzles.

The Sermon on the Mount and the Sermon at the Temple

The drama of Christ's birth in the Book of Mormon begins in earnest five years before it occurs in the New Testament, when Samuel the Lamanite stands on the Zarahemla city wall and gives a very specific prophecy:

> And behold, he said unto them: Behold, I give unto you a sign. *For five years more cometh, and behold, then cometh the Son of God* to redeem all those who shall believe on his name. And behold, this will I give unto you for a sign at the time of his coming. For behold, there shall be great lights in heaven, insomuch that in the night before he cometh there shall be no darkness, insomuch that it shall appear unto man as if it was day. (Hel 14:2–3, emphasis mine)

Over the next five years, Samuel's prophecy works its way into the culture as a test. If the sign is not given within five years of Samuel's statement, the church's enemies reason, then everyone will know for sure that the Christian movement is based on a lie. "There was a day set apart by the unbelievers," Mormon writes, "that all those who believed in those traditions should be put to death except the sign should come to pass" (3 Ne 1:9). Mormon exploits this trope for maximum dramatic tension by having the sign come just in the nick of time. When Nephi fears that all of the members of his church will be killed, he implores God in prayer, and God tells him, "On this night shall the sign be given. And on the morrow come I into the world" (3 Ne 1:13). When the sign appears, the wicked fall to the ground as if dead, "for they knew that the great plan of destruction which they had laid for those who believed in the words of the prophets had been frustrated" (3 Ne 1:16).

After the signs appear, the Nephite-Lamanite population follows a familiar pattern of conversion and collapse. First, a large percentage of the population "believe and [are] converted to the Lord" and are baptized into the church (3 Ne 1:22–23). For several years they live in peace in the cities, with both Nephite and Lamanite dissenters joining the Gadianton Robbers, who "dwel[l] upon the mountains" (3 Ne 1:27). Over time, the people "forget those signs and wonders which they had heard" (3 Ne 2:1), and the Gadianton Robbers become powerful nonstate actors capable of waging war on the Nephites and the Lamanites simultaneously (3 Ne 2:11). After years of protracted warfare, the Nephites defeat the robbers (2 Ne 5: 4), but the fight permanently damages their society.

Thirty years after the signs of Christ's birth appeared, Nephite society begins to collapse. The church falls victim to socioeconomic inequality. "The people began to be distinguished by ranks according to their riches and their chance for learning," writes Nephi. "Some were ignorant because of their poverty; and others did receive great learning because of their riches" (3 Ne 6:12). The text does not specify exactly how these socioeconomic conditions affect the church, but Nephi does suggest a connection when he writes that "there became a great unequality in all the land, insomuch that the church began to be broken up" and that "in the thirtieth year the church was broken up in all the land save it were among a few of the Lamanites which were converted unto the true faith" (3 Ne 6:14). The few remaining Christians are subjected to extreme persecution, including judicial murders in which "those which testified of the things pertaining to Christ ... [are] taken and put to death secretly by the judges" even though "this [is] contrary to the laws of the land" (3 Ne 6:23–24).

The breakup of the Nephite church occurs together with the collapse of the Nephite government, which begins when the extrajudicial executions of the Christian faithful come to light and the judges who carried them out are put on trial. Officials of both church and state—"almost all the lawyers and the high priests"—enter into a covenant with the families of the guilty judges to "combine against all righteousness" and to "destroy the governor, and to establish a king over the land that the land should be no more be at liberty" (3 Ne 6:27–30). They successfully assassinate the chief judge, but they fail to establish a kingdom (3 Ne 7:1). Rather, when the chief judge dies, "the people [are] divided one against another. And they ... separate one from another into tribes, every man according to his family and his kindred and friends. And thus they ... destroy the government of the land" (3 Ne 7:2).

Soon after the massive physical destruction that occurs after Christ's crucifixion in the Old World, the city of Zarahemla burns with its inhabitants (3 Ne 8:8, 24), the city of Moroni sinks into the sea (3 Ne 8:9), the city of Moronihah is buried under a mountain (3 Ne 8:10), "many great and notable cities [are] sunk, and many [are] burned, and many [are] shook till the buildings thereof had fallen to the earth" (3 Ne 8:14). The entire land—the known world, from the perspective of the Nephites and the Lamanites—is irrevocably changed by three hours of relentless earthquakes:

> And thus the face of the whole earth became deformed because of the tempests and the thunderings and the lightnings and the quaking of the earth. And behold, the rocks were rent in twain; yea, they were broken up upon the face of the whole earth, insomuch that they were found in broken fragments and in seams and in cracks, upon all the face of the land. And it came to pass that when the thunderings and the lightnings and the storm and the tempest and the quakings of the earth did cease—for behold, they did last for about the space of three hours; and it was said by some that the time was greater; nevertheless all these great and terrible things were done in about the space of three hours—and then behold, there was darkness upon the face of the land. (3 Ne 8:17–19)

In chapter 9 the text shifts to a first-person narrative from the viewpoint of "a voice heard among all the inhabitants of the earth" (3 Ne 9:1) that catalogs even more destruction. "Behold, that great city Zarahemla have I burned with fire and the inhabitants thereof," the voice thunders. "And behold, that great city Moroni have I caused to be sunk in the depths of the sea and the inhabitants thereof to be drowned. And behold, that great city Moronihah have I covered with earth and the inhabitants thereof, to hide their iniquities and their abominations from before my face" (3 Ne 9:3–5). The voice goes on to list another dozen cities that he destroyed because of "the wickedness and abominations" of the people, and he makes it clear that those who survived were spared because they were more righteous than those who were destroyed (3 Ne 9:7–13). When the destruction is complete, the voice proclaims his identity: "Behold, I am Jesus Christ the Son of God. I created the heavens and the earth and all things that in them is [sic]. I was with the Father from the beginning. I am in the Father and the Father in me; and in me hath the Father glorified his name" (3 Nephi 9:15).

After the widespread destruction of Nephite and Lamanite cities, Mormon—writing four hundred years later as the final redactor—steps into the narrative to explain that the events we were reading about fulfill specific biblical prophecies:

And now whoso readeth, let him understand; he that hath the scriptures, let him search them and see and behold if all these deaths and destructions by fire and by smoke and by tempests and by whirlwinds and by the opening of the earth to receive them and all these things is not unto the fulfilling of the prophecies of many of the holy prophets. Behold, I say unto you: Yea, many have testified of these things at the coming of Christ and were slain because they testified of these things—yea, the prophet Zenos did testify of these things, and also Zenoch spake concerning these things—because they testified particular concerning us, which is the remnant of their seed. (3 Ne 10:14–16)

Modern readers of the Book of Mormon know that Zenos and Zenoch are part of the primordial Bible that the Book of Mormon posits but not part of the Christian Bible that currently exists. They are among the "plain and precious" things that have been removed. Whether he knows it or not, Mormon's invocation of these two prophets to explain the destruction of the Nephite-Lamanite civilization is deeply ironic because it underscores once again the Book of Mormon's argument against the Christian Bible. Not only did Zenoch and Zenos understand things about the coming of Christ that were not preserved; they "testified particularly concerning us [meaning the people of the Book of Mormon], which is the remnant of their seed." These missing prophets, in other words, spoke directly of Mormon's people. Their omission from the current Christian Bible creates the need for, while hiding the existence of, the Book of Mormon.

Christ's first appearance in the Book of Mormon has all the pomp and spectacle of a big-budget Broadway show. It begins with a voice coming out of the sky: a "small voice . . . did pierce them that did hear to the center, insomuch that there were no part of their frame that it did not cause to quake" (3 Ne 11:3). Unclear at first, the voice becomes progressively clearer, and the people finally hear God the Father say, "Behold my Beloved Son, in whom I am well pleased, in whom I have glorified my name. Hear ye him" (3 Ne 11:7). Then the people see "a Man descending out of heaven, and he [is] clothed in a white robe." They are terrified of this figure, whom they believe to be an angel, and they huddle in fear. Then Christ "stretche[s] forth his hand and [speaks] unto the people, saying: Behold, I am Jesus Christ—of which the prophets testified—that should come into the world" (3 Ne 11:8–10). He invites them to thrust their hands into his side and to feel the nail prints in his hands and feet (3 Ne 11:15). And he then gets down to business.

The first order of business is instruction. Christ teaches many of the same things in the Book of Mormon that he taught in the New Testament. Almost immediately on arrival, he gives an address to the crowd that reproduces verbatim about 80 percent of the Sermon on the Mount from the book of Matthew in the King James Bible.[45] Latter-day Saints often refer to this as the "Sermon at the Temple" because it takes place "round about the temple which was in the land Bountiful" (3 Ne 11:1).[46] The discrepancies between the two sermons occasionally have doctrinal significance,[47] but more often they reflect differences in their settings and audiences.[48] Yet the contextual differences between the two sermons affect their meanings dramatically. In the New Testament, Jesus is a relatively poor itinerant preacher who was just beginning to attract followers. In the Book of Mormon, he is a fearsome god who just destroyed most of the known world and then descended to earth in a pillar of light.

The Book of Mormon expands significantly on one point of doctrine that appears in both the Sermon on the Mount and the Sermon at the Temple when Christ says, "Think not that I am come to destroy the law, or the prophets: I am not come to destroy, but to fulfil" (Mat 5:17/3 Ne 12:17). This is a particularly vexed passage in the New Testament because it gives a crucial piece of information for the Christian community—how the gospel of Christ fits into the framework of the law of Moses—and the word that the text uses for "to fulfill," πληρῶσαι, can mean different things. It has been interpreted to mean that Christ "uphold[s] or confirm[s]" the law, that he fulfills the law through obedience, that he gives "deeper insight into the law's intended meaning," that the law is "transcended by Jesus' teaching being a more perfect picture of the nature of God's will," or that fulfillment of the law consists of "a realisation of what the law anticipated."[49]

This lack of clarity caused significant contention in the early church and even divisions between the apostles leading to the Council of Jerusalem described in Acts 15, which decided that non-Jewish converts to Christianity were not subject to circumcision or other aspects of Mosaic law.[50] In the Book of Mormon, Christ seems to realize the potential for such confusion, and he moves proactively to prevent it. After giving the Sermon at the Temple, Jesus perceives that the people were confused about the law of Moses (3 Ne 15:2), so he gives a much more detailed explanation. "The law in me is fulfilled," he tells them, "therefore it hath an end" (3 Ne 15:5). And then he says that "the covenant which I have made with my people is not all fulfilled, but the law which was given unto Moses hath an end in me" (3 Ne 15:8). Christ makes it very clear that the law of Moses is no longer in force. Its purpose was to prepare people for the coming of Christ (3 Ne 15:10), so, now that he has come, its purpose has come to an end.

Christ's in-depth explanation of the law of Moses—the only part of the Sermon on the Mount/Sermon at the Temple that he significantly expands on in the Book of Mormon—makes little sense in a nineteenth-century context. Most of the questions about Christianity and the Mosaic law had long been settled by 1830, and very few Christians believed that Christians had to undergo circumcision, observe Jewish dietary laws, or perform animal sacrifices.[51] But if we consider Christ's remarks in the context of Third Nephi's overall ecclesiology—its discussion of how the Nephites and Lamanites should set up a church to function after Christ's departure—it makes far more sense. The question of how to incorporate Mosaic law into Christian ecclesiology was an extremely divisive question for the New Testament church. One might conclude from these divisions that Christ's occasional comments about the law of Moses in the New Testament did not give sufficient information for the apostles to implement ecclesiastical policies in his absence. Given the Book of Mormon's mission of reconstructing the Bible as the book that should have been written and passed on to posterity, this this is precisely the kind of clarification that would be important.[52]

Much of what Christ does and says in the Book of Mormon can be explained by focusing on the ecclesiology of the Nephite-Lamanite church—and on the need for more specific instructions than we find in the New Testament for organizing a Christian church. The instruction begins in the first moments of the visit, when Christ specifically ordains Nephi and eleven other people, gives them the authority to baptize in his name, and walks them through the precise steps of conducting a valid baptism (3 Ne 11:18–21, 12:1). Christ also institutes a communion ritual with bread and wine (3 Ne 18:1–11) and gives rules about who should and should not partake of it (3 Ne 18:27–29). And near the end of his visit he gives a lengthy discourse on the proper name of the church. "Verily, verily, I say unto you: Why is it that the people should murmur and dispute because of this thing?" he asks when the question of the church's name comes up. "Have they not read the scriptures, which sayeth: Ye must take upon you the name of Christ, which is my name. For by this name shall ye be called at the last day" (3 Ne 27:4–5).[53]

Each of the issues that Christ brings up—the correct mode of baptism, the proper authority to perform ordinations, the nature of the Eucharist, and the proper name of the church—divided Christians for generations. In each case, the New Testament leaves room for multiple interpretations because the ecclesiastical intentions of Christ must be intuited from statements that he makes for reasons other than organizing a church.[54] Christ's clear instructions for developing a church have their intended effect. The book of 4 Nephi reports that, after Christ departs, everybody in the land, both Nephites and Lamanites, joins the church and lives in righteousness. This perfect society lasts for two hundred years before divisions creep back into the population (4 Ne 1:24).

The coming of Christ in the Book of Mormon, then, actually was the eschatological event that people expected, but did not get, in the New Testament. The social and physical collapses that preceded his coming in the Book of Mormon correspond closely to the signs that the Jews of Christ's time associated with the arrival of the Messiah.[55] And the results are also the same: Christ brings an end to the world as it existed, and, as the Messiah was supposed to do, he inaugurates an era of universal peace and prosperity under the leadership of wise and moral leaders whom everybody willingly follows. Most Christians, including most Latter-day Saints, have exported the messianic expectations of Second Temple Judaism to the Second Coming of Christ. But nearly everything about Christ's appearance in the Book of Mormon—the violence that precedes it, the dramatic spectacle of his appearance, the fundamental disruption of society that accompanies it, and the paradisiacal era that follows—meets the expectations that Christians associate with Christ's coming at the end of time. The similarities, as Christopher Blythe writes, are "unmistakable."[56]

The coming of Christ in the Book of Mormon is an apocalypse, but it is not *the* apocalypse. It is not even the only apocalypse in the Book of Mormon; there are two others: the end of the Jaredite civilization in the Book of Ether and the destruction of Nephite society in the books of Mormon and Moroni. Other than the presence of Christ, these three social collapses have very similar shapes, and they can probably be understood as a single type. The fact that such a type recurs throughout the text underscores an important difference between the Bible and the Book of Mormon. The biblical narrative is oriented toward a final eschatological event, which is foreseen in the Old Testament and only partly fulfilled in the New Testament. The final apocalypse is postponed to an end of time, when the Messiah will come back in all the ways he did not come the first time. The Book of Mormon, on the other hand, operates on the fundamentally typological assumption that history cycles through similar events, including apocalypses, and that everything that has happened will at some time happen again. In the final chapter we will look carefully at the way the Book of Mormon quietly subverts—even as it partly embraces—the Bible's understanding of a final apocalypse.

CHAPTER EIGHT

Last Things

> The Bible is a familiar model of history. It begins at the
> beginning . . . and ends with a vision of the end . . . the
> first book is Genesis, the last Apocalypse. Ideally, it is a
> wholly concordant structure, the end is in harmony with
> the beginning, the middle with beginning and end. The
> end, Apocalypse, is traditionally held to resume the whole
> structure, which it can do only by figures predictive of that
> part of it which has not been historically revealed.
>
> —Frank Kermode, *The Sense of an Ending*

> For he that diligently seeketh shall find, and the mysteries
> of God shall be unfolded to them by the power of the
> Holy Ghost as well in these times as in times of old and
> as well in times of old as in times to come wherefore, the
> course of the Lord is one eternal round.
>
> —1 Nephi 10:19

It is fitting that the last chapter should talk about last things—about the ways in which both the Bible and the Book of Mormon talk about the things that will happen at the end of the world. Discussions about last things usually fit into the branch of theology called "eschatology," a term derived from the Greek word *eschaton*, which means "last." The topic of Christian eschatology is endlessly fascinating, and endlessly complicated, because a hundred generations of Christians have struggled to create a coherent picture of the world's end by piecing together messianic prophecies from the Old Testament, cryptic statements by Jesus and Paul from the New Testament, and the very strange, very disturbing images found in the book of Revelation. With different combinations and emphases, these source texts produce very different understandings of what the end of the world will look like and of when (or if) it will occur. Speculation has run rampant for two thousand years, with each generation inventing a new formula for calculating the end of the world and a new description of what awaits us.

This chapter focuses on three of the most important eschatological concepts in the Christian tradition: The Parousia, the Apocalypse, and the Millennium. Each of these terms comes up frequently in discussions of Christian theology, but they are not interchangeable, and they are not all part of every Christian's eschatological toolkit. They are also used in different ways, at different times, by different people. In order to make sense of how the Book of Mormon revises or clarifies the Bible's eschatological narratives, we must first define the way each term will be used in this chapter:

- *Parousia* comes from a Greek word meaning "coming" or "presence" and is used in Christian theology almost exclusively to refer to the Second Coming of Christ. Christians believe that many of the Old Testament prophecies about the Messiah that were not fulfilled during Christ's lifetime will be fulfilled in the Second Coming, when Christ will come in power and glory, judge the righteous and the unrighteous, and usher in a new version of reality.

- *Apocalypse* comes from the Greek word for "revelation" or "disclosure." In both the Jewish and the Christian traditions, apocalypse is a genre of prophecy in which an angel or other supernatural interlocutor uses elaborate symbols to reveal something in a dream or a vision. The most well-known examples of apocalyptic literature are the book of Revelation and chapters 7–12 of the book of Daniel. Contemporary scholars draw a distinction between the use of "apocalypse" as a genre and the use of "apocalyptic" as an eschatological framework. Apocalyptic eschatology, which is a feature of many scriptural genres, is characterized by, among other things, an "urgent expectation of the end of earthly conditions in the immediate future" and "the end as a cosmic catastrophe."[1] When preceded by a definite article, *the* Apocalypse refers to a catastrophic sequence of events that will end the world as we understand it. Not all examples of the apocalyptic genre manifest an apocalyptic eschatology.[2] "Truly apocalyptic apocalypses," suggests Michael Stone, who recommends abandoning the terms altogether to eliminate this ambiguity, "are the exception rather than the rule."[3]

- *Millennium* comes from the Latin word for "thousand" and refers to a period of peace and harmony that some Christians believe will occur in conjunction with the Parousia. The idea that this period will last for a thousand years comes from a single passage in Revelation in which John describes seeing those "which had not worshipped the beast . . . and they lived and reigned with Christ a thousand years. But the dead lived not again until the thousand years were finished" (Rev 20:4–5). Some Christians take this reference literally and believe that Christ will usher in a thousand years of peace and prosperity. Others see it figuratively and see the Millennium as a future society of any duration in which people will live in accordance with the principles that Christ taught in the New Testament.

In many Christian traditions, these three concepts have been rolled up into a single eschatological event. According to the belief system that theologians call "premillennialism," all three things will happen in rapid sequence at some point in the future: First, there will be a series of wars and calamities that bring the world to the brink of disaster, and, when things are at the lowest point for the forces of righteousness, Jesus Christ will come back to claim the world. As Timothy Weber describes it in the *Oxford Handbook of Eschatology*, "Christ's coming [Parousia] will be dramatic and sudden; he will break out of the clouds with his warrior saints to defeat his enemies at the Battle of Armageddon [Apocalypse] then establish his own kingdom, which will endure for a thousand years" and be a "golden age of peace, righteousness, and justice [Millennium]."[4] This sequence is normally considered a single event that can be referred to as "the Apocalypse," "the Second Coming," or "the Millennium." Were it the only eschatological belief in Christendom, then there would be no need to separate its three parts into different types.

But the three concepts don't have to go together, and in some Christian theologies they don't. In another system, called "postmillennialism," human beings must create a peaceful society before Christ can come again and the Millennium (which may or may not be a thousand years) refers to a natural consequence of people being converted to Christ. Postmillennial theology sees human nature as perfectible by means of "ordinary grace" rather than as fallen and redeemable only through direct divine intervention. Postmillennial ideas fueled many of the utopian religious movements in eighteenth- and nineteenth-century America and continue to influence some strands of liberal Protestantism today.[5] Postmillennialist eschatology rejects the notion of an apocalypse in which the world becomes so wicked that God destroys it. Rather, it believes that the world will become so good that people create the Kingdom of God on earth (Millennium) and that, when we do, Christ will return in person to ratify its creation (Parousia).

Still another system, sometimes called "amillennialism," posits that Christ will come during a series of apocalyptic events and will initiate a final judgment that will separate the wheat from the tares (Matt 13:24–30). He will send the wicked to hell and the righteous to heaven, with no intervening period in which an ideal society will exist on earth. Amillennialists understand the thousand years in Revelation 20 as referring to "the reign of Christ and all the saints living and dead between the first and second comings."[6] The "Kingdom of God" in this theology refers only to a spiritual reality, and it would be foolish and arrogant to believe that human beings can create such a thing themselves in a fallen world. William F. Buckley's famous slogan "don't immanentize the Eschaton" was an amillennial critique of post-millennial utopian attempts to create heaven on earth by means of human agency.[7] Amillennialism states that there will be a climactic end of the world (Apocalypse) followed by the Second Coming of Christ (Parousia), but, as the name suggests, it does not accept an eschatological Millennium.

Clearly, each of the three concepts can stand alone in eschatological terms; Christians can and do incorporate some or all them into their beliefs about the end of time. All three can also stand alone in typological terms in that scriptures within the same canon can contain narrative types of one, two, or all three of them. In the remainder of this chapter I argue that the Book of Mormon (and, in one case, the Pearl of Great Price) engages with the New Testament's eschatology by creating its own types of the Apocalypse, the Parousia, and the Millennium. These types sometimes occur together. In order to understand how the Book of Mormon reframes the Christian Bible's understanding of the last days, we must first look at the way these individual types operate, both alone as themselves and together as prophetic descriptions of the end of time.

The Coming of Christ in the Book of Mormon

"Christianity began with the announcement that time and history were about to end," writes the religious historian Paula Frederiksen. "As history . . . persistently failed to end on time—the Church, of necessity, had to come to terms with its own foundational prophecy."[8] The famous theologian and humanitarian Albert Schweitzer put it even more directly: "The whole history of 'Christianity,' down to the present day, that is to say, the real inner history of it, is based on the delay of the Parousia."[9] For many scholars such as Frederickson and Schweitzer, the situation is dire, indeed. Jesus was an apocalyptic preacher who foretold the imminent end of the world. His followers believed him and called him the Christ, or the Messiah. His followers did not form a permanent institution. What would be the point of starting a church when the world was just about to end? When Jesus died without ushering in a new era, his disciples reoriented their beliefs to expect an imminent return—after all, he had already been resurrected, so how long should it take to come back? As the Parousia kept not happening, Christians began to develop hierarchies, bureaucracies, and institutions capable of sustaining believers in a world that was not going to end any time soon.

The main body of Schweitzer's famous work *The Quest of the Historical Jesus* consists of Schweitzer summarizing and interrogating more than a hundred years of attempts by German scholars to understand the historical Jesus. He begins with the work of Hermann Samuel Reimarus, a German scholar and professor who died in 1768 without publishing his major work, a group of incomplete essays about the historical Jesus and the origins of Christianity. These essays were published posthumously under the title *Wolfenbütteler Fragmente* (Fragments by an Anonymous Writer) and, Schweitzer argues, they became the foundational work of a long German tradition of studying the historical Jesus from a secular perspective. Reimarus saw Jesus as an apocalyptic prophet and Christianity as a fraudulent religion based entirely on its founder's unfulfilled promise to return.

As Schweitzer presents it, Reimarus saw the non-occurrence of the Parousia as a fatal flaw in the Christian tradition. "Inasmuch as the non-fulfilment of its eschatology is not admitted, our Christianity rests upon a fraud," Schweitzer summarizes, "the sole argument which could save the credit of Christianity would be a proof that the Parousia had really taken place at the time for which it was announced; and obviously no such proof can be produced." Schweitzer does not entirely endorse this view; he calls Reimarus's work "a polemic, not an objective historical study." But he does not entirely reject it, either. "We have no right simply to dismiss it in a word," he argues, as Reimarus "was the first to grasp that the world of thought in which Jesus moved was essentially eschatological." And because of Schweitzer's attention, Reimarus's argument has stood as a challenge to the integrity of the Christian tradition that many consider decisive.

In a magnificent 2014 article in the *Journal of Book of Mormon Studies* titled "Saving Christianity," Heather Hardy explicitly takes up this challenge as articulated by Schweitzer by presenting Christ's visit to the Nephites and Lamanites as a fulfillment of Reimarus's condition for saving the credit of Christianity:

> As far as we know, Jesus's postresurrection ministry to the Nephites is the only reported incident that comprehensively fits the description of "eschaton," a concept that has otherwise been pieced together from prophetic expectation rather than from actual enactment. Presented in greater clarity than in the prophecies offered by either the mortal Jesus or by others, the narrative of Christ's coming to the Nephites provides a type for each of the components of his still-future, universal, and glory-filled second coming: the calamitous judgment of the wicked, the descent of the risen Lord from heaven, and the establishment of the kingdom of God.[10]

Hardy goes on to point out that the Book of Mormon's description of Christ's visit meets the Bible's criteria for the Parousia in three ways. First, it is preceded by "earthquakes, famines and pestilences, the preaching and persecution of prophets, and signs from heaven."[11] Second, it includes a judgment in which the wicked are destroyed and the righteous preserved.[12] And finally, Christ ends the political and social orders that had prevailed in the New World for six centuries and inaugurates a new order that "results in two hundred years of peace, prosperity, and social harmony" (4 Ne 1:1–22).[13]

If Hardy is correct, then the entire history of Christianity must be rewritten to account for the fact that the Parousia was not delayed at all; it was just in a different place than people expected. Of course, rewriting the history of Christianity—and of traditional interpretations of the Christian Bible—is precisely what the Book of Mormon tells us that it wants to do. If Hardy has correctly identified the intent of the text, and I believe she has, then we can add the Parousia to the long list of Christian concepts whose meaning, according to the Book of Mormon, has been obscured by the Bible's lack of clarity and limited geographical scope. Indeed, one of the flaws of the Christian Bible that the Book of Mormon claims to address is its regional bias—its reduction of the entire world to a small region of the Levant where it sets every spiritually significant event in the world's history. By setting the Parousia in a location other than Roman Judea, the Book of Mormon highlights both the lack of clarity with which the Bible predicts Christ's coming and the regional biases that have kept people looking for Christ in Jerusalem for two millennia.

But if the Second Coming happened two thousand years ago, what does that do to the Book of Mormon's other eschatological pronouncements? Does it mean that the Book of Mormon does not predict a coming of Christ that still lies in our future? Should Latter-day Saints and those in other Restoration denominations settle in for a long, Parousia-less haul with no end in sight? There is no evidence that Joseph Smith and the first generation of Mormons believed this, and there is overwhelming evidence that they were as apocalyptic as the first generation of Christians and expected the Apocalypse, the Second Coming, and the start of the Millennium to occur in their lifetimes.[14] The first Mormons brought much of this apocalyptic fervor to Mormonism because it was part of the American Protestant world that they inhabited.[15] And, while the Book of Mormon speaks frequently about Christ's first coming in Jerusalem and about his visit to the Nephites and Lamanites after his resurrection, it speaks only vaguely and cryptically about a third coming at the end of time. But Christ does make two concrete references in 3 Nephi to a future day when he would "come in glory," making it difficult to read his visit to the Nephites as his final trip to the earth.[16] Other than these two references, though, almost nothing in the Book of Mormon speaks of a final eschatological event in which Christ will come and put an end to the world once and for all. As Grant Hardy suggests, "Book of Mormon prophecies are concerned with general conditions in the last days rather than the culminating event that will bring them to a conclusion."[17]

Apocalypse as a Recurring Type

For all of the apocalyptic and millennial fervor surrounding the coming forth of the Book of Mormon, it is not a particularly eschatological text. It is, however, a *generally* eschatological text. Rather than pointing toward a final series of events that will bring an end to all human history everywhere, the Book of Mormon depicts the collapse of several civilizations, focusing on the typology of the events and the factors that they have in common. Thus, the Book of Mormon demonstrates the recursive nature of events that other religious traditions have always depicted as singular and final. It speaks not of a single Apocalypse but of the spiritual forces that put societies on the path to destruction again and again.

As we saw in Chapter 7, Christ's appearance in the Book of Mormon came with all of the world-ending destruction that the Jews associated with the coming of the Messiah. Christ's visit followed a series of major wars that produced a complete social collapse. Societies stopped functioning, and the people reverted to a Hobbesian war of all against all. This social collapse was followed by the cataclysmic natural disasters that occurred after Christ's crucifixion as recorded in 3 Nephi 8–9—disasters far worse than the minor earthquake that Matthew records at the same time (Matt 27:51–53).[18] The disasters also include a type of judgment: The wicked are destroyed, and the more righteous part of the people survive (3 Ne 10:12). The series of apocalyptic events destroys the world as it existed from the beginning of Mosiah through the seventh chapter of 3 Nephi, and it dramatically changes society in ways that we will explore in the next two sections, but it does not quite bring an end to the world. More than three hundred years later, when Mormon begins his own brief record, he is in the midst of another societal collapse. The world has once again divided into Nephites and Lamanites, and "there [are] sorceries and witchcrafts and magics; and the power of the evil one [is] wrought upon all the face of the land" (Morm 1:19). In true typological fashion, almost everything that happened before Christ's visit happens again. The Nephites and the Lamanites become equally wicked (4 Ne 1:45), the Gadianton Robbers once again become a threat (Morm 1:18), and the people fight multiple major wars punctuated by only brief periods of peace (Morm 1:8–14, 2:1–29, 3:4–10, 4:1–22). After more than fifty years of near-constant battles, Mormon gathers the Nephite forces for a final clash:

> And it came to pass that in the three hundred and eightieth year the Lamanites did come again against us to battle. And we did stand against them boldly. But it was all in vain, for so great were their numbers that they did tread the people of the Nephites under their feet. And it came to pass that we did again take to flight. And they whose flight were swifter than the Lamanites did escape; and they whose flight did not exceed the Lamanites were swept down and destroyed. And now behold, I Mormon do not desire to harrow up the souls of men in casting before them such an awful scene of blood and carnage as was laid before mine eyes. (Morm 5:6–8)

The Lamanites continue to pursue the Nephites until only twenty-four of Mormon's people remain, including his son, Moroni (Morm 6:11). Then Mormon's record stops (Morm 7:10) and, in the next verse, we read, "Behold, I Moroni do finish the record of my father Mormon" (Morm 8:1). As we later discover, Moroni waited sixteen years before completing his father's record.[19] We should not find this surprising, given that, during those sixteen years, Moroni was fighting in a civilization-ending war and then moving around and hiding while carrying heavy metal plates everywhere he went. From this point to the end, everything in the Book of Mormon was either written or edited by Moroni.

Moroni had custody of the Nephite records for at least thirty-six years, from the time he received them from his father in 384 CE until his last entry, which states, "More than four hundred and twenty years has passed away since the sign was given of the coming of Christ" (Moro 10:1). Everything that Moroni says is directed to an unknown future audience, because he has no contemporaries to address. He is the last Nephite, and the last Christian believer, in his world. He knows that he is creating a time capsule. All he can do is protect the records and add in occasional tidbits of information as he thinks about them. Consequently, Moroni's literary output is modest. He completes his father's record and adds some very short chapters of his own. If we do not include two long epistles that he copied into the official record, then Moroni's contribution to the Book of Mormon as an author is minuscule—about six thousand words, or 2 percent of the text.

Moroni's most extensive contribution to the Book of Mormon, though, is his abridgment of the Jaredite record that we know as the book of Ether. The Jaredites were the previous inhabitants of the Book of Mormon's promised land. According to their records, they migrated to the New World when God confounded the languages at the Tower of Babel. The records are introduced into the Book of Mormon long before Moroni abridges them. When the Nephites first discover Zarahemla, the people of that city bring Mosiah$_1$ a stone with strange writings, which he is able to translate. He discovers them to be the record of Coriantumr, the last king of the Jaredites, who survived the war and was discovered by the Zarahemlans' ancestors (Omni 1:21). When Ammon's expedition finds the lost Nephite colony in the book of Mosiah, Limhi tells Ammon that, while searching for Zarahemla, his people discovered "a land which was covered with bones . . . and was also covered with ruins of buildings of every kind" (Mosiah 8:8). From that land, Limhi's people brought back twenty-four plates of pure gold with unintelligible writing on them (Mosiah 8:9). When everybody is back safely in Zarahemla, Mosiah$_2$ translates the plates with divine assistance and discovers "an account of the people which was destroyed from the time that they were destroyed back to the building of the great tower, at the time the Lord confounded the language of the people" (Mosiah 28:17). When he shared the account with others, it "did cause the people of Mosiah to mourn exceedingly." Mormon then interjects that the account "shall be written hereafter" for "it is expedient that all people should know the things which are written in this account" (Mosiah 28:18–19).

Despite Mosiah's prediction, Mormon does not include the Jaredite record in his abridgment of the Book of Mormon, either because he found Mosiah's translation, which was already part of the record, to be sufficient or, more likely, because he died before he could complete an abridgement of the book of Ether. The task falls to Moroni, and this raises important interpretive questions. Engraving seventeen thousand words on metal plates would be difficult even in the best of times. For Moroni—homeless, stateless, in hiding, and on the run—the cost of abridging and recording the book of Ether would have been enormous. And it could not have been justified simply by a desire to preserve the records of an ancient culture. Mosiah$_2$ had already translated the record, and it was already on the plates that Moroni was hauling around. In order to make sense of the Book of Ether, we must look to the story Moroni wanted to tell about his own people and determine how the abridgment he made contributes to that story.

The Jaredite record tells the story of a civilization that thrived for at least a thousand years and possibly much longer.[20] Moroni's abridgment of this record focuses almost entirely on the first and the last generations of Jaredites, whose stories bore striking resemblances to those of the first and the last generations of Nephite civilization. Like Lehi, Jared and his brother and their families were led by God out of the world of the Bible and into a land that had been prepared especially for them. Through divine intervention, both escaped Old World calamities (the Babylonian captivity for the Lehites, the confounding of the languages for the Jaredites). And both created large civilizations that eventually were destroyed by the same evil forces. As Grant Hardy argues, Moroni creates a version of the Jaredite record that "brings the two people into conjunction by using both parallel narrative elements and distinctive phrasal borrowing from the Nephite account."[21] As table 3 demonstrates, Moroni's version of the Jaredite story replicates (or is replicated by) the trajectory of Nephite-Lamanite civilization on almost every point.

Moroni's abridgment of the Jaredite record matches the Nephite experience as closely as it does because Moroni himself was interested primarily in the parallels. "Moroni is *not* especially interested in the Jaredite record for its own sake," explains Rosalynde Frandsen Welch. "He passes over aspects of Jaredite experience that do not connect with Nephite experience. He shows little curiosity about the specifics of religious belief and practice. He has no comment on Jaredite society, culture, or politics beyond the appearance of evil conspiracies for personal gain, which Moroni connects to Nephite secret combinations."[22] This likely reflects the fact that Moroni, the last survivor of a civilization that has collapsed, was not engaging in academic history. He was trying to isolate the reasons why civilizations fail so he could pass that information on to the next civilization that would read his record. Moroni takes just a few pages to narrate what comes between the first and the last generation of Jaredite settlers, a span of as much as two thousand years, or the time between the birth of Christ and the present day. "Aside from the first and the last major figures," Grant Hardy explains, "his treatment of the twenty-seven intervening kings reads like a lightly edited chronicle, checking off generations one by one in a much more truncated form than we see in biblical narratives like First and Second Kings."[23]

By placing the highly compressed version of the Jaredite record immediately after the final battle that destroyed the Nephites but before his final messages to his future readers, Moroni dramatically changes the nature of his own story. Rather than representing the end point of a linear progression toward a final catastrophic event, Moroni's narrative becomes one more recurrence of a type—something that has happened before and will continue to happen in the future because it is hard-wired into the nature of reality. This, in turn, has implications for how we read the Bible's prophecies in Revelation and elsewhere about an eschatological event that will bring the world to an end and usher in Christ's final millennial reign. The Book of Mormon actually shows us three world-ending events: the destruction of Zarahemla that occurred immediately before the appearance of Jesus Christ, the final

Table 3. Parallel histories of the Jaredite and the Nephite-Lamanite civilizations

Jaredite Narrative		Nephite-Lamanite Narrative	
Ether 1:33–37	A small group of people are saved from an imminent catastrophe associated with Babylon (the confounding of languages at the tower of Babel).	1 Ne 1–2	A small group of people are saved from an imminent catastrophe associated with Babylon (the destruction of Jerusalem and the Babylonian captivity).
Ether 1:40–42	God tells the brother of Jared that his friends and family will be led to "a land which is choice above all the land of the earth." Their continued possession of the land will be conditioned on their righteousness (Ether 2:9).	1 Ne 2:20	God tells Nephi that his family will be led to "a land which is choice above all other lands." Their continued possession of the land will be conditioned on their righteousness (2 Ne 1:5).
Ether 2:1–5	The people of Jared wander in the wilderness for several years before coming to a great body of water that they need to cross.	1 Ne 2–7	The people of Lehi wander in the wilderness for several years before coming to a great body of water that they need to cross.
Ether 2:16–3:5	With the Lord's help, the brother of Jared builds eight barges to carry his friends and family across the water.	1 Ne 17–18	With the Lord's help, Nephi builds a ship to carry his friends and family across the water.
Ether 1:25–26	The brother of Jared experiences a panoramic vision in which he sees "all the inhabitants of the earth which had been and also all that would be."	1Ne 11–14	Nephi experiences a panoramic vision in which he sees the future of his descendants and the descendants of his brethren in Jerusalem. The vision includes the birth of Christ and the coming forth of the Book of Mormon.
Ether 6:22–24	The people desire a king, but the brother of Jared resists, saying that a king would lead the people into captivity. Jared persuades him to anoint one of his sons king, and a monarchy soon develops in the land.	2 Ne 5:18	The people want Nephi to be their king, but Nephi is "desirous that they should have no king." Nonetheless he does for them that which [is] in [his] power." And a monarchy soon develops in the land.

Table 3. continued

Jaredite Narrative		Nephite-Lamanite Narrative	
Ether 7:15–20	The descendants of Jared and his brother split into two different kingdoms who frequently fight against each other.	2 Ne 5:1–25	The descendants of Lehi and Ishmael split into two different cultural groups who frequently fight against each other.
Ether 7:23–26	The people become corrupt after the first generation of immigrants die, and prophets are sent to call the people to repentance.	Enos 1:22; Jarom 1:10	The people become corrupt after the first generation of immigrants die, and prophets are sent to call the people to repentance.
Ether 8:13–18	Akish introduces secret combinations into the Jaredite culture through which people covenant together to "gain power and to murder and to plunder and to lie and to commit all manner of wickedness and whoredoms."	Hel 2:3–14	Kishcumen and Gadianton introduce secret combinations into the culture when they establish a band of robbers and murderers who swear oaths to each other "to murder and to rob and to get power."
Ether 8–10	The people fight a series of disastrous civil wars that create an almost constant state of warfare.	Alma 2–3; 44–63; Hel 1–2, 10–11	The people fight a series of disastrous civil wars that create an almost constant state of warfare.
Ether 9:30–35	During a time of war, a great drought comes upon the land, and "when the people [see] that they must perish, they beg[i]n to repent of their iniquities and cry unto the Lord." When the people repent sufficiently, the Lord sends rain and the people are saved.	Hel 11:4–17	During a time of war, Nephi, using the sealing power that God bestowed on him, calls forth a great famine. When the people see that "they were about to perish by famine" they "beg[i]n to remember the Lord their God." They repent, and the Lord sends rain to end the famine.

Table 3. continued

Jaredite Narrative	Nephite-Lamanite Narrative	
Ether 10:32–33 The secret combinations resurface and become a substantial political power. They adopt the old plans and administer oaths as the ancients had, and seek again to destroy the kingdom.	3 Ne 2:11–12	The Gadianton Robbers resurface and become a substantial political power. They "slay so many of the people and . . . lay waste to so many cities and . . . spread so much death and carnage throughout the land that it [becomes] expedient that all the people . . . should take up arms against them."
Ether 13:15–15:12 The different factions of Jaredites clash in an epic final battle that completely destroys the civilization.	Morm 1–7	The Nephites and the Lamanites meet in an epic final battle in which all of the Nephites are killed and the civilization collapses.
Ether 15:33–34 A single prophet, Ether, manages to avoid being killed during the final battle. He hides during the day and compiles the Jaredite record on metal plates and conceals them, to be found by a subsequent civilization and translated by the gift and power of God.	Morm 8–9; Moro 1–7, 10	A single prophet, Moroni, manages to avoid being killed during the final battle. He hides from the Lamanite armies and compiles the Nephite record on metal plates, including the major abridgment that his father made. He conceals the record to be found by a subsequent civilization and translated by the gift and power of God.

collapse of Nephite society, and, immediately after that, the narrative of the Jaredite collapse hundreds of years earlier.

But in the Book of Mormon, final collapses—though certainly final for the people and societies that experience them—are, literally, not the end of the world. In each case, the world starts over again, and the stories of apocalyptic collapse become cautionary tales for the civilizations that come next. As a case in point, the Lamanite destruction of Nephite civilization serves as a special kind of type that Jared Hickman has called an "Amerindian Apocalypse." In the narrative's "prophetically extended temporal frame," Hickman argues, "the resurgence of the Lamanites' Amerindian descendants in antebellum America, by more bloodshed if necessary, is imagined."[24] Hickman quotes a remarkable speech by Jesus Christ in 3 Nephi stating that, if the Gentiles of the future do not repent, then God will empower "a remnant of the house of Jacob" (meaning the Native American Indians) to sweep the Europeans off the continent and "establish in this land, unto the fulfilling of the covenant which I made with your father Jacob . . . a New Jerusalem."[25]

But should this occur, it will not be the final apocalypse, for the Native peoples will survive it and build yet another new civilization that contains the seeds of yet another apocalypse. Because of the Jaredite narrative, the Book of Mormon's temporal frame stretches all the way back to the primeval history in the early part of Genesis. And because of its prophecies, it extends as far into the future as the Second Coming. In effect, it encompasses the entire history of the world within the geographical frame of the American continent. Apocalypses take place throughout this timeline for the Jaredites, the Nephite-Lamanite-Mulekite civilization of Zarahemla, the postmillennial Nephites, the European Gentiles, and whatever civilization exists before the coming of Christ. The Apocalypse is not a singularity in the Book of Mormon, as it is in the Bible; it is a recurring type of which the one foretold by John at Patmos is simply a single instance. Whether the type will be fulfilled once and for all—and the cycle of the birth, collapse, and rebirth of civilizations replaced by a permanent civilization built on the ethical principles of Jesus Christ—depends, as we will see in the next section, on the choices that human beings make.

The Kingdom of God (Some Assembly Required)

Nineteenth-century Mormonism, though definitely millennial, does not fall neatly into the premillennial and the postmillennial models that scholars use to describe millennial movements. On one hand, the early Mormons were profoundly influenced by the premillennialist apocalypticism of the

Second Great Awakening. The first Latter-day Saints saw the coming forth of the Book of Mormon and the Restoration of the Gospel as signs of the last days, and they even identified Jackson County, Missouri, as the site of the New Jerusalem, where the faithful would gather. They believed, as Janeice Johnson writes, that the Book of Mormon would "unlock all manner of biblical things" and "prepar[e] the way for the final eschaton."[26] These are all hallmarks of premillennial belief, and, in *The Millenarian World of Early Mormonism*, Grant Underwood flatly rejects previous scholars' attempts to categorize Joseph Smith's Mormons as postmillennialists because they believed in working to build the Kingdom of God. Mormon eschatology, he argues, exhibits "a much closer kinship to millenarian apocalypticism than it does to allegorist postmillennialism."[27]

Underwood's view, though, substantially discounts the importance to both Mormons and postmillennial Christians of a Kingdom of God that must be built and not simply waited for.[28] The early Mormons were thoroughgoing utopians who had very specific ideas about what they needed to do to create the kingdom. Even as they anticipated a Second Coming, they did everything they could to immanentize the Eschaton. They set up communal societies in Ohio, Missouri, and Illinois. In Utah, Brigham Young set up communities of the "United Order of Enoch." The earliest Mormons seized on Isaiah's notion of a redeemed Jerusalem called Zion and turned it into both a blueprint and a rallying cry for the Kingdom that was theirs to build:

> The building up of Zion is a cause that has interested the people of God in every age; it is a theme upon which prophets, priests and kings have dwelt with peculiar delight; they have looked forward with joyful anticipation to the day in which we live; and fired with heavenly and joyful anticipations they have sung and written and prophesied of this our day; but they died without the sight; we are the favored people that God has made choice of to bring about the Latter-day glory; it is left for us to see, participate in and help to roll forward the Latter-day glory.[29]

Passages like this make it very clear that, while early Mormonism followed the typical premillennial expectations of other nineteenth-century religious movements, its understanding of the Kingdom of God was much closer to the postmillennial view that human beings could, through their own efforts and the better angels of their natures, create an ideal political kingdom.

The first Mormons invested tremendous energy in building Zion, although they believed that the Parousia was imminent and that Christ would soon come and set up an ideal society. They did not believe that Christ was waiting for them to create a perfect world before he came. But they knew that, even if Christ were to come down and magic a perfect society into existence for them, they would be able to keep that society for only as long as they and their descendants remained genuinely converted to Christ. If they stopped treating each other as Christ taught them to, they could lose the Kingdom of God forever. They knew this because it is exactly what happened in the Book of Mormon.

If that text had ended halfway through 4 Nephi it would have followed the Bible's end-of-the-world script to the letter, and there would have been nothing more to the story. After a series of massive upheavals and natural cataclysms destroyed the social order, the resurrected Christ literally came down from the sky and set up a new society built around the principles of the Kingdom of God as articulated in the New Testament. Everybody loved and worshipped God, and "every man did deal justly one with another" (4 Ne 1:2). The people had all of their possessions in common, and "therefore there were not rich and poor, bond and free, but they were all made free and partakers of the heavenly gift" (4 Ne 1:4). There "was no contention in the land because of the love of God which did dwell in the hearts of the people" (4 Ne 1:15). Even the previous ethnic designations were obliterated, and there were "no manner of -ites" (4 Ne 1:17). "These 'partakers of the heavenly gift,'" writes Marilyn Arnold, "actually lived the ideal that utopian societies have managed to achieve only in their dreams."[30] Mormon concurs when he concludes, "Surely there could not be a happier people among all the people which had been created by the hand of God" (4 Ne 1:16).

Mormon devotes only nineteen verses in 4 Nephi to a description of this ideal society, but it lasts for two hundred years—more time than is covered by the books of Mosiah, Alma, Helaman, and 3 Nephi combined. He devotes the rest of 4 Nephi to describing its undoing. One by one, the people stopped living the laws and customs that built their society. First, a group of religious dissenters began to call themselves "Lamanites" again, restoring the old ethnic divisions as voluntary affiliations and creating a social division where none had existed (4 Ne 1:20). Then wealthy people began wearing "costly apparel, and all manner of fine pearls and of the fine things of the world" (4 Ne 1:24). Soon they stopped holding their possessions in common and "began to be divided into classes" and "build up churches unto themselves to get gain" (4 Ne 1:25–26). All of the old ethnic divisions came back as elective affinity groups, and they fought with each other as fiercely as the old groups did before Christ came (4 Ne 1:35–39). Eventually, even the religious differences between Nephites and Lamanites vanished, and "both . . . had become exceedingly wicked one like unto another" (4 Ne 1:45). Finally, the Gadianton Robbers returned with their secret combinations

(4 Ne 1:46), and the world reverted to the Hobbesian hellscape that it had been before the Parousia. As so often happens, the people ended up with the government, and the society, that they deserved.

Soon after the Book of Mormon was published, Joseph Smith created another narrative about people creating Zion by their own actions: the City of Enoch, an ancient society so righteous that all of its inhabitants were taken into heaven without tasting death. The story is told in the sixth and seventh chapters of the book of Moses—Joseph Smith's inspired revision of the first six books of Genesis. The hero of this story, Enoch, is a minor character in the Old Testament—the son of Jared and the father of Methuselah—whose lifespan of 365 years is less than half that of the other patriarchs because he "walked with God: and he was not; for God took him" (Gen 5:21–24). The letter to the Hebrews explains a little bit more, saying that "by faith Enoch was translated that he should not see death; and was not found, because God had translated him: for before his translation he had this testimony, that he pleased God" (Heb 11:5). These intriguing references have given birth to a large body of literature about Enoch in the Jewish, Christian, and Masonic traditions. Enoch was considered the author of the apocryphal (and apocalyptic) book of Enoch—actually five distinct works of early Enochian literature—which is quoted in the New Testament (Jude 1:14).[31] Two other apocryphal books—2 Enoch and 3 Enoch—have survived to the present day. In these books, Enoch is portrayed as a great patriarch, the inventor of writing, and the first great astronomer.[32] In the Kabbalistic tradition, he became the archangel Metatron and the guardian of mystical knowledge.[33] In Masonry, Enoch was an early Mason who constructed a secret vault in which he deposited the great wisdom of the world.[34]

In the book of Moses, Enoch travels to a new land where people are extremely wicked. God tells Enoch that he is angry with this people and, if they do not repent soon, they will be destroyed (Moses 6:26–30). God commands Enoch to preach repentance to the people and, when Enoch protests that he is "slow of speech," God tells him, "open thy mouth, and it shall be filled, and I will give thee utterance" (Moses 6:31–32). Enoch—who, like Nephi and Abinadi, has a complete understanding of the role that Christ will play in human salvation—teaches the people about the atonement:

> And the Lord called his people Zion, because they were of one heart and one mind, and dwelt in righteousness; and there was no poor among them. And Enoch continued his preaching in righteousness unto the people of God. And it came to pass in his days, that he built a city that was called the City of Holiness, even Zion. And it came to pass that Enoch talked with the

Lord; and he said unto the Lord: Surely Zion shall dwell in safety forever. But the Lord said unto Enoch: Zion have I blessed, but the residue of the people have I cursed. And it came to pass that the Lord showed unto Enoch all the inhabitants of the earth; and he beheld, and lo, Zion, in process of time, was taken up into heaven. And the Lord said unto Enoch: Behold mine abode forever. (Moses 7:18–21)

In this dramatic expansion of the Enoch story, Smith reframes the narrative as one of an entire city that repents of its wickedness and establishes a society that meets the three criteria of Zion: (1) the people are not divided into tribes or factions but are united as one people; (2) they are righteous and obey God's commandments; and (3) there are no poor among them. The Nephite-Lamanite society of 4 Nephi meets these same criteria, which were the principles on which nineteenth-century Mormons tried to set up their experimental communities. In March 1832 Smith presented a revelation to the leaders of the church calling for the creation of Zion in Kirtland, Ohio. After this revelation, the Saints set up a company called the United Firm to handle the economic affairs of this new society:

> For verily I say unto you, the time has come, and is now at hand; and behold, and lo, it must needs be that there be an organization of my people, in regulating and establishing the affairs of the storehouse for the poor of my people, both in this place and in the land of Zion—For a permanent and everlasting establishment and order unto my church, to advance the cause, which ye have espoused, to the salvation of man, and to the glory of your Father who is in heaven; That you may be equal in the bonds of heavenly things, yea, and earthly things also, for the obtaining of heavenly things. For if ye are not equal in earthly things ye cannot be equal in obtaining heavenly things. (D&C 78:3–5)[35]

If we think of the Millennium exclusively as a single period of exactly one thousand years during which humans will live on earth in a perfect society, then there can be no doubt that the Mormon tradition sees the Millennium as a future eschatological event. But if we see it as an instance of God's temporal kingdom—the millenniumness of a certain time rather than *the* Millennium—then we must acknowledge that both the Book of Mormon and the Restoration tradition see it as a recurring type—something that occurs multiple times in the scriptural record and constitutes a reasonable goal that human beings can work toward at any time. This does not map well onto the traditional models of pre-, post-, and amillennial theologies. But it does have a close counterpart among contemporary Bible scholars in the work of John Dominic Crossan, who posits that the historical Jesus always intended to represent the Kingdom of God as a political model already within the grasp of human beings.

Crossan's is a minority view. Most contemporary scholars agree with at least the broad outlines of Schweitzer's argument that the historical Jesus was an apocalyptic preacher who believed that the world would soon end and be replaced by a physical kingdom presided over by God. Crossan and others have long argued that Jesus spoke of a "sapiential" rather than an eschatological kingdom. Unlike an eschatological kingdom, a sapiential kingdom is created from inside. Rather than promising to destroy human civilizations and replace them with a divine government, Crossan argues, Jesus gave people a set of constitutive rules that would allow them to create the Kingdom of God:

> The sapiential Kingdom looks to the present rather than the future and imagines how one could live here and now within an already or always available divine domination. One enters that Kingdom by wisdom or goodness, by virtue, justice, or freedom. It is a style of life for now rather than a hope of life for the future. This is therefore an ethical Kingdom, but it must be absolutely insisted that it could be just as eschatological as was the apocalyptic Kingdom. Its ethics, for instance, challenge contemporary morality to its depths. It would be a gross mistake to presume that in my terminology, a sapiential kingdom of God was any less world-negating than an apocalyptic one.[36]

Crossan's final point is crucial. He does not say that the Kingdom of God is not eschatological. But he does not believe that Jesus followed John the Baptist and other Jewish apocalyptic preachers in his day in saying that the kingdom would come about by "the overpowering action of God moving to restore justice and peace to an earth ravished by oppression."[37] After once following John, Crossan suggests, Jesus rejected the idea of an apocalyptic kingdom and told people that they could start building the kingdom themselves by following the principles he taught.[38] The sapiential kingdom can be described as "eschatological if we want it to be." It can bring an end to the social and governmental systems that prevail in the absence of God's kingdom—systems based on force, oppression, greed, and corruption—but whether it does so is entirely up to us. Crossan labels his view of the kingdom "sapiential eschatology," which he differentiates sharply from "apocalyptic eschatology." The latter "is a world-negation stressing imminent divine intervention: we wait for God to act," he explains. "Sapiential eschatology is a world-ending negation emphasizing immediate divine imitation: God waits for us to act."[39]

Crossan bases his statements about Jesus's intentions by appealing to versions of texts and noncanonical gospels that he considers to be earlier, and therefore more reliable, than the canonized sources.[40] His conclusions have often been controversial among Bible scholars, and he has frequently debated colleagues who see the Kingdom of God as Jesus described it in the New Testament as primarily otherworldly and apocalyptic.[41] But Crossan's argument is much easier to reconcile with the Book of Mormon, the book of Moses, and the early Mormon experience than the idea of Jesus as a believer in an imminent eschatological singularity whose timing he clearly did not understand. In the Book of Mormon, the Kingdom of God is a recurring type rather than a fixed apocalypse. In the most dramatic occurrence of the type, Christ's visit to the New World actually does produce an apocalypse; Christ sweeps away the *ancien régime* and establishes a political order based on unity, righteousness, and the conquest of poverty. This solves the people's problems for a time, but the problems don't stay solved. Although Christ destroys Babylon, he cannot build Zion—or, at least, he cannot build it by himself. And the Book of Mormon gives us no reason to believe that things will be different the next time around. It is simply in the nature of Zion that we can build it any time we want it more than anything else in the world. And, after we build it, we can lose it the minute we start to want other things more than the Kingdom of God.

The passage of thousands of years with the end of the world just around the corner has not only affected the theology of the Christian world but it has shaped the ways Christian-influenced cultures see such basic things as time and narrative, building them around what Frank Kermode famously called "the sense of an ending." The Bible, Kermode explains, "begins at the beginning . . . and ends with a vision of the end," giving the biblical narrative a "wholly concordant structure" in which "the end is in harmony with the beginning, the middle with beginning and end."[42] Because all human beings are born, and die, in the middle of the story, we appeal to larger narratives in order to give structure and meaning to our existence. As middle-dwellers, human beings "make considerable imaginative investments in coherent patterns which, by the provision of an end, make possible a satisfying consonance with the origins and with the middle."[43] If Kermode is correct, then all the artifacts of our culture—literature, art, music, ceremonies, institutions, and political structures—bear the stamp of an expected endpoint derived from a worldview that posits a final and irrevocable end to human history.

In its final canonical form, the Christian Bible presents history as a linear journey toward a known, definite end. This view is not entirely consistent with the typological assumptions that underlie the connections between the Old and the New Testaments. Typology posits a cyclical view of history in which similar types of incidents recur because they form part of the fabric of reality. Most ancient cultures saw time and history this way, as Mircea Eliade explains in *The Myth of the Eternal Return*. "The archaic man," he explains, "acknowledges no act which has not been previously posited and lived by someone else.... His life is the ceaseless repetition of gestures initiated by others."[44]

Types in the Bible recur to a point, but they cannot recur endlessly simply because the world of the Christian Bible is not an endless world. This is not the case with the Book of Mormon. Fairly early on, Nephi tells us that "the course of the Lord is one eternal round" (1 Ne 10:19). Alma confirms the point by using the same language in two different places (Alma 7:20, 37:12). And the typological structure, which the Book of Mormon uses to connect its themes, characters, and narrative arcs to those of the Christian Bible, also connects it to a fundamental understanding of reality that the Bible, with its uncompromising eschatological certainty, rejects. Whereas the Bible speaks of the last days in definite articles—the Parousia, the Apocalypse, and the Millennium—the Book of Mormon presents us with multiple types of these events that happened in the past, combined with the expectation that they will happen again in the future. And the Book of Mormon leaves open the possibility that, even after the final apocalypse and the long-awaited Millennium, there may be future apocalypses and future millennia after that, in places and with people who have never been the subjects of scriptural prophecy before. In an eternal round, not only are all things possible—all things are possible again.

At first glance, the way the Book of Mormon incorporates the concepts of Parousia, Apocalypse, and Millennium seems to mirror the biblical accounts of these phenomena closely, often by quoting or invoking the same words. Like the Bible, the Book of Mormon foresees an end of days that will consist of a great final battle, the victorious return of Jesus Christ. In his own apocalyptic vision, Nephi sees the beginnings of the last days, when "the wrath of God is poured out upon the mother of harlots" and "the work of the Father shall commence in preparing the way for the fulfilling of his covenants" (1 Ne 14:17). Immediately thereafter, he sees one of the apostles of Jesus, whom he later identifies as John (1 Ne 14:27). This apostle, Nephi says, "shall see and write the remainder of these things" and "shall also write concerning the end of the world. Wherefore the things which he shall write are just and true" (1 Ne 14:21–23). With these words, Nephi in effect adds the book of Revelation to the Book of Mormon in toto, framing it as a continuation of the vision that he saw when he asked to know the meaning of his father's dream.

In his second book Nephi quotes liberally from the writings of Isaiah that the Christian tradition has long considered prophecies of Christ's first and second comings.[45] But not only does Nephi use the Bible's own words to invoke its eschatological timeline as interpreted by the Christian tradition; he incorporates the very book he is writing—the Book of Mormon—into this timeline as a sign of the Second Coming. Nephi prophesies that in the last days "the Lord God shall bring forth unto you the words of a book, and they shall be the words of them which have slumbered. And behold, the book shall be sealed" (2 Ne 27:1, 6–7). After introducing the sealed book, Nephi, without any notice to the reader, shifts to a close paraphrase of Isaiah 29, which speaks of a "book that is sealed, which men deliver to one that is learned . . . and he saith, I cannot; for it is sealed" (Isa 29:11/2 Ne 27:15–17)—a passage that incorporates events that occurred during the Book of Mormon's translation.[46] Nephi continues to quote Isaiah, prophesying that the Lord will work "a marvelous work and a wonder" in the world (Isa 29:14/2 Ne 27:26)—a phrase that Latter-day Saints generally interpret as foretelling the Restoration of the Gospel or the Latter-day Saint movement itself.[47] Christ himself picks up this language in 3 Nephi when he says that one of the signs of the last days will be "a great and a marvelous work" that will be done through a servant (3 Ne 21:9) and again when he says that "there shall be a great and marvelous work . . . before that judgment day" (3 Ne 28:32).

As such passages demonstrate, the entire Book of Mormon narrative depends on a standard Christian model of the last days, including the major elements discussed in this chapter—a great final battle, the Second Coming of Christ, and a period of millennial peace. In many cases, the Book of Mormon replicates key chapters from the Bible verbatim or otherwise interpolates them into its narrative. And it takes the extra step of constructing its own publication as an event that will set the Bible's eschatological clock in motion. In these ways, the Book of Mormon's reading of the Bible is faithful, even complementary, describing the last days and the Second Coming in terms completely consistent with the biblical record.

But the Book of Mormon also makes a fundamental change to the Bible's eschatological narrative by casting it as a cyclical story rather than a linear one. Both works of scripture foresee a tragic, civilization-destroying last battle that will precede the coming of Christ. But in the Book of Mormon, this will be the fourth such battle in its extended narrative. Likewise, the coming of the resurrected Christ has already happened once. When it happens again, it will be part of a cycle. And even the millennial period of peace and prosperity that will, according to some Christians, follow Christ's visit has, according to the Book of Mormon, already happened once, and it did not turn out to be the final destiny of humankind. We can hardly overstate the extent to which this changes the same biblical narrative that, on another level, the Book of Mormon follows so precisely. If events such as the Apocalypse, the Parousia, and the Millennium are parts of cycles that recur throughout history, then there is no reason to see them as final, or eschatological, at all, because history does not progress from start to finish, from creation to apocalypse. Rather, it cycles through different themes and different events that are part of "one eternal round." Ironically, perhaps, this is precisely the view of history that makes typological representation possible.

The way the Book of Mormon's eschatological narrative simultaneously depends on and undermines the Bible illustrates, as clearly as one might want, the central argument of this book: The Book of Mormon approaches the Bible as a text that it must attach itself to with a faithful reading of the text while simultaneously undermining it with a subversive rereading. In this way, the Book of Mormon casts the Bible as a credible but incomplete record of God's dealings with humanity and as a necessary but not sufficient repository of the divine word. Much as the New Testament did with the Hebrew Bible, the Book of Mormon incorporates the Bible into its own text via the steady flow of allusions, direct quotations, and typological references. And, also like the New Testament, it radically reshapes its predecessor by discovering itself in the text. The Bible does not change as part of the Restoration canon, but the way we read it as part of that canon must change dramatically with the new context that the Book of Mormon creates. To acknowledge this, we must claim no more than the Book of Mormon claims for itself, but once we acknowledge it, we can never read one of the texts without feeling the overwhelming and at times disconcerting pull of the other.

Notes

Introduction

1. The five Book of Mormon stories referenced in this paragraph can be found in 1 Nephi 16:14–23; Enos 1:1–27; Mosiah 11:20–17:20; and Alma 17:26–31.

2. The largest Restoration denomination, the Church of Jesus Christ of Latter-day Saints, accepts as canonical the King James Version of the Bible, the Book of Mormon, a collection of writings and revelations known as the Doctrine and Covenants, and a collection of biblical and historical writings called the Pearl of Great Price (including the book of Abraham, the book of Moses, an extension of the book of Matthew, and Joseph Smith's story of the coming forth of the Book of Mormon, which, through the PoGP, has itself become canonical). The second-largest denomination includes the KJV as revised by Joseph Smith, the Book of Mormon, and a more expansive version of the Doctrine and Covenants.

3. Two good studies of the Book of Mormon that use an ancient context to illuminate the text rather than polemicize on its behalf are John Sorenson, *An Ancient American Setting for the Book of Mormon* (Deseret Book, 1996) and Brant Gardner, *Traditions of the Fathers: The Book of Mormon as History* (Kofford, 2015).

4. The setting of the Book of Mormon in a nineteenth-century American context is showcased in the recent collection *Americanist Approaches to the Book of Mormon*, edited by Elizabeth A. Fenton and Jared Hickman (Oxford University Press, 2019). Among the contributors to this volume are Eran Shalev, Peter Coviello, and Elizabeth Fenton, each of whom has published a book that reads the Book of Mormon from a nineteenth-century perspective. See Eran Shalev, *American Zion: The Bible as a Political Text from the Revolution to the Civil War* (Yale University Press, 2012); Peter Coviello, *Make Yourselves Gods: Mormons and the Unfinished Business of American Secularism* (University of Chicago Press, 2019); and Elizabeth A. Fenton, *Old Canaan in a New World: Native Americans and the Lost Tribes of Israel* (NYU Press, 2020).

5. New Critics practiced "close reading," in which "the poem or literary text is treated as a self-sufficient verbal artifact. In this general orientation, the literary text as such was generally viewed as a privileged site for shaping and disseminating cultural values held to be essential attribute[s] of the aesthetic specificity of poetry." See Leroy Searle, "New Criticism," in *The Johns Hopkins Guide to Literary Theory and Criticism*, ed. Michael Groden, Martin Kreiswirth, and Imre Szeman (Johns Hopkins University Press, 2005), 692.

6. R. John Williams, "The Ghost and the Machine: Plates and Paratext in The Book of Mormon," in *Americanist Approaches to the Book of Mormon*, ed. Elizabeth A. Fenton and Jared Hickman (Oxford University Press, 2019), 46.

7. Mary C. Callaway, "Canonical Criticism," in *To Each Its Own Meaning: An Introduction to Biblical Criticisms and Their Application*, ed. Steven L. McKenzie and Stephen R. Hayes (Westminster John Knox Press, 1999), 147.

8. John Barton, *Reading the Old Testament: Method in Biblical Study* (Darton, Longman and Todd, 1996), 102.

9. Barton, *Reading the Old Testament*, 82.

10. James L. Crenshaw, "Ecclesiastes: Odd Book In," *Bible Review* 6 (1990): 30–31.

11. See T. A. Perry, *Dialogues with Kohlet* (Pennsylvania State University Press, 1993).

12. Adam Miller, *Nothing New Under the Sun: A Blunt Paraphrase of Ecclesiastes* (CreateSpace, 2016), i–ii.

13. Barton, *Reading the Old Testament*, 82–83.

14. Frank Kermode, "The Canon," in *The Literary Guide to the Bible*, ed. Robert Alter and Frank Kermode (Belknap Press of Harvard University Press, 1999), 605.

15. John E. Hartley, "Job II: Ancient Near Eastern Background," in *Dictionary of the Old Testament: Wisdom, Poetry and Writings*, ed. Tremper Longman and Peter Enns, 346–61 (InterVarsity, 2008).

16. The term "canonical criticism" was introduced by James Sanders in *Torah and Canon* (Fortress, 1972). This is generally the name used in introductory texts to biblical studies (see Calloway, "Canonical Criticism," 142–55; Barton, *Reading the Old Testament*, 130–71). Brevard Childs, who is usually seen as the founder of the school, objected to the term, preferring instead "the canonical method." He writes, "Canonical criticism implies that the canonical approach is considered another historical critical technique which can take its place alongside of source criticism, form criticism, rhetorical criticism, and similar methods. I do not envision the approach to canon in this light. Rather, the issue at stake in relation to the canon turns on establishing a stance from which the Bible can be read as sacred scripture." *Introduction to the Old Testament as Scripture* (Fortress, 1970), 82.

17. Brevard Childs, *Biblical Theology in Crisis* (Westminster, 1970), 99.

18. James Barr, *Holy Scripture: Canon, Authority, Criticism* (Westminster, 1983), 130–71; Dale A. Brueggemann, "Brevard Childs' Canon Criticism: An Example of Post-critical Naiveté," *Journal of the Evangelical Theological Society* 32, no. 3 (1989): 311–26.

19. For a reading of Satan/the serpent as a trickster figure, see Hershey H. Friedman and Steve Lippman, "Satan the Accuser: Trickster in Talmudic and Midrashic Literature," *Thalia: Studies in Literary Humor* 18 (March 1999): 31–41.

20. Stephen Greenblatt, *The Rise and Fall of Adam and Eve* (Norton, 2017), 39–63.

21. On this point see Tyggve N. D. Mettinger, *The Eden Narrative: A Literary and Religio-Historical Study of Genesis 2–3* (Eisenbrauns, 2007), 49–52.

22. John Milton, *Paradise Lost* (1667) and *Paradise Regained* (1671).

23. Laurie F. Maffly-Kipp, ed., introduction to *The Book of Mormon* (Penguin, 2009), xx.

24. The 1879 edition of the Book of Mormon, edited by Orson Pratt, adopted a chapter-and-verse style that mirrored the Bible, and the 1920 edition, edited by James E. Talmage, adopted the double-column text common in nearly all editions of the Bible. See Paul C. Gutjahr, *The Book of Mormon: A Biography* (Princeton University Press, 2012), 95–97.

25. The full chapters quoted in the Book of Mormon are Isaiah 2–14 (2 Ne 12–24), Isaiah 48–49 (1 Ne 20–21), Isaiah 50–51 (2 Ne 7–8), Isaiah 53 (Mosiah 14), Isaiah 54 (3 Ne 22), Matthew 5–7 (3 Ne 12–14), and Malachi 3–4 (3 Ne 24–25).

26. Maffly-Kipp, introduction to *The Book of Mormon*, xx.

27. The seven older brother–younger brother pairs in Genesis are as follows: Cain and Abel (Gen 4:2–15), Ham and Japheth (Gen 9–10), Ishmael and Isaac (Gen 21), Jacob and Esau (Gen 25, 27), Reuben and Joseph (Gen 37, 39–47; Deut 33:13; 1 Chr 5:2), Er and Pharez (Gen 30), and Ephraim and Manasseh (Gen 48:13–19). See Michael Austin, "The Genesis Narrative and the Primogeniture Debate in Seventeenth-Century England," *Journal of English and Germanic Philology* 98, no. 1 (January 1999): 17–39.

28. See Chapter 4 for a list of the seven iterations of the Exodus type in the Book of Mormon.

29. Elizabeth A. Fenton, "Open Canons: Sacred History and American History in The Book of Mormon," *J19: The Journal of Nineteenth-Century Americanists* 1, no. 2 (2013): 345.

30. Fenton, "Open Canons," 345–46.

31. See Michael Austin, *Useful Fictions: Evolution, Anxiety, and the Origins of Literature* (University of Nebraska Press, 2010), 17–40.

32. The term "Smith-Rigdon" distinguishes the early Mormon movement from the other major restorationist movement at the time, the Stone-Campbell movement. See Steven L. Shields, "Joseph Smith and Sidney Rigdon: Co-Founders of a Movement," *Dialogue* 52, no. 3 (Fall 2019): 1–18.

33. On the theological, rather than simply the canonical, importance of the King James Bible, see Jan J. Martin, "The Theological Value of the King James Language in the Book of Mormon," *Journal of Book of Mormon Studies* 27 (2018): 88–124.

Chapter 1. A Theory of Types

1. I am grateful to my friend and blog partner Kevin Barney for the overall comparison between the Book of Mormon and the Aeneid, which he developed in a post on the By Common Consent blog: https://bycommonconsent.com/2017/09/23/the-bom-and-the-aeneid.

2. The Latin phrase *graecia capta ferum victorem cepit* can be found in Horace, Epistles 2.1, 156–57.

3. Homer, *The Odyssey*, trans. Robert Fagles (Penguin, 1996), 274–75.

4. The traditional site for the scenes with Scylla and Charybdis is the Strait of Messina, between the easternmost tip of Sicily and the Italian mainland.

5. Virgil, *The Aeneid*, trans. Robert Fagles (Penguin, 2008), 117.

6. William L. Davis has done extensive work on early nineteenth-century sermon culture in the United States and its influence on the Book of Mormon. See *Visions in a Seer Stone: Joseph Smith and the Making of the Book of Mormon* (University of North Carolina Press, 2020), 33–58, 89–121.

7. Northrop Frye, *The Great Code: The Bible and Literature* (Harcourt Brace Jovanovich, 1982), 79.

8. For commentary on the New Testament's direct citations and allusions to the Old Testament, see Gregory K. Beale, *Handbook on the New Testament Use of the Old Testament: Exegesis and Interpretation* (Baker Academic), 2012.

9. Leonhard Goppelt, *Typos: The Typological Interpretation of the Old Testament in the New*, trans. Donald H. Madvig (Eerdmans, 1982), 198.

10. Sacvan Bercovitch, *The American Jeremiad* (University of Wisconsin Press, 1978), 40–44.

11. Nearly all American Christians in the nineteenth century—Catholic and Protestant alike—accepted the typological connections between the Old and the New Testaments, and many also saw America as an extension of the typology of the Old Testament. See ibid., 176–210..

12. Eric Auerbach, *Scenes from the Drama of European Literature: Six Essays* (Meridian, 1959), 53.

13. Auerbach, *Scenes from the Drama of European Literature*, 52.

14. No extant Old Testament source has been identified for this prophecy.

15. R. T. France, *Matthew: An Introduction and Commentary*. Tyndale New Testament Commentaries (InterVarsity, 2008), 63.

16. Walter Arend, *Die Typischen Scenen Bei Homer* (Weidmann, 1933). Arend's work, though extremely important in Europe, has never been translated into English.

17. Mark David Usher, *Homeric Stitchings: The Homeric Centos of the Empress Eudocia* (Rowman & Littlefield, 1998), 84.

18. Rick M. Newton, "The Aristotelian Unity of Odysseus's Wanderings," in *Approaches to Teaching Homer's* Iliad *and* Odyssey, ed. Kostas Myrsiades, 195–238 (Modern Language Association, 1987).

19. Robert Alter, *The Art of Biblical Narrative* (New York: Basic Books, 1981),

52. Alter responds here to work done by Robert Culley in *Studies in the Structure of Hebrew Narrative* (Fortress and Scholars, 1976), 41–43.

20. Ruth 2:9. For an interpretation of the type-scene see Alter, *Art of Biblical Narrative*, 58.

21. See Andrew E. Arterbury, "Breaking the Betrothal Bonds: Hospitality in John 4," *Catholic Biblical Quarterly* 72, no. 1 (2010): 63–83; R. Alan Culpepper, *Anatomy of the Fourth Gospel: A Study in Literary Design* (Fortress, 1983), 136; Lyle Eslinger, "The Wooing of the Woman at the Well: Jesus, the Reader and Reader-Response Criticism," *Literature and Theology* 1 (1987): 167–83; Calum M. Carmichael, "Marriage and the Samaritan Woman," *New Testament Studies* 26 (1979–80): 32–46.

22. See Mark D. Thomas, *Digging in Cumorah* (Signature, 1999), 138–39.

23. See Michael Austin, "How the Book of Mormon Reads the Bible: A Theory of Types," *Journal of Book of Mormon Studies* 26 (January 2017): 48–81, 61–65.

24. The nine specific references to typology in the Book of Mormon occur in the following verses: Mosiah 3:15, Mosiah 13:10, Mosiah 13:31, Alma 13:16, Alma 25:10, Alma 25:15, Alma 33:39, Alma 37:45, and Ether 13:6.

25. The Record of Zeniff, which comprises Mosiah 9–22, contains the record of the Nephite offshoot group that colonized the Land of Nephi under the leadership of Zeniff, Noah, and Limhi. It is separated narratively from the rest of Mormon's record by the presumption of a different narrative voice. See Gary L. Sturgess, "The Book of Mosiah: Thoughts About Its Structure, Purposes, Themes, and Authorship," *Journal of Book of Mormon Studies* 4, no. 2 (1995): 107–35.

26. On the relation between repetition scenes in Homer and Virgil see Elizabeth Minchin, "Poet, Audience, Time, and Text: Reflections on Medium and Mode in Homer and Virgil," in *Between Orality and Literacy: Communication and Adaptation in Antiquity*, ed. Carl A. Anderson and Ruth Scodel, 267–88 (Brill, 2014).

27. Simone Caroti, "Science Fiction, Forbidden Planet, and Shakespeare's *The Tempest*," *CLCWeb: Comparative Literature and Culture* 6, no. 1 (2004): https://doi.org/10.7771/1481-4374.1214.

28. Judy Klitsner, *Subversive Sequels in the Bible* (Maggid, 2011), xxv.

29. Klitsner, *Subversive Sequels in the Bible*, xxi.

30. Klitsner, *Subversive Sequels in the Bible*, xix–xx.

31. Klitsner, *Subversive Sequels in the Bible*, xxii–xxiii.

32. Steven N. Zwicker, *Dryden's Political Poetry: The Typology of King and Nation* (Brown University Press, 1972).

33. For a book-length study of how neotypes worked in the seventeenth and eighteenth centuries, see Michael Austin, *New Testaments: Cognition, Closure, and the Figural Logic of the Sequel, 1660–1740* (University of Delaware Press, 2012).

34. Bercovitch, *American Jeremiad*, 93–131.

35. The last possibility—that universal archetypes are the result of natural selection acting on a narrative-based cognitive structure—is one that I explore at some length in Michael Austin, *Useful Fictions: Evolution, Anxiety, and the Origins of Literature* (University of Nebraska Press, 2010).

36. Since 1979 the headnote to Genesis 49 in the official LDS edition of the Bible has read, "Joseph is a fruitful bough by a well—His branches (the Nephites and La-manites) will run over the wall."

37. Modern editions of the Book of Mormon change the words that the biblical Joseph spoke from "fruit of thy loins" to "fruit of my loins."

38. Carl Jung, Gerhard Adler, and Richard Francis Carrington Hull, *Collected Works of C. G. Jung*, vol. 9, pt. 1, *Archetypes and the Collective Unconscious*, 2nd ed. (Princeton University Press, 1969), 183.

39. This passage from 2 Nephi forms the basis of Genesis 50:24–38, which Joseph Smith included in his revision of the Bible and which is included as an appendix in the current LDS Bible.

Chapter 2. Stories of the Fall

1. Augustine, *The Literal Meaning of Genesis 9:6*, in Augustine, *On Genesis*, ed. Edmund Hill and John E. Rotelle, trans. Edmund Hill (New City, 2002), 379.

2. Augustine wrote the short volume *On Genesis: A Refutation of the Manichees*, in 388/9. From 393 and 395 he worked on a commentary to be called "Literal Commentary on Genesis," but he left it unfinished, and it survives as *Unfinished Literal Commentary on Genesis*. His major work on the topic, *The Literal Meaning of Genesis*, was composed between 401 and 416. All three commentaries appear in *On Genesis*. Augustine also wrote extended commentaries on Genesis in both *Confessions* and *City of God*.

3. Augustine, *On Genesis*, 380.

4. For a fascinating discussion of late medieval conjectures about Augustine and prelapsarian sexuality, see Alastair Minnis, *From Eden to Eternity: Creations of Paradise in the Later Middle Ages* (University of Pennsylvania Press, 2020), 37–54.

5. Augustine, *On Genesis*, 385.

6. Augustine, *On Genesis*, 386.

7. For Augustine's commentary on this verse, see *Literal Meaning of Genesis 6:37* (*On Genesis*, 322).

8. Terryl Givens, *Wrestling the Angel: The Foundations of Mormon Thought; Cosmos, God, Humanity* (Oxford University Press, 2015), 185.

9. Givens, *Wrestling the Angel*, 184.

10. Sterling M. McMurrin, *The Theological Foundations of the Mormon Religion* (University of Utah Press, 1965), 66–67.

11. For a careful examination of LDS scriptures, including Joseph Smith's inspired revision of the Bible (JST), relating to the Fall and the Atonement, see Kathleen Flake, "Translating Time: The Nature and Function of Joseph Smith's Narrative Canon," *Journal of Religion* 87, no. 4 (October 2007): 511–20.

12. The story of Persephone eating the pomegranate seeds occurs in Homeric Hymn 2, "Hymn to Demeter," lines 384–417; for Gilgamesh and the serpent, see the Epic of Gilgamesh, tablet 11, lines 307–311.

13. In his discussion of the sacred tree archetype, Mircia Eliade notes that "the tree represents—whether ritually and concretely, or in mythology and cosmology, or simply symbolically—the living cosmos, endlessly renewing itself. Since inexhaustible life is the equivalent of immortality, the tree-cosmos may therefore become, at a different level, the tree of 'life undying.'" *Patterns in Comparative Religion*, trans. Rosemary Sheed (Sheed & Ward, 1958), 267. See also Michaela Bauks, "Sacred Trees in the Garden of Eden and Their Ancient Near Eastern Precursors," *Journal of Ancient Judaism* 3, no. 3 (2012): 267–301.

14. Bruce W. Jorgensen's paper "The Dark Way to the Tree: Typological Unity in the Book of Mormon" was originally delivered at the December 1977 meeting of the Utah Academy of Sciences, Arts, and Letters and published in the academy's journal, *Encyclia*, 54, pt. 2 (1977): 16–24. It was reprinted in the volume *Literature of Belief: Sacred Scripture and Religious Experience*, ed. Neal E. Lambert, 217–31 (Religious Studies Center, Brigham Young University, 1981). My citations are to the latter publication.

15. Jorgensen, "Dark Way to the Tree," 222.

16. Corbin T. Volluz makes the argument that the tree in Lehi's dream was literally the tree of life mentioned in Genesis 2:9 and again in Genesis 3:24. See "Lehi's Dream of the Tree of Life: Springboard to Prophecy," *Journal of Book of Mormon Studies* 2, no. 2 (1993): 14–38.

17. The term "lone and dreary world" is frequently used in LDS discourse to describe the state of Adam and Eve's existence after they are cast out of Eden, as James Talmage explains in his classic book *House of the Lord* (Deseret News Press, 1912): "The Temple Endowment . . . includes a recital of the most prominent events of the creative period, the condition of our first parents in the Garden of Eden, their disobedience and consequent expulsion from that blissful abode, [and] their condition in *the lone and dreary world* when doomed to live by labor and sweat" (99–100).

18. For a specifically archetypal approach to all of the symbols in Lehi's dream see Charles Swift, "'I Have Dreamed a Dream': Lehi's Archetypal Vision of the Tree of Life," in *The Tree of Life: From Eden to Eternity*, ed. John W. Welch and Donald W. Parry, 129–49 (Deseret Book, 2011).

19. Matthew L. Bowen, "Not Partaking of the Fruit: Its Generational Consequences and Its Remedy," in *The Things Which My Father Saw: Approaches to Lehi's Dream and Nephi's Vision* (2011 Sperry Symposium), ed. Daniel L. Belnap, Gaye Strathearn, and Stanley A. Johnson (Religious Studies Center, Brigham Young University; Deseret Book, 2011), 240.

20. See Terryl Givens, *The Pearl of Greatest Price* (Oxford University Press, 2019), 27–42.

21. See Daniel K. Judd, "The Fortunate Fall of Adam and Eve," in *No Weapon Shall Prosper: New Light on Sensitive Issues*, ed. Robert L. Millet (Religious Studies Center, Brigham Young University; Deseret Book, 2011), 318–19.

22. In the 1830 edition of the Book of Mormon, the name "Jesus Christ" appears once, in 1 Nephi 12:28. This was removed in the 1837 edition and all subsequent ones. The name "Christ" does not appear until 2 Ne 10:3, which reads, "Wherefore,

as I said unto you, it must needs be expedient that Christ—for in the last night the angel spake unto me that this should be his name—should come among the Jews." But the term "Messiah," which is the Hebrew equivalent of "Christ," or "anointed one," appears in the very first chapter, in a description of Lehi's prophecies in Jerusalem (1 Ne 1:19). The name "Jesus" occurs for the first time in 2 Ne 25:19: "For according to the words of the prophets, the Messiah cometh in six hundred years from the time that my father left Jerusalem; and according to the words of the prophets, and also the word of the angel of God, his name shall be Jesus Christ, the Son of God."

23. My primary concern here is with the way the Book of Mormon attaches itself to the canonical descriptions of Josiah's reforms in 2 Kings 22–23 and 2 Chronicles 34–35, which included a restoration of the temple, rediscovery of the law of Moses, the destruction of temples and altars dedicated to other gods, the execution of Baalist priests, and the forcible suppression of any form of worship not compatible with the law of Moses. The reality of the Josianic reforms was likely very different because the biblical narrative was constructed during the Babylonian captivity and likely incorporated a later understanding of monotheism and Judaism. See Thomas Römer, *The Invention of God*, trans. Raymond Guess (Harvard University Press, 2016), 191–209.

24. See Jared M. Halverson, "Lehi's Dream and Nephi's Vision as Apocalyptic Literature," in *The Things Which My Father Saw: Approaches to Lehi's Dream and Nephi's Vision* (2011 Sperry Symposium), ed. Daniel L. Belnap, Gaye Strathearn, and Stanley A. Johnson, 53–69 (Religious Studies Center, Brigham Young University; Deseret Book, 2011).

25. Modern versions of the Book of Mormon replace "mother of God" in verse 18 with "mother of the Son of God" and "Eternal Father" in verse 21 with "Son of the Eternal Father." Both changes were made in the 1837 edition and likely reflect Joseph Smith's movement away from trinitarianism. The changes are not strictly necessary, however, as Mormon theology considers Jesus Christ to be Jehovah (Yahweh), the God of the Old Testament and creator of the world who was born as a human infant and crucified for the sins of the world. See David B. Seely, "Jehovah, Jesus Christ," *Encyclopedia of Mormonism* (Macmillan, 1992), 720–21.

26. The angel's response to Nephi, "Yea, and the most joyous to the soul" (1 Ne 11:23) affirms that Nephi was correct to say that the tree in Lehi's dream represented the love of God. But the brevity of the response, and the fact that the angel moves on to an even more elaborate vision of Christ, both suggest that Nephi still doesn't grasp the scale of God's condescension.

27. Augustine, for example, writes, "Our Lord Jesus Christ in His condescension entered the Virgin's womb (*Christus uterum virginis dignatus intravit*), without stain impregnated a woman's members, without corruption made His Mother fertile, and, when formed, came forth from her, preserving intact His Mother's body so that He might fill with the honor of maternity and with the holiness of virginity her from whom He deigned to be born." *Sermons on the Liturgical Seasons*, trans. Mary Sarah Muldowney, R.S.M. (Fathers of the Church, 1959), 144.

28. Charles J. Doe, ed., *Jonathan Edwards in the Pulpit* (Curiosmith, 2012), 78–79.

29. An 1836 edition of Watts's hymns lists three psalms with God's condescension in the subtitles: Psalm 8, "God's Condescension in conferring Honour upon Man" (61) and "Christ's Condescension and Glorification" (62); Psalm 113, "The Majesty and Condescension of God" (225); and Psalm 144, "Vanity of Man and Condescension of God" (275). Hymn 46 likewise is subtitled "God's Condescension to Human Affairs" (401). See Samuel Worchester, ed., *The Psalms, Hymns, and Spiritual Songs, of the Rev. Isaac Watts, D. D., To which are Added, Select Hymns, from Other Authors; and Directions for Musical Expression* (Crocker & Brewster, 1834).

30. According to the Book of Mormon's timeline, Nephi saw his vision before the party of Lehi separated into Nephites and Lamanites. However, he created his record much later, toward the end of his life, after the two groups had been separate for generations.

31. John A. Widtsoe, *Evidences and Reconciliations* (Bookcraft, 1960), 155.

32. Grant Hardy, "Prophetic Perspectives and Prerogative: How Lehi and Nephi Applied the Lessons of Lehi's Dream," in *The Things Which My Father Saw: Approaches to Lehi's Dream and Nephi's Vision* (2011 Sperry Symposium), ed. Daniel L. Belnap, Gaye Strathearn, and Stanley A. Johnson (Religious Studies Center, Brigham Young University; Deseret Book, 2011), 205.

33. Hardy, "Prophetic Perspectives," 205, 207.

34. Nephi identifies Nazareth as the home of the virgin in 1 Ne 11:13. Nazareth is not mentioned anywhere in the Old Testament or in the rabbinic literature; if it existed at all in Nephi's time, it would have been too small to be worth mentioning in any official records.

35. Leonhard Goppelt, *Typos: The Typological Interpretation of the Old Testament in the New* (Wipf & Stock, 2002), 129.

36. James D. G. Dunn, *The Theology of Paul the Apostle* (Eerdmans, 2006), 241.

37. "In LDS doctrine, to be damned means to be stopped, blocked, or limited in one's progress. Individuals are damned whenever they are prevented from reaching their full potential as children of God." Richard Holzapfel, "Damnation," *Encyclopedia of Mormonism* (Macmillan, 1992), 353.

Chapter 3. Curses from God

1. Thomas Mann, *Joseph and His Brothers*, trans. John E. Woods (New York: Everyman's Library, 2005), xxxii.

2. In defining "demythologization," Bultmann writes, "Can Christian proclamation today expect men and women to acknowledge the mythical world picture as true? To do so would be both pointless and impossible. It would be pointless because there is nothing specifically Christian about the mythical world picture, which is simply the world picture of a time now past that was not yet formed by scientific thinking. It would be impossible because no one can appropriate a world picture by sheer resolve, since it is already given with one's particular historical situation." Rudolph Bultmann, *New Testament Mythology and Other Basic Writings* (Fortress, 1984), 3.

3. Wolf-Daniel Hartwich, "Religion and Culture in *Joseph and His Brothers*," in *The Cambridge Companion to Thomas Mann*, ed. Ritchie Robertson (Cambridge University Press, 2002), 152.

4. Mann, *Joseph and His Brothers*, 6–7.

5. Israel Finkelstein and Neil A. Silberman, *The Bible Unearthed* (Free Press, 2001), 98–122.

6. From internal textual evidence, modern commentators conclude that the books from 1 Nephi through Omni were taken intact from the Small Plates of Nephi; the content of Words of Mormon through Mormon 7 were taken from the Large Plates of Nephi, which were used by scribes from Nephi through Mormon. The book of Ether was translated from another set of plates dating back to the Tower of Babel and presumably written in the universal ancestral language, and the Brass Plates of Laban, which provided many of the extensive quotes from Isaiah and other Old Testament prophets, were written in Hebrew and taken by the Lehites from Jerusalem. In addition, the final three chapters of Mormon and the book of Moroni were added after the final abridgment by Mormon's son, Moroni, who ultimately buried the plates for a future generation to discover. See Rex C. Reeve Jr., "The Book of Mormon Plates," in *First Nephi: The Doctrinal Foundation*, ed. Monte S. Nyman and Charles D. Tate Jr., 99–111 (Religious Studies Center, Brigham Young University, 1988).

7. For a fuller exploration of the challenges that Mormon and Moroni faced as narrators see Grant Hardy, *Understanding the Book of Mormon: A Reader's Guide* (Oxford University Press, 2010), 92–97 (Mormon) and 218–22 (Moroni).

8. David Rohrbacher, *The Historians of Late Antiquity* (Routledge, 2002), 225. One common folk story in these accounts, which probably comes from Eunapius, is that the Huns and the Goths once lived on opposite sides of a great lake that they both considered the end of the world. They did not know of each other's existence until an ox was chased by insects across the lake, and when the Huns discovered that they were not the only people in the world, they decided to conquer the new land (225).

9. See, for one example, E. A. Thompson, *A History of Attila and the Huns* (Clarendon, 1948), which contains this particularly delightful, if vicious, assessment: "We should remember, however, that Zosimus also made use of the history of Eunapius, who was endowed with more than a due share of human frailties. We must therefore be careful to distinguish between those parts of Zosimus' work which are based on Eunapius and those which paraphrase Olympiodorus. Of Eunapius himself we need say nothing here: would that we could avoid him throughout" (9).

10. For a book-length discussion of the universal nature of Genesis 1–11, see Dru Johnson, Craig G. Bartholomew, and David J. H. Beldman, *The Universal Story: Genesis 1–11* (Lexham, 2018).

11. Theodore Hiebert, "The Tower of Babel and the Origin of the World's Cultures," *Journal of Biblical Literature* 126, no. 1 (2007): 29—58.

12. The argument that biblical texts, like Renaissance texts, must be read according to the cultures of the writers rather than the subjects of the stories is made at great length in Gary A. Rendsburg, "The Genesis of the Bible," inaugural lecture of the Blanche

and Irving Laurie Chair in Jewish History at Rutgers University, October 28, 2004, http://jewishstudies.rutgers.edu/component/docman/doc_view/117-the-genesis -of-the-bible?Itemid=158.

13. Walter Brueggemann, *Genesis: Interpretation; a Bible Commentary for Teaching and Preaching* (John Knox, 1982), 60.

14. For an overview of rabbinic debates about this passage see David M. Goldenberg, "The Words of a Wise Man's Mouth Are Gracious" (Qoh 10:12), *Festschrift for Gunter Stemberger*, ed. Mauro Perani (Walter de Gruyter, 2005), 257–66. For specific modern arguments featuring sodomy or castration, see Anthony Phillips, "Uncovering the Father's Skirt," *Vetus Testamentum* 30 (1980): 38–43; Frederick W. Bassett, "Noah's Nakedness and the Curse of Canaan: A Case of Incest," *Vetus Testamentum* 21 (1971): 232–37; and John Sietze Bergsma and Scott Walker Hahn, "Noah's Nakedness and the Curse of Canaan (Genesis 9:20–27)" *Journal of Biblical Literature* 121 (2005): 25–40.

15. This is a key argument in Howard Eilberg-Schwartz, *God's Phallus and Other Problems for Men and Monotheism* (Beacon, 2001), 91–97.

16. This is one of the alternatives explored by O. Palmer Robinson in "Current Critical Questions Concerning the 'Curse of Ham' (Gen 9:20–27)," *Journal of the Evangelical Theological Society* 41, no. 2 (1998): 177–88.

17. Devora Steinmetz, "Vineyard, Farm, and Garden: The Drunkenness of Noah in the Context of Primeval History," *Journal of Biblical Literature* 113, no. 2 (1994): 194.

18. Steven L. McKenzie, *How to Read the Bible: History, Prophecy, Literature; Why Modern Readers Need to Know the Difference, and What It Means for Faith Today* (Oxford University Press, 2011), 37.

19. See David M. Goldenberg, *The Curse of Ham: Race and Slavery in Early Judaism, Christianity, and Islam* (Princeton University Press), 2003; and the same author's more recent *Black and Slave: The Origins and History of the Curse of Ham* (De Gruyter, 2017). See also Stephen R. Haynes, *Noah's Curse: The Biblical Justification of American Slavery* (Oxford University Press, 2002); and David M. Whitford, *The Curse of Ham in the Early Modern Era: The Bible and the Justifications for Slavery* (Routledge, 2009).

20. Goldenberg, *Black and Slave*, 154–55.

21. Goldenberg, *Curse of Ham*, 178–79

22. Official Declaration 2, which ended the policy forbidding African American men from holding the priesthood and placing other restrictions on anyone of African descent, was read at the General Conference of the Church of Jesus Christ of Latter-day Saints and formally canonized. Since 1981 it has been part of the Doctrine and Covenants, one of four books of scripture considered canonical by the Utah-based church.

23. For the argument that "blackness" should be read metaphorically, rather than as a literal description of skin color, see Brant Gardner, *Traditions of the Fathers: The Book of Mormon as History* (Kofford, 2015), 159–61; and Armaund L. Mauss, *All Abraham's Children: Changing Mormon Conceptions of Race and Lineage* (University

of Illinois Press, 2003), 127–28. The argument that an intended nineteenth-century etiology of Native Americans would have used "red" instead of "black" to describe skin color is the main point of Jeremy Talmage's "Black, White, and Red All Over: Skin Color in the Book of Mormon," *Journal of Book of Mormon Studies* 28 (2019): 46–68. The argument that changes in skin color in the Book of Mormon might be seen as multigenerational effects of intermarriage was made most clearly by Eugene England in the essay "Lamanites and the Spirit of the Lord" (*Dialogue* 18, no. 4 [Winter 1985]: 25–32), in which he states that some passages in the Book of Mormon "make most sense as descriptions of natural processes resulting from changed life style and intermarriage . . . rather than as the wholesale and sudden genetic intervention of a race-conscious God" (30). John A. Tvedtnes explored the possible differences between the "curse" and the "mark" in "The Charge of 'Racism' in the Book of Mormon," *Review of Books on the Book of Mormon* 15, no. 2 (2003): 186–88.

24. For a brief introduction to the book of Moses and the Joseph Smith translation of the Bible, see Terryl Givens and Brian M. Hauglid, *The Pearl of Greatest Price: Mormonism's Most Controversial Scripture* (Oxford University Press, 2019), 37–42.

25. The Bible mentions four sons as the lineage of Ham: Cush, Mizraim, Phut, and Canaan (Gen 10:6). Adding the daughter, Egyptus, to the line makes five descendants of Noah who carry the curse of Cain through the maternal and the paternal line. This virtually guarantees that, by the time of the Exodus a thousand years later, every human being on earth would have a least one ancestor from a cursed lineage. And indeed, if all human beings really descended from three brothers who lived four thousand years ago, then all people on earth would now have millions of ancestors from all three lines in their family tree. The curse narratives never had much to do with tracing actual descent, which, given the time scales involved, would be both meaningless and futile.

26. For a complete analysis of passages in the Pearl of Great Price dealing with racial issues, see Matthew L. Harris and Newell G. Bringhurst, eds., *The Mormon Church and Blacks: A Documentary History* (University of Illinois Press, 2015), 11–14.

27. See Goldenberg, *Curse of Ham,* 139–200.

28. Nancy Bentley, "Kinship, The Book of Mormon, and Modern Revelation," in *Americanist Approaches to the Book of Mormon*, ed. Elizabeth A. Fenton and Jared Hickman (Oxford University Press, 2019), 247.

29. Max P. Mueller, *Race and the Making of the Mormon People* (University of North Carolina Press, 2018), 40–41.

30. The Thirteen Articles of Faith were originally composed by Smith in an 1842 letter to John Wentworth, editor of the *Chicago Democrat.* In 1851 they were included in the first edition of the Pearl of Great Price, which was formally canonized in 1880.

31. *History of the Church* 1:118; see also Doctrine and Covenants 28:8; 32:2–3 and *History of the Church* 1:125.

32. See, e.g., Doctrine and Covenants 49:24–25: "But before the great day of the Lord shall come, Jacob shall flourish in the wilderness, and the Lamanites shall blossom as the rose. Zion shall flourish upon the hills and rejoice upon the mountains, and shall be assembled together unto the place which I have appointed."

33. Although the Book of Mormon has been seen since its publication, by Mormons and non-Mormons alike, as an attempt to explain the origins of Native Americans, nothing in the text suggests that the narrative takes place in the Americas. The text itself is silent on both the location of its setting and the identity of its main characters' descendants. As Richard Bushman explains, "The Book of Mormon deposited its people on some unknown shore—not even definitely identified as America—and has them live out their history in a remote place in a distant time, using names that had no connection to modern Indians." *Joseph Smith: Rough Stone Rolling* (Knopf, 2005), 97.

34. Goldenberg, *Black and Slave*, 178–82.

35. https://www.churchofjesuschrist.org/study/manual/gospel-topics-essays/race-and-the-priesthood?lang=eng.

36. https://www.churchofjesuschrist.org/study/manual/gospel-topics-essays/book-of-mormon-and-dna-studies?lang=eng.

37. Eldin Ricks, "The Small Plates of Nephi and the Words of Mormon," in *The Book of Mormon: Jacob Through Words of Mormon, To Learn with Joy*, ed. Monte S. Nyman and Charles D. Tate Jr., 209–19 (Religious Studies Center, Brigham Young University, 1990).

38. Grant Hardy, *Understanding the Book of Mormon* (Oxford University Press, 2010), 59–60, 37.

39. Fatima Saleh and Margaret Olsen Hemming, *The Book of Mormon for the Least of These* (By Common Consent Press, 2020), 67.

40. John L. Sorenson, *An Ancient American Setting for the Book of Mormon* (Deseret Book, 1996), 89–90.

41. The book of Jarom describes the Lamanites as "exceedingly more numerous" than the Nephites (Jarom 1:6). The book of Mosiah says that the Nephites and the Mulekites combined were "not half so numerous" as the Lamanites (Mosiah 25:3). The book of Alma describes Lamanites as "more numerous, yea, by more than double the number of the Nephites." The book of Helaman reports that "so numerous were the Lamanites that it became impossible for the Nephites to obtain more power over them" (Hel 4:19).

42. For a detailed analysis of population figures from the Book of Mormon, see John C. Kunich, "Multiply Exceedingly: Book of Mormon Population Sizes," in *New Approaches to the Book of Mormon*, ed. Brent Metcalfe, 231–67 (Signature, 1993).

Chapter 4. Reimagining the Exodus

1. Michael Walzer, *Exodus and Revolution* (Basic Books, 1986), ix.

2. Edward W. Said, "Michael Walzer's 'Exodus and Revolution': A Canaanite Reading," *Arab Studies Quarterly* 8, no. 3 (Summer 1986): 289–303.

3. Said, "Michael Walzer's 'Exodus and Revolution,'" 290.

4. Said, "Michael Walzer's 'Exodus and Revolution,'" 302.

5. Daniel L. Hawk, "The Truth About Conquest: Joshua as History, Narrative, and Scripture," *Interpretation* 66, no. 2 (2012): 130.

6. Gareth Lloyd Jones, "Sacred Violence: The Dark Side of God," *Journal of Beliefs & Values* 20, no. 2 (1999): 186.

7. See John Coffey, *Exodus and Liberation: Deliverance Politics from John Calvin to Martin Luther King Jr.* (Oxford University Press, 2014), 4–5.

8. Coffey surveys the many uses of Exodus by both slaves and abolitionists in ibid. (79–177) and the uses in the civil rights movement (181–214). See also Gary S. Selby, *Martin Luther King and the Rhetoric of Freedom: The Exodus Narrative in America's Struggle for Civil Rights* (Baylor University Press, 2008).

9. David Brion Davis, "Exiles, Exodus, and Promised Lands," *Tanner Lectures on Human Values* 27 (2007): 138.

10. For a useful primary source and contextualization of the Exodus typology in Puritan thought see Sacvan Bercovitch's discussion of Samuel Danforth's 1670 *Brief Recognition of New England's Errand into the Wilderness* in Bercovitch, *The American Jeremiad* (University of Wisconsin Press, 1978), 10–17.

11. Alfred A. Cave, "Canaanites in a Promised Land: The American Indian and the Providential Theory of Empire," *American Indian Quarterly* 12, no. 4 (Autumn 1988): 277.

12. The extent to which the New World was populated when Lehi's family arrived has been a subject of some debate in Mormon apologetics, with most commentators agreeing that there must have been other inhabitants, based on a wealth of archeological and DNA evidence accumulated since the publication of the Book of Mormon. But there is scant evidence in the text that the Lehites met indigenous inhabitants when they arrived at the start of the sixth century BCE. See Matthew Roper, "Nephi's Neighbors: Book of Mormon Peoples and Pre-Columbian Populations," *FARMS Review* 15, no. 2 (2003): 91–128; Brant A. Gardner, "The Other Stuff: Reading the Book of Mormon for Cultural Information," *FARMS Review* 13, no. 2 (2001): 29–37; and John L. Sorenson, "When Lehi's Party Arrived in the Land, Did They Find Others There?" *Journal of Book of Mormon Studies* 1, no. 1 (1992): 1–34.

13. The record of Chemish, the third of the five authors of the book of Omni, contains only a single verse explaining that his brother didn't write on the plates until the day he handed them over: "Now I, Chemish, write what few things I write, in the same book with my brother; for behold, I saw the last which he wrote, that he wrote it with his own hand; and he wrote it in the day that he delivered them unto me. And after this manner we keep the records, for it is according to the commandments of our fathers. And I make an end" (Omni 1:9).

14. George S. Tate, "The Typology of the Exodus Pattern in the Book of Mormon," in *Literature of Belief: Sacred Scripture and Religious Experience*, ed. Neal E. Lambert (Religious Studies Center, Brigham Young University, 1981), 249.

15. The scholarly literature concerning the Deuteronomists, and on the various forms of the documentary hypothesis that include "the Deuteronomist" (D) as one of the four principal sources of the Pentateuch, is immense. In addition to the book of Deuteronomy, Deuteronomistic sources are generally considered the principal authors of the "Deuteronomistic History," consisting of the books of Joshua, Judges,

1 Samuel, 2 Samuel, 1 Kings, and 2 Kings. An excellent, highly readable summary can be found in Stephen A. Geller's essay "The Religion of the Bible," in *The Jewish Study Bible*, ed. Adele Berlin, Mark Zvi Brettler, and Michel Fishbane, 2021–40 (Oxford University Press, 2004), esp. 2031–33.

16. This verse is unpacked in detail in Kimberly Matheson Berkey and Joseph M. Spencer, "'Great Cause to Mourn': The Complexity of the Book of Mormon's Presentation of Gender and Race," in *Americanist Approaches to the Book of Mormon*, ed. Elizabeth A. Fenton and Jared Hickman (Oxford University Press, 2019), 309–12.

17. Tate, "Typology of the Exodus Pattern," 257.

18. Tate, "Typology of the Exodus Pattern," 258–59.

19. Discussions of the Exodus typology in the Book of Mormon include Noel B. Reynolds, "The Political Dimension in Nephi's Small Plates," *BYU Studies Quarterly* 27, no. 4 (Fall 1987): 15–37; Terrance L. Szink, "Nephi and the Exodus," in *Rediscovering the Book of Mormon*, ed. John L. Sorenson and Melvin J. Thorne, 35–51 (Deseret Book and FARMS, 1991); Alan Goff, "Boats, Beginnings, and Repetitions," *Journal of Book of Mormon Studies* 1, no. 1 (1992): 67–84; S. Bruce J. Boehm, "Wanderers in the Promised Land: A Study of the Exodus Motif in the Book of Mormon and Holy Bible," *Journal of Book of Mormon Studies* 3, no. 1 (1994): 187–203; Mark J. Johnson, "The Exodus of Lehi Revisited," *Journal of Book of Mormon Studies* 3, no. 2 (1994) 123–26; Richard D. Rust, *Feasting on the Word: The Literary Testimony of the Book of Mormon* (Deseret Book, 1997), 207–10; Kent Brown, "The Exodus Pattern in the Book of Mormon," in *From Jerusalem to Zarahemla: Literary and Historical Studies of the Book of Mormon*, ed. Kent Brown, 75–98 (Religious Studies Center, Brigham Young University, 1998).

20. There has been significant discussion among LDS scholars who see the Book of Mormon as a historical document about the likelihood that the American continent was populated, a view that the Church of Jesus Christ of Latter-day Saints appeared to endorse in 2006 when it changed wording in the introduction to the official version of the Book of Mormon describing the Lamanites as "the principal ancestors of the American Indians" to read "among the ancestors of the American Indians." This is primarily a historical rather than a textual argument, though there is some internal textual evidence to support this view. No characters other than the Mulekites and the Jaredites are explicitly labeled by the text as anything other than descendants of the Lehite migration. See Brant A. Gardner, *Traditions of the Fathers: The Book of Mormon as History* (Kofford, 2015), 119–50; Roper, "Nephi's Neighbors"; Sorenson, "When Lehi's Party Arrived."

21. Mormon tradition labels this group "Mulekites," after the proposed original ancestor, Mulek—an analog to "Nephite" and "Lamanite." This term does not appear in the text, though, where they are simply called "the People of Zarahemla" in Omni and are subsequently grouped with the Nephites.

22. "The White Man's Burden" was originally published in the February 1899 issue of *McClure's*.

23. Jared Hickman, "The Book of Mormon as Amerindian Apocalypse," *American Literature* 86, no. 3 (September 2014): 448.

24. Peter Coviello, *Make Yourselves Gods: Mormons and the Unfinished Business of American Secularism* (University of Chicago Press, 2019), 146.

25. Edward Said, *Culture and Imperialism* (Knopf, 1994), 66–67.

26. Dan Belnap, "'And it came to pass . . .': The Sociopolitical Events in the Book of Mormon Leading to the Eighteenth Year of the Reign of the Judges," *Journal of Book of Mormon Studies* 23 (2014): 120.

27. Mohammad Khosravi Shakib, "The Position of Language in Development of Colonization," *Journal of Languages and Culture* 2, no. 7 (July 2011): 117–23.

28. Prominent LDS author Orson Scott Card has suggested that the native Zarahemlans may have invented a royal Israelite ancestry in an attempt to claim superior descent and, therefore, a right to rule over the Nephites and that, once established, "the story of Mulek served a very useful purpose" because it "allowed the people to merge, not with the hostility of conquerors over the conquered, though that in fact is what the relationship fundamentally was, but rather with the idea of brotherhood." Orson Scott Card, "The Book of Mormon—Artifact or Artifice?" in *A Storyteller in Zion* (Bookcraft, 1993), 31–32.

29. John L. Sorenson, "The "Mulekites," *BYU Studies Quarterly* 30, no. 3 (1990): 16–17.

30. Gardner, *Traditions of the Fathers*, 223.

31. Alma, Mosiah, and Helaman all have sons named after them. By convention, the LDS tradition refers to Alma's son as "Alma the Younger," though this is not a designation used by the text. When there is any possibility of confusing these names, I will employ the scholarly convention of using subscript numbers to indicate whether I am referring to the father or the son of the same name.

32. Most scholars believe that the book of Mosiah was the first book that Joseph Smith dictated after losing the 116 manuscript pages in the summer of 1828, making it the first book in the current Book of Mormon. The priority of Mosiah has been accepted by both Mormon and non-Mormon scholars as the most likely theory of compositional sequence. See Brent Metcalfe, "The Priority of Mosiah: A Prelude to Book of Mormon Exegesis," in *New Approaches to the Book of Mormon*, ed. Brent Metcalf, 395–444 (Signature, 1993); Terryl Givens, *By the Hand of Mormon: The American Scripture That Launched a New World Religion* (Oxford University Press, 2003), 36; Royal Skousen, *The Book of Mormon: The Earliest Text* (Yale University Press, 2009), xii; Grant Hardy, *Understanding the Book of Mormon: A Reader's Guide* (Oxford University Press 2010), 10; Paul C. Gutjahr, *The Book of Mormon: A Biography* (Princeton University Press, 2012); Gardner, *Traditions of the Fathers* 213.

33. Belnap, "'And it came to pass,'" 119.

34. The text is not clear with regard to how much say the people actually had in their government or what "the voice of the people" actually means. Chief judges seem to have been appointed for life or until they resigned, and, on at least some occasions, the chief judgeship passed from father to son. Chief judges also seem to choose their own successors. For example, when Alma decided to resign as chief judge and retain only the office of high priest, he "selected a wise man who was among the elders of the

church, and gave him power according to the voice of the people" (Alma 4:16), suggesting, perhaps, popular ratification of official appointments rather than democratic elections. The "wise man," Nephihah, ruled until he died and was succeeded by his son, much as a king would have been (Alma 50:39). Richard Bushman has written that "despite Mosiah's reforms, Nephite government persisted in monarchical practices, with life tenure for the chief judges, hereditary succession, and the combination of all functions in one official." See "The Book of Mormon and the American Revolution," *BYU Studies Quarterly* 17, no. 1 (1976): 18.

35. For an application of Alma 1 to nineteenth-century debates about universal salvation, see Dan Vogel, "Anti-Universalist Rhetoric in the Book of Mormon," in *New Approaches to the Book of Mormon*, ed. Brent Metcalf, 21–52 (Signature, 1993).

36. Kylie Turley highlights an additional layer of irony in this scene in that Alma "likely dressed and spoke like Nehor only a few years earlier." As Nehor no doubt knew, Alma, as a young man, was a religious dissenter and opponent of the church that he now headed. "Nehor's boldness," she suggests, "may be the brash assumption that Alma has not really changed or that a changed Alma can be bullied and humiliated by a reminder of his past." *Alma 1–29: A Brief Theological Introduction* (Maxwell Institute, 2020), 38.

37. David Gore, *The Voice of the People: Political Rhetoric in the Book of Mormon* (Maxwell Institute, 2019), 69.

38. Michael S. Carter, "A 'Traiterous Religion': Indulgences and the Anti-Catholic Imagination in Eighteenth-Century England," *Catholic Historical Review* 99, no. 1 (2013): 57. See also Mark Goldie, "Priestcraft and the Birth of Whiggism," in *Political Discourse in Early Modern Britain*, ed. Nicholas Phillipson and Quentin Skinner (Cambridge University Press, 1993), 209–31.

39. Royal Skousen and other scholars have asserted, based on the spellings of "Amlicite" and "Amalekite" in the original manuscript versions of the Book of Mormon, that the two terms refer to the same people. See Royal Skousen, "Alma 2:11–12," in *Analysis of Textual Variants of the Book of Mormon Part Three: Mosiah 17–Alma 20* (Foundation for Ancient Research and Mormon Studies, Brigham Young University, 2006), 1605–9.

40. Concerning this verse, Fatimah Salleh and Margaret Olsen Hemming note: "This disturbing description implies some kind of torture or shaming in his death. While the text is vague enough that readers are left without clarity regarding exactly what happened to this man, it is apparent that the Nephites enacted some pretty awful kind of violence. It also seems to have been done in anger, as a reaction to the tragedy of Gideon's death, rather than out of a sense of fairness." *The Book of Mormon for the Least of These* (By Common Consent Press, 2022), 2:131.

41. Grant Shreve, "Nephite Secularization; or, Picking and Choosing in The Book of Mormon," in *Americanist Approaches to the Book of Mormon*, ed. Elizabeth A. Fenton and Jared Hickman (Oxford University Press, 2019), 213.

42. I will argue in Chapter 6 that something similar possibly happens in Helaman 5:1–4, when Alma$_1$'s great-grandson, Nephi$_2$, "yielded up the judgment seat" to someone named Cezoram, but this is not stated directly in the narrative.

43. In the book of Alma, the people who are described as being in favor of a king rather than the reign of the judges almost favor restoring the Zarahemlan monarchy that ended when King Zarahemla ceded power to Mosiah. It is unlikely that this group would want to replace Alma with one of the sons of Mosiah, thus restoring the Nephite monarchy. The term "dissenter" or "Nephite dissenter" is used more than a dozen times in the Book of Mormon to describe people in Zarahemla who do not accept the Nephite church or otherwise oppose Nephite orthodoxy. In most cases, the "dissenters" end up allying with the Lamanites against the Nephites. See Alma 61:17, 62:6, 63:14; Helaman 1:15, 4, 11:4–25; and 3 Nephi 1:28.

44. Bill Ashcroft and Gareth Griffiths, *Key Concepts in Post-Colonial Studies* (Routledge, 2014), 25–26.

45. For example, one of the cities that the Amalickiahite-Lamanite army takes possession of during the war is the city of Mulek, named after the original ancestor of the people of Zarahemla and likely still populated by native Zarahemlans (Alma 51:26). When the Nephites begin to retake occupied cities, the Lamanites "[retreat] with all their army in the city of Mulek and [seek] protection in their fortifications" (Alma 52:2). And after Captain Moroni retakes Mulek, the narrative describes it as "one of the strongest holds of the Lamanites in the Land of Nephi" (Alma 53:6). This repeated emphasis on the importance of Mulek to the Lamanite army suggests that at least some its population, if not all of it, supported Amalickiah's rebellion and would therefore provide a safe place for allied armies to retreat.

46. Coriantumr was also the name of the last survivor of the Jaredite civilization, which hints at the possibility of a deeper relationship between Mulekites and Jaredites than the text presents.

47. Royal Skousen concludes that the Amalekites were not an otherwise unidentifiable group of religious dissidents but were in fact Amlici's own group, the Amlicites. This means that both major groups of Nephite dissenters in the book of Alma are orthographically related to the mysterious Amalekites in Alma 21–27. See Skousen, *Analysis of Textual Variants*, 1606.

Chapter 5. Divided Kingdoms

1. For a brief description of the historical development of his interpretation, see Joseph M. Spencer, "The Sticks of Judah and Joseph: Reflections on Defending the Kingdom," in *They Shall Grow Together: The Bible in the Book of Mormon*, ed. Charles Swift and Nicholas J. Frederick (Deseret Book and BYU Religious Studies Center, 2022), 304–9.

2. A Jewish rebuttal to the LDS interpretation of this passage from Ezekiel can be found at the Jews for Judaism website: https://jewsforjudaism.org/knowledge/articles/the-stick-of-judah-and-the-stick-of-joseph. A Catholic rebuttal can be found at the Catholic Answers site: https://www.catholic.com/qa/what-are-mormons-referring-to-when-they-talk-about-the-stick-of-joseph. And a rebuttal from the Evan-

gelical perspective can be found on the Mormonism Research Ministry's "God Loves Mormons" page at https://www.mrm.org/ezekiel-37.

3. Several Mormon scholars, most notably Keith Messervy, have argued in LDS publications that Ezekiel's "sticks" were actually wooden tablets of a sort known to exist in the ancient Near East. See Messervy's articles "Ezekiel's Sticks," *Ensign* (September 1977), 22–27; "Ezekiel's Sticks and the Gathering of Israel," *Ensign* (February 1987), 4–13. The anthropologist Brian Keck refutes this argument in "Ezekiel 37, Sticks, and Babylonian Writing Boards: A Critical Reappraisal," *Dialogue* 23, no. 1 (1990), 126–38.

4. See John B. Whitley, "The Literary Expansion of Ezekiel's 'Two Sticks' Sign Act (Ezekiel 37:15–28)," *Harvard Theological Review* 108, no. 2 (2015): 307–24; C. L. Crouch, "Dueling Dynasties: A Proposal Concerning Ezekiel's Sign-Act of the Two Sticks," *Journal for the Study of the Old Testament* 45, no. 1 (2020): 3–19.

5. Spencer, "Sticks of Judah and Joseph," 311.

6. Spencer, "Sticks of Judah and Joseph," 310. Spencer specifically rejects the idea that Doctrine & Covenants 27:5—in which God describes the Book of Mormon as "containing the fulness of my everlasting gospel, to whom I have committed the keys of the record of the stick of Ephraim"—equates the Book of Mormon with the stick of Ephraim. Rather, he argues, the "Stick of Ephraim" can be seen (as most Bible Scholars see it) as the descendants of the Tribes of Joseph, with the Book of Mormon as their record. "This revelation thus in no way asks the Saints—whether early in the Church's history or today—to understand Ezekiel's 'stick of Ephraim' as being a book or a record. It asks them and us to understand Ezekiel's 'stick of Ephraim' as having a book or a record that belongs most appropriately to them" (310).

7. On apocalypticism in the Book of Mormon see Christopher Blythe, *Terrible Revolution: Latter-day Saints and the American Apocalypse* (Oxford University Press, 2020), 16–24.

8. The Jews were expelled by Edward I in 1290. In 1656 Cromwell, in response to a petition from Menasseh ben Israel, convened a council to discuss the matter of permitting Jewish immigration to England. The council did not authorize the resolution, which Cromwell appeared to favor, but the Lord Protector did issue a statement authorizing the Jews who were already in England to meet in their own houses and practice their religion "without fear of molestation." This proclamation is generally seen as the beginning of the readmission of Jews to England. See Kathy Lavezzo, *The Accommodated Jew: English Antisemitism from Bede to Milton* (Cornell University Press, 2016), 348–54; David Katz, *Philo-Semitism and the Readmission of the Jew to England, 1603–1655* (Clarendon, 1982), 20–29.

9. See Sacvan Bercovitch, *The American Jeremiad* (University of Wisconsin Press, 1978), 73–78; Michael Hoberman, *New Israel/New England: Jews and Puritans in Early America* (University of Massachusetts Press, 2011), 13–17.

10. The text of the Book of Mormon does not specifically identify the American Indians as the descendants of the Lamanites. It does, though, insist that the Lamanites

will have descendants in the last days, and its original title page declares that the book is "written to the Lamanites, which are a remnant of the House of Israel: and also to Jew and Gentile." From its first publication, paratextual elements of the Book of Mormon—introductions, official summaries, illustrations, and other materials that have accompanied its publication—have equated American Indians and Lamanites, and several canonized passages in the Doctrine & Covenants make the connection clear (D&C 28:8–9, 32:1–2). From 1891 to 2006 the introduction printed in the Book of Mormon stated that "the Lamanites are the principal ancestors of the American Indians." In 2006 this was changed to "are among the ancestors of the American Indians."

11. John W. Welch, "Lehi's Last Will and Testament: A Legal Approach," in *The Book of Mormon: Second Nephi; The Doctrinal Structure*, ed. Monte S. Nyman and Charles D. Tate Jr. (Religious Studies Center, Brigham Young University, 1989), 69.

12. Welch, "Lehi's Last Will," 72–73.

13. Nephi acknowledges at least two sisters in 2 Nephi 5:6: "Wherefore, it came to pass that I, Nephi, did take my family, and also Zoram and his family, and Sam, mine elder brother and his family, and Jacob and Joseph, my younger brethren, and also my sisters, and all those who would go with me." Simple deduction suggests that these daughters married the two sons of Ishmael mentioned in 1 Ne 7:6, because there were no other possible marriage partners in the Lehite party. See Sidney B. Sperry, "Did Father Lehi Have Daughters Who Married the Sons of Ishmael?" *Journal of Book of Mormon Studies* 4, no. 1 (1995), 235–38. (Reprint of an article previously published in the *Improvement Era*, September 1953, 642, 694.)

14. Along with Welch's article, see John L. Sorenson, *An Ancient American Setting for the Book of Mormon* (Deseret Book, 1996), 313; and John L. Sorenson, John A. Tvedtnes, and John W. Welch, "Seven Tribes: An Aspect of Lehi's Legacy," in *Reexploring the Book of Mormon: A Decade of New Research*, ed. John W. Welch (FARMS, 1992), 93.

15. Welch, "Lehi's Last Will," 69.

16. In the Old Testament, this is the period of narrative silence, during which Israel was ruled by scattered tribal judges and military culture heroes. It corresponds to the Late Bronze Age Collapse, during which most of the cultures in the Mediterranean region suffered severe political and economic setbacks that led to a sharp decrease in literacy and recordkeeping. For a discussion of how the Late Bronze Age Collapse impacted the people of the southern Levant, see Eric H. Cline, *1177 B.C.: The Year Civilization Collapsed* (Princeton University Press, 2014), 89–96. In the Book of Mormon, it corresponds to the time between the end of Nephi's narrative on the Small Plates of Nephi and Mormon's narrative on the Large Plates of Nephi. The narrative gap may be in some measure attributable to the loss of the first 116 manuscript pages that Joseph Smith produced and then lent to Martin Harris. Scholarly consensus holds that Smith dictated the Words of Mormon and the Book of Mosiah after Harris lost the 116 pages, which he reported to have been part of the Large Plates of Nephi and which may have contained more details from the period between Nephi and Mosiah.

17. In her exceptional account of the first three of these short books, Sharon Harris concludes that the primary function of the plates during this time period, when the custodians present very little in the way of history or doctrine, was to preserve the genealogical record during a time when it would otherwise have been lost. See Sharon Harris, *Enos, Jarom, Omni: A Brief Theological Introduction* (Maxwell Institute, 2020), 88–97.

18. The story of the division of Israel is narrated in 1 Kings 12 and in 2 Chronicles 10, with both texts using almost exactly the same language.

19. Mark Leuchter, *The Levites and the Boundaries of Israelite Identity* (Oxford University Press, 2017), 160.

20. See Karel Van der Toorn, *Scribal Culture and the Making of the Hebrew Bible* (Harvard University Press, 2007), 154–60; Jeffrey C. Geoghegan, "'Until This Day' and the Preexilic Redaction of the Deuteronomistic History," *Journal of Biblical Literature* 122, no. 2 (2003): 226; Gerhard von Rad, *Studies in Deuteronomy* (SCM Press, 1953), 60–69.

21. See Israel Finkelstein and Neil A. Silberman, "Temple and Dynasty: Hezekiah, the Remaking of Judah and the Rise of the Pan-Israelite Ideology," *Journal for the Study of the Old Testament* 30, no. 3 (Mar. 2006): 266.

22. Finkelstein and Silberman, "Temple and Dynasty," 279.

23. Mary Douglas, *Jacob's Tears: The Priestly Work of Reconciliation* (Oxford University Press, 2006), 15.

24. Zvi Ben-Dor Benite, *The Ten Lost Tribes: A World History* (Oxford University Press, 2013), 17.

25. Dan Cohn-Sherbok, *The Jewish Messiah* (T&T Clark, 1997), 1–20.

26. Esdras (Ezra) claims that the ten lost tribes decided to "leave the multitude of peoples and proceed to a more remote region where no human species ever lived and there perhaps observe their ordinances which they did not observe in their land." The text even gives the name of the new land, "Arazareth," and affirms that getting there "required a long track of a year and a half" (2 Esdras 13:40–46). Translation, with extensive commentary, by Jacob M. Myers in the *Anchor Bible*, vol. 42, *I and II Esdras* (Doubleday, 1974), 306. Though 2 Esdras is considered apocryphal by most Christian denominations—only the Ethiopian Orthodox Tewahedo Church accepts it as canonical scripture—it is printed in the Apocrypha section of many bibles, including the original King James Version of 1611. This passage has been quoted frequently in Christian history and has become something of a starting place for "lost tribe" hunters.

27. The story of a younger son who outshines or outmaneuvers an older brother is one of the most recognizable type-scenes in Genesis and occurs no fewer than seven times: Cain and Abel (Gen 4:2–15), Shem, Ham, and Japheth (Gen 9–10), Ishmael and Isaac (Gen 21), Jacob and Esau (Gen 25, 27), Joseph and his brothers (Gen 37, 39–47; Deut 33:13; 1 Chr 5:2), Er and Pharez (Gen 30), and Ephraim and Manasseh (Gen 48:13–19). Robert Alter, explaining these type-scenes, concludes that "the entire Book of Genesis is about the reversal of the iron law of primogeniture, about the election through some devious twist of destiny of a younger son to carry on the line." *The*

Art of Biblical Narrative (Basic Books, 1981), 6. The account of Nephi in the Book of Mormon is very much in line with these other type-scenes.

28. Grant Hardy, *Understanding the Book of Mormon: A Reader's Guide* (Oxford University Press, 2010), 42.

29. For summaries of early church teachings about Joseph and Christ, see A. W. Argyle, "Joseph the Patriarch in Patristic Teaching," *Expository Times* 67, no. 7 (1956): 199–201; Kristian S. Heal, "Joseph as a Type of Christ in Syriac Literature," *Brigham Young University Studies* 41, no. 1 (2002): 29–49.

30. Meir Sternberg, *The Poetics of Biblical Narrative* (Indiana University Press, 1987), 84–85.

31. The title page of the original 1830 edition reads, "And now if there be fault, it be the mistake of men." This was changed in the 1837 edition to, "And now if there are faults, they are the mistakes of men." The sentiment is repeated at the very end of the book of Mormon, the primary redactor: "And if there be faults they be the faults of a man" (Morm 8:17).

32. For a strong feminist reading of this passage, see Kimberly M. Berkey and Joseph Spencer, "'Great Cause to Mourn': The Complexity of the Book of Mormon's Presentation of Gender and Race," in *The Book of Mormon: Americanist Approaches*, ed. Jared Hickman and Elizabeth Fenton, 298–320 (Oxford University Press, 2019), esp. 305–8.

33. Deidre Nicole Green, *Jacob: A Brief Theological Introduction* (Maxwell Institute and Brigham Young University, 2020), 47.

34. See Helaman 7:24, 13:1; 3 Nephi 6:14; Alma 27:27. See also Richard O. Cowan, "The Lamanites—A More Accurate Image," in *The Book of Mormon: Helaman Through 3 Nephi 8, According to Thy Word*, ed. Monte S. Nyman and Charles D. Tate Jr. (Religious Studies Center, Brigham Young University, 1992), 251–64.

35. In fairness to Zeniff, he does begin his tale with a description of a time in his early career in which he "was sent as a spy among the Lamanites that I might spy out their forces, that our army might come upon them and destroy them—but when I saw that which was good among them I was desirous that they should not be destroyed." At considerable danger to his own life, he resists the order to take part in a massacre (Mosiah 9:1–2). By including this part of the story Mormon shows that, as prejudiced as Zeniff was against the Lamanites, he was downright progressive compared to other Nephites.

36. Max P. Mueller, *Race and the Making of the Mormon People* (University of North Carolina Press, 2018), 50.

37. Mueller, *Race and the Making of the Mormon People*, 51.

38. Jared Hickman, "The Book of Mormon as Amerindian Apocalypse," *American Literature* 86, no. 3 (2014): 452.

39. Armand L. Mauss, *All Abraham's Children: Changing Mormon Conceptions of Race and Lineage* (University of Illinois Press, 2003), 116.

40. Hugh Nibley, "Teachings of the Book of Mormon, Semester 2: Transcripts of Lectures Presented to an Honors Book of Mormon Class at Brigham Young University, 1988–1990" (Maxwell Institute, 2004), 71, 321.

41. Stephen D. Ricks, "Anti- Nephi-Lehi," in *Book of Mormon Reference Companion*, ed. Dennis L. Largey (Deseret Book, 2003), 67, quoted in the "Book of Mormon Student Manual: Religion 121–122" (Church of Jesus Christ of Latter-day Saints, 2009), 207.

42. Royal Skousen, *Analysis of Textual Variants of the Book of Mormon Part Four: Alma 21–55* (Maxwell Institute, 2009), 2037.

43. For a complete breakdown of the different verses and versions, see my *Buried Treasures*, 175–79, also available on the By Common Consent blog at https://bycommon consent.com/2016/07/17/what-were-the-anti-nephi-lehies-against-and-why-does -it-matter-today-bom2016/.

44. A Google n-gram search accessed on June 19, 2021, turned up seven books published between 1825 and 1830 containing the word "antidiluvian" and five more using "anti-diluvian." By contrast, ninety-seven books contained the word spelled "antediluvian." To the extent that this is a representative selection, it would suggest that the variant spelling was used, very roughly, 10 percent of the time.

45. In 3 Ne 3:28, Mormon reports that "the Nephites began to reckon their time from this period when the sign was given, or from the coming of Christ," which appears to hold true for the rest of the Book of Mormon, making the dates align precisely with the Western use of Christ's presumed birth year as the dividing point between BC and AD, or the modern rendering of time as either before the Christian era (BCE) or Christian era (CE).

46. Mueller, *Race and the Making of the Mormon People*, 37.

47. Mauss, *All Abraham's Children*, 49.

Chapter 6. Prophets and Prophecy

1. The King James version of the Bible refers to Abraham and Moses as prophets in, respectively, Genesis 20:7 and Deuteronomy 34:10. Samuel, Nathan, and Ahijah are frequently referred to as prophets in their role as counselors to Saul, David, and Solomon (see 1 Sam 3:20, 2 Sam 7:2, and 1 Kgs 11:20). Elijah and Elisha are the two primary prophets that oppose the kings of Israel during the reigns of Ahab and Ahaziah (1 Kgs 17–2 Kgs 13).

2. The Talmud recognizes seven biblical women as prophetesses: Sarah, Miriam, Deborah, Hannah, Abigail, Huldah, and Esther. Five women are labeled prophetesses in the *Tanakh*: Deborah (Judg 4:4), Miriam (Exod 15:20), Huldah (2 Kgs 22:14), Noadiah (Neh 6:14), and the unnamed prophetess in Isaiah 8:3. See H. G. M. Williamson, "Prophetesses in the Hebrew Bible," in *Prophecy and the Prophets in Ancient Israel: Proceedings of the Oxford Old Testament Seminar*, ed. John Day, 65–76 (T&T Clark, 2010).

3. Joseph Blenkinsopp, *Sage, Priest, Prophet: Religious and Intellectual Leadership in Ancient Israel* (Westminster John Knox Press, 1995), 115.

4. The *Nevi'im* is traditionally divided into the "former prophets" and the "latter prophets." The books of the former prophets include Joshua, Judges, 1 and 2 Samuel, and 1 and 2 Kings, and the prophets include Samuel, Nathan, Ahijah, Elijah, and

Elisha. The latter prophets—Isaiah, Ezekiel, Jeremiah, and "the Twelve"—are also called the "literary prophets" because their prophetic writings are part of the Hebrew Bible, whereas the former prophets are known only through the historical chronicles.

5. Blenkinsopp, *Sage, Priest, Prophet*, 116.

6. Max Weber, *The Sociology of Religion*, trans. Ephraim Fischoff (Beacon, 1964), 46.

7. Blenkinsopp, *Sage, Priest, Prophet*, 116.

8. Max Weber and Talcott Parsons, *The Theory of Social and Economic Organization* (Free Press, 1982), 341.

9. Weber and Parsons, *The Theory of Social and Economic Organization*, 329–41.

10. Weber and Parsons, *The Theory of Social and Economic Organization*, 358–59.

11. Weber and Parsons, *The Theory of Social and Economic Organization*, 369.

12. The other charismatic leader whom Weber mentions is Kurt Eisner, the German revolutionary who founded the short-lived People's State of Bavaria in 1918. Weber does qualify his labeling of Joseph Smith somewhat, noting that he "cannot be classified this way with absolute certainty since there is a possibility that he was a very sophisticated type of deliberative swindler" (*Sociology of Religion*, 359).

13. See C. Jetter, "Continuing Revelation and Institutionalization: Joseph Smith, Ralph Waldo Emerson and Charismatic Leadership in Antebellum America," *Studies in Church History* 57 (2021): 233–53; Eric W. Schoon and A. Joseph West, "From Prophecy to Practice: Mutual Selection Cycles in the Routinization of Charismatic Authority," *Journal for the Scientific Study of Religion* 56, no. 4 (December 2017): 781–97; Omri Elisha, "Sustaining Charisma: Mormon Sectarian Culture and the Struggle for Plural Marriage, 1852–1890," *Nova Religio* 6, no. 1 (2002): 45–63; and Douglas Davies, "Jural and Mystical Authority in Religions: Exploring a Typology," *Diskus* 3, no. 2 (1995): 1–12.

14. Thomas F. O'Dea, *The Mormons* (University of Chicago Press, 1957), 156.

15. Richard Bushman, in an article applying Weber's theory of charisma to the LDS Church, argues that Joseph Smith originally created the church with both charismatic and bureaucratic authority and that, therefore, there was no need for a routinization of charisma by Smith's successors because the routinization was already built into the charismatic structure. See Richard Lyman Bushman, "Joseph Smith and Power," in *A Firm Foundation: Church Organization and Administration*, ed. David J. Whittaker and Arnold K. Garr, 1–13 (Religious Studies Center, Brigham Young University; Deseret Book, 2011).

16. Bengt Holmberg, *Paul and Power: The Structure of Authority in the Primitive Church as Reflected in the Pauline Epistles* (Wipf and Stock, 2004), 162.

17. Holmberg, *Paul and Power*, 173–74.

18. Holmberg, *Paul and Power*, 174.

19. Most scholars believe that the book of Mosiah was the first book that Joseph Smith dictated after losing 116 manuscript pages in the summer of 1828, making it the first book in the current Book of Mormon. The priority of Mosiah has been accepted by Mormon and non-Mormon scholars as the most likely theory of compositional sequence. See Brent Metcalfe, "The Priority of Mosiah: A Prelude to Book of Mormon

Exegesis," in *New Approaches to the Book of Mormon*, ed. Brent Metcalfe, 395–444 (Signature, 1993); Terryl L. Givens, *By the Hand of Mormon: The American Scripture That Launched a New World Religion* (Oxford University Press, 2003), 36; Royal Skousen, *The Book of Mormon: The Earliest Text* (Yale University Press, 2009), xii; Grant Hardy, *Understanding the Book of Mormon: A Reader's Guide* (Oxford University Press, 2010), 10; Paul C. Gutjahr, *The Book of Mormon: A Biography* (Princeton University Press, 2012); and Brant A. Gardner, *Traditions of the Fathers: The Book of Mormon as History* (Kofford, 2015), 213.

20. Avram R. Shannon identifies only five figures in this portion of the Book of Mormon as "prophets": Abinadi, Alma the Younger, Ammon, Nephi₂, and Samuel the Lamanite. A sixth person, the second King Mosiah, is identified (though not by name) as a "seer" in a passage that states that "a seer is a revelator and a prophet also" (Mosiah 8:13–16). "Prophets and Prophecy in the Book of Mormon," in *Samuel the Lamanite: That Ye Might Believe*, ed. Charles Swift, 3–24 (Religious Studies Center, Brigham Young University, 2021). Shannon also identifies the Jaredite Ether as a named prophet in Mormon's narrative, albeit one who lived centuries before the events that Mormon describes.

21. The exception to the statement, "Abinadi is the closest thing in the Book of Mormon to an Old Testament Prophet," of course, is Lehi, the original ancestor of the Nephites and the Lamanites, who *was* an Old Testament prophet. Lehi prophesied in Jerusalem at the same time as Jeremiah and Ezekiel; however, he functions differently in the Book of Mormon.

22. Roger Terry makes the intriguing suggestion that Abinadi is the son of Abinadom and the brother of Amaleki, one of the authors of the book of Omni, who first introduced the expedition to the land of Nephi and wrote, "And I, Amaleki, had a brother, who also went with them; and I have not since known concerning them" (Omni 1:30). See Roger Terry, "Scripture Notes: Unearthing Abinadi's Genealogy," *Sunstone* (June 11, 2013) https://www.sunstonemagazine.com/scripture-notes -unearthing-abinadis-genealogy/.

23. Joseph M. Spencer, *An Other Testament: On Typology* (Maxwell Institute, 2016), 142.

24. Spencer, *An Other Testament*, 143.

25. Spencer, *An Other Testament*, 144.

26. The first verse of Isaiah 53, the line "Who hath believed our report?" is quoted in John 12:38 and Romans 10:16; Isaiah 53:4—"He Himself took our infirmities and bore our sicknesses"—is quoted in Matthew 8:17. And Isaiah 53:7 is quoted, with slight differences, in Acts 8:32: "He is brought as a lamb to the slaughter, and as a sheep before her shearers is dumb, so he openeth not his mouth." The verse in Acts (in the KJV) switches "lamb" and "sheep" to read, "He was led as a sheep to the slaughter; and like a lamb dumb before his shearer, so opened he not his mouth."

27. Frank F. Judd Jr. has speculated that the charge could have also been the capital crime of false prophecy (Deut 18:20). See "Conflicting Interpretations of Isaiah in Abinadi's Trial" in *Abinadi: He Came Among Them in Disguise*, ed. Shon D. Hopkin (Religious Studies Center, Brigham Young University, 2018), 85.

28. The British anthropologist Robin Dunbar famously set at 150 the number of people who can form a group whose members all know and interact with each other. This has come to be known as "Dunbar's Number." Dunbar himself co-authored research applying this number to religious congregations. See R. Bretherton and R. Dunbar, "Dunbar's Number Goes to Church: The Social Brain Hypothesis as a Third Strand in the Study of Church Growth," *Archive for the Psychology of Religion* 42, no. 1 (2020): 63–76.

29. Grant Shreve, "Nephite Secularization," in *Americanist Approaches to the Book of Mormon*, ed. Elizabeth A. Fenton and Jared Hickman (Oxford University Press, 2019), 214–15.

30. For a careful analysis of how these events shaped Alma's subsequent career see Kylie Turley, "Alma's Hell: Repentance, Consequence, and the Lake of Fire and Brimstone," *Journal of Book of Mormon Studies* 28 (2019): 1–45.

31. I am indebted to my friend William Davis for recognizing the similarities between Abinadi and Stephen and for pointing out relevant details that support the comparison.

32. Alma 46:6 refers to Helaman and his brethren as "high priests over the church" but does not single out Helaman as *the* high priest of the church, as his father and grandfather were. During the war with Amalickiah, he commanded the "2000 stripling warriors," or the children of Lamanite converts who joined on the side of the Nephites and fought without a single fatality (see Alma 56).

33. In LDS usage, the "sealing power" stems from Christ's words to Peter in Matthew 16:19: "And I will give thee the keys of the kingdom of heaven: and whatsoever thou shalt bind on earth shall be bound in heaven: and whatsoever thou shalt loose on earth shall be loosed in heaven." It derives its name from the fact that its most common use is to marry people in the temple "for time and all eternity" (See D&C 132:7–19), but the actual power is much more expansive, as Nephi demonstrates when he uses it to cause, and later to end, a famine. See Kimberly Matheson Berkey, *Helaman: A Brief Theological Introduction* (Maxwell Institute, 2020), 63–67, for a description of the sealing power given to Nephi compared to other LDS uses of the term.

34. For a treatment of Nephi and Samuel as narrative foils to each other, see Berkey, *Helaman*, 94–96.

35. Berkey, *Helaman*, 95.

36. Laura Thiemann Scales, "'The writing of the fruit of thy loins': Reading, Writing, and Prophecy in the Book of Mormon," in *Americanist Approaches to the Book of Mormon*, ed. Elizabeth A. Fenton and Jared Hickman (Oxford University Press, 2019), 185.

Chapter 7. "We Talk of Christ, We Rejoice in Christ"

1. Among the most intriguing historical arguments about the Book of Mormon's foreknowledge of Christ comes from Alana Smith, who invokes Walter Benjamin's historical materialist view of "Messianic Time" to suggest that "the Nephites awaiting the coming of Jesus model messianic time for millenarian, nineteenth-century read-

ers, who, especially if socially or economically marginalized at the time of America's increasing industrialization, may be struggling to adapt to capitalism's empty, homogeneous time." Alana Smith, "Messianic Time in the Book of Mormon," *Journal of Book of Mormon Studies* 27 (2018): 203.

2. For the argument that the Book of Mormon contains only information about Christ that is available in the New Testament, see Melodie Moench Charles, "Book of Mormon Christology" in *New Approaches to the Book of Mormon: Explorations in Critical Methodology*, ed. Brent Lee Metcalfe (Signature, 1993), 89–90.

3. For a comparison of the Restoration movements of Joseph Smith and Alexander Campbell, see RoseAnn Benson's "Campbellites and Mormonites: Competing Restoration Movements," in *Interpreter* 31 (2019): 233–44.

4. Alexander Campbell, *Delusions: An Analysis of the Book of Mormon; with an Examination of Its Internal and External Evidences, and a Refutation of Its Pretences to Divine Authority* (1832), 13, 7.

5. Campbell, *Delusions*, 15. The page numbers refer to the original edition of the Book of Mormon (1830).

6. Frederik S. Kleiner, *Experiment upon the Word* (By Common Consent Press, 2022), 39–40.

7. Modern editions of the Book of Mormon are published with an editorial apparatus that includes headnotes for each chapter that give some context and periodic footnotes giving approximate dates for major events in the text. The 1830 edition that Campbell read had no such tools.

8. Robert Owen and Alexander Campbell, *Debate on the Evidences of Christianity: Containing an Examination of the Social System, and of All the Systems of Scepticism of Ancient and Modern Times, Held in the City of Cincinnati, for Eight Days Successively, Between Robert Owen . . . and Alexander Campbell; with an Appendix by the Parties; Complete in One Volume* (Groombridge, 1839), 202–3.

9. Samuel M. Brown, *Joseph Smith's Translation: The Words and Worlds of Early Mormonism* (Oxford University Press, 2020), 130.

10. See Revelation 13:1–6; Daniel 2:31–35.

11. Sigmund Mowinckel, *He That Cometh* (Blackwell, 1954), 4.

12. Joseph A. Fitzmyer, *The One Who Is to Come* (Eerdmans, 2007), 11; Dan Cohn-Sherbok, *The Jewish Messiah* (T&T Clark, 1997), 16–18.

13. Fitzmyer, *One Who Is to Come*, 137.

14. For a survey of Christian responses to Peter's use of Psalm 16, see Gregory V. Trull, "Views on Peter's Use of Psalm 16:8–11 in Acts 2:25–32," *Bibliotheca Sacra* 161, no. 642 (April 2004): 194–214. Cambridge University professor Monique Cuany has recently argued that the traditional interpretation of the speech—that Peter uses this psalm as evidence that the Messiah would be resurrected—cannot be correct. She argues that Peter's only point in doing so was to reference "the widespread belief that God protects the life of the faithful and that he will eventually rise the righteous." Monique Cuany, "The Divine Necessity of the Resurrection: A Re-assessment of the Use of Psalm 16 in Acts 2," *New Testament Studies* 66 (2002): 403.

15. Jesus Christ quotes Psalm 110:1 in reference to himself in Matthew 22:43–44,

Mark 12:36, Mark 14:62, and Luke 20:41–44 and alludes to it in Matthew 26:64, Mark 14:62, and Luke 22:69. It is also quoted or alluded to in 1 Corinthians 15:25, Ephesians 1:20, Colossians 3:1, and Hebrews 8:1.

16. See Fitzmyer, *One Who Is to Come*, 44–45; S. E. Gillingham, "The Messiah in the Psalms," in *King and Messiah in Israel and the Ancient Near East: Proceedings of the Oxford Old Testament Seminar*, ed. John Day, 209–37 (Bloomsbury, 2013).

17. See Barry C. Davis, "Is Psalm 110 a Messianic Psalm?" *Bibliotheca Sacra* 157 (April–June 2000): 160–73.

18. See David Klinghoffer, *Why the Jews Rejected Jesus: The Turning Point in Western History* (Harmony, 2013), 101–3.

19. Rosemary R. Ruether, *Faith and Fratricide: The Theological Roots of Anti-Semitism* (Alexander Street, 2017), 161.

20. Eusebius of Caesarea, *The Proof of the Gospel: Being the Demonstratio Evanelica*, trans. W. J. Ferrar (Macmillan, 1920), 1:63–70.

21. The Book of Mormon blames the Jews for misinterpreting their scriptures in terms even harsher than those in the Bible. Consider the words of Nephi's brother, Jacob: "But behold, the Jews were a stiffnecked people; and they despised the words of plainness, and killed the prophets, and sought for things that they could not understand. Wherefore, because of their blindness, which blindness came by looking beyond the mark, they must needs fall; for God hath taken away his plainness from them, and delivered unto them many things which they cannot understand, because they desired it" (Jacob 4:14). The Book of Mormon differs from the Bible by attributing greater foreknowledge to the Jews of Christ's time.

22. Modern translations of the Book of Mormon use "Zenock," rather than "Zenoch," in this and other passages.

23. For a comparison of Jacob 5 and Romans 11:13–24, see James E. Faulconer, "The Olive Tree and the Work of God: Jacob 5 and Romans 11," in *The Allegory of the Olive Tree*, ed. Stephen D. Ricks and John Welch, 347–72 (Deseret Book, 1994).

24. Brown, *Joseph Smith's Translation*, 129.

25. Modern editions of the Book of Mormon substitute "the fullness of the gospel of the Lord" for "the fullness of the Gospel of the Lamb."

26. Modern editions of the Book of Mormon use "a great and abominable church" rather than "that great and abominable church," shifting from the indefinite article to a demonstrative pronoun and diminishing the anti-Catholic bias that was often perceived in the original phrasing.

27. Nicholas A. Frederick and Joseph M. Spencer suggest that the great and abominable church in Nephi's vision is abominable primarily because it removed the plain and precious parts of the Bible. "Remnant or Replacement? Outlining a Possible Apostasy Narrative," *BYU Studies Quarterly* 60, no. 1 (2021): 112.

28. See Lori Driggs, "Nephi's Vision and the Loss and Restoration of Plain and Precious Truths," in *The Things Which My Father Saw: Approaches to Lehi's Dream and Nephi's Vision*, ed. Daniel L. Belnap, Gaye Strathearn, and Stanley A. Johnson, 70–91 (Religious Studies Center, Brigham Young University; Deseret Book, 2011).

29. The set phrase "plain and precious" occurs nine times in the Book of Mormon, eight times in 1 Nephi 13: "plain and precious things" occurs in 1 Nephi 13:28, 13:29 (twice), and 13:40; "plain and precious parts" occurs in 1 Nephi 13:34 and 1 Nephi 19:3; 1 Nephi 13:34 reads, "I will bring forth unto them, in mine own power, much of my gospel, which shall be plain and precious"; 1 Nephi 13:35 reads, "they shall write many things which I shall minister unto them, which shall be plain and precious."

30. Book of Mormon scholar Rebecca A. Roesler has made the intriguing argument that the Small Plates of Nephi—which contain the only record of Nephi that we have in the Book of Mormon (the record on the Large Plates having produced the 116 manuscript pages that were lost and not retranslated by Joseph Smith)—did not become part of the Nephite record used by the characters in the middle period of the Book of Mormon. To support this argument, Roesler cites multiple revelations about Christ that are given and received in this middle period that replicate information on the Small Plates of Nephi without acknowledging their existence, as if the information that they contain was not available. If this is true (and the argument is compelling), then it becomes a further example of the way clarity can be lost in a scriptural canon via centuries of transmission. See Rebecca A. Roesler, "Plain and Precious Things Lost: The Small Plates of Nephi," *Dialogue* 52, no. 2 (Summer 2019): 85–106.

31. The full chapters from Isaiah in the record of Nephi consist of four blocks of text: Isaiah 48–49 in 1 Nephi 20–21; Isaiah 50–51 in 2 Nephi 7–8; Isaiah 2–14 in 2 Nephi 12–24; and Isaiah 29 in 2 Nephi 27. Three more full chapters are reprinted in other parts of the Book of Mormon: Isaiah 52 in Mosiah 14; Isaiah 53 in 3 Nephi 20; and Isaiah 54 in 3 Nephi 22. Individual verses and passages from Isaiah are quoted throughout the text.

32. In *The Isaiah Variants in the Book of Mormon* (Foundation for Ancient Research and Mormon Studies, 1981), John A. Tvedtnes examines all of the Isaiah passages in the Book of Mormon and concludes that "over 40% of the verses are identical with KJV. . . . [O]f the 478 times that Isaiah verses are cited in BM, 201 read as in KJV, while 207 are variants, 58 are paraphrases, and another 11 must be listed as variants and/or paraphrases" (6). Of the 394 Isaiah passages in 1 and 2 Nephi, 162 (41.12 percent) are verbatim quotes from the KJV and 232 (58.88 percent are either variants or paraphrases (6–19). Less than two dozen of the changes that Tvedtnes surveys affect the meaning of the text in any material way (111–14).

33. A version of this story is archived on the urban legend site Mormon Monsters at http://mormonmonsters.blogspot.com/2009/09/scriptures-saved-mormon-soldier-from.html.

34. For reflections on the difficulty of Isaiah see Joseph Spencer, *The Vision of All: Twenty-five Lectures on Isaiah in Nephi's Record* (Kofford, 2016), 1–11.

35. Boyd K. Packer, "The Things of My Soul," in *Conference Reports of The Church of Jesus Christ of Latter-day Saints* (April 1986), 59.

36. The full text of Isaiah 2–12 is included in 2 Nephi 12–24. The text in these chapters is similar to but not identical to that found in the KJV. However, the text

itself attributes the differences to Nephi's having a different (and more correct) version of Isaiah's original writings.

37. Grant Hardy, *Understanding the Book of Mormon: A Reader's Guide* (Oxford University Press, 2010), 61.

38. Spencer, *Vision of All*, 230.

39. Bradley Kramer, *Gathered in One: How the Book of Mormon Counters Anti-Semitism in the New Testament* (Kofford, 2019), 43–44.

40. Quoted in John F. A. Sawyer, *The Fifth Gospel: Isaiah in the History of Christianity* (Cambridge University Press, 1996), 1.

41. Scholars agree that the Hebrew word *almah* (הָעַלְמָה), which the KJV translates as "virgin," would be better rendered "young woman" or, perhaps, "single young woman." It conveys a sense of sexual maturity but not of sexual abstinence. See Brevard S. Childs, *Isaiah* (Westminster John Knox Press, 2001), 65–66. The Hebrew Bible uses a different word, *bethulah* (הַבְּתוּלָה) to denote virginity, as in "And Amnon was so vexed, that he fell sick for his sister Tamar; for she was a virgin" (2 Sam 13:2). The sexual (or, rather, not-sexual) connotation of the term traces back to Matthew, who quotes the passage from Isaiah in Matthew 1:23, using the term *parthenos* (παρθένος), which does connote virginity in the modern sense of sexual abstinence.

42. Side-by-side comparisons of the Book of Mormon and KJV chapters from Isaiah can be found online on the blog Isaiah in The Book of Mormon (http://isaiahbom .blogspot.com/p/full-list-of-c.html) and in print in John A. Tvedtnes, "The Isaiah Variants in the Book of Mormon" (Foundation for Ancient Research and Mormon Studies, 1981). Shorter commentary can be found in John A. Tvedtnes, "Isaiah Variants in the Book of Mormon," in *Isaiah and the Prophets: Inspired Voices from the Old Testament*, ed. Monte S. Nyman and Charles D. Tate Jr., 165–78 (Religious Studies Center, Brigham Young University, 1984); Royal Skousen, "Textual Variants in the Isaiah Quotations in the Book of Mormon," in *Isaiah in the Book of Mormon*, ed. Donald W. Parry and John W. Welch, 369–90 (Foundation for Ancient Research and Mormon Studies, 1998); and David P. Wright, "Isaiah in the Book of Mormon: Or Joseph Smith in Isaiah," in *American Apocrypha: Essays on the Book of Mormon*, 157–234 (Signature, 2002).

43. It is clear from 3 Ne 9:13 that the more wicked part of the population was killed during the great upheaval while the more righteous part survived: "O all ye that are spared because ye were more righteous than they, will ye not now return unto me, and repent of your sins, and be converted, that I may heal you?"

44. For an overview of Jewish expectations of the Messiah in the generations before Christ, see Cohen-Sherbok, *Jewish Messiah*, 43–60; Klinghoffer, *Why the Jews Rejected Jesus*, 33–38; Fitzmeyer, *One Who Is to Come*, 82–133.

45. See "Track Changes: The Sermon on the Mount—Book of Mormon vs. New Testament" at the Thoughts on Things and Stuff blog: https://thoughtsonthingsandstuff .com/track-changes-the-sermon-on-the-mount-book-of-mormon-vs-new-testament/.

46. See John W. Welch, *The Sermon at the Temple and the Sermon on the Mount: A Latter-Day Saint Approach* (Deseret Book, 1999).

47. An example of a textual discrepancy with significant doctrinal implications is the final verse of the first chapter of the Sermon on the Mount, which Matthew renders as, "Be ye therefore perfect, even as your Father which is in heaven is perfect" (Matt 5:48). In the Sermon at the Temple, this becomes, "Therefore I would that ye should be perfect even as I, or your Father who is in heaven is perfect" (3 Ne 5:48). From this discrepancy Latter-day Saints conclude that Christ did not claim to be perfect before his resurrection but did when he appeared in the Book of Mormon after his resurrection, because a resurrected physical body is necessary for perfection. See Russell M. Nelson, "Perfection Pending," in *Conference Reports of the Church of Jesus Christ of Latter-day Saints* (September–October 1995), 115–16.

48. As an example of a contextual difference, five verses in Matthew 5 begin with the phrase "Ye have heard" (Matt 5:21, 27, 33, 38, 43). In 3 Nephi these are replaced by "Ye have heard that it hath been said by them of old time, and it is also written before you" (12:21); "Behold, it is written by them of old time" (12:27), "And again it is written" (12:33); "And behold, it is written" (12:38); and "And behold it is written also" (12:43). John Welch has argued that this reflected the fact that the Nephites were "cut off from most sources of oral or customary Israelite law" and therefore "saw the law primarily as a written body." See Welch, *Sermon at the Temple*, 132.

49. Bradley Trout, "Matthew 5:17 and Matthew's Community," *Hervormde teologiese studies* 72, no. 3 (2016): 2. See also P. la G. Du Toit, "The Fulfilment of the Law According to Matthew 5:17: A Dialectical Approach," *Acta Theologica* 38, no. 2 (2018): 49–69; and F. P. Viljoen, "The Foundational Statement in Matthew 5:17–20 on the Continuing Validity of the Law," *In die Skriflig* 45, nos. 2–3, (2011): 385–407.

50. See J. Julius Scott Jr., "The Church's Progress to the Council of Jerusalem According to the Book of Acts," *Bulletin for Biblical Research* 7 (1997): 205–24.

51. Christian views of the law of Moses vary somewhat, but most Christian theologians invoke some version of the view that the moral aspects of the law such as the Ten Commandments are still in effect for Christians, but the ceremonial aspects—including circumcision, dietary laws, and animal sacrifice—are not. See Michael Wyschogrod, "Christianity and Mosaic Law," *Pro Ecclesia* 2, no. 4 (Fall 1993): 451–59.

52. Kimberly Matheson Berkey points out that, whereas Matthew emphasizes the fact that Jesus preserves the totality of Mosaic law, saying that "one jot or one tittle shall in no wise pass from the law, till all be fulfilled" (Matt 5:17), Nephi$_3$ uses the same words to describe the totality of Christ's fulfillment of the law (3 Ne 1:25). "Temporality and Fulfillment in 3 Nephi 1," *Journal of Book of Mormon Studies* 24 (2015): 59–60.

53. This passage from the Book of Mormon underlies recent efforts of the Church of Jesus Christ of Latter-day Saints to eliminate use of the word "Mormon" in reference to itself. In 2018 President Russell M. Nelson issued a statement that all aspects of the church should use the name that Christ "has revealed for His Church, even the Church of Jesus Christ of Latter-day Saints" (official statement, August 16, 2018, https://newsroom.churchofjesuschrist.org/article/name-of-the-church). This necessitated numerous alterations to official documents. The website where the statement

first appeared was renamed from "mormonnewsroom.com" to "newsroom.churchofje-suschrist.org," and the Mormon Tabernacle Choir was renamed the Tabernacle Choir at Temple Square. In a conference talk the following month, Nelson quoted 3 Ne 27:4 as the impetus for the change.

54. In the King James Version, Christ speaks of a "church" only twice: "And I say also unto thee, That thou art Peter, and upon this rock I will build my church; and the gates of hell shall not prevail against it" (Matt 16:18); and "And if he shall neglect to hear them, tell it unto the church: but if he neglect to hear the church, let him be unto thee as an heathen man and a publican" (Matt 18:17).

55. Cohn-Sherbok, *Jewish Messiah*, 43–60, esp. 44–45.

56. Christopher J. Blythe, *Terrible Revolution: Latter-day Saints and the American Apocalypse* (Oxford University Press, 2020), 17.

Chapter 8. Last Things

1. John J. Collins, *The Apocalyptic Imagination*, 3rd ed. (Eerdmans, 2016), 15.

2. Nephi's vision (1 Ne 11–14), which is discussed at length in Chapter 2, is often referred to as "Nephi's Apocalypse" because it contains most of the elements usually found in the apocalypse genre such as angelic visitors, otherworldly settings, and teaching through symbols. It is not, however, a work of apocalyptic eschatology when placed in its canonical Book of Mormon context. Though it does talk about the last days in some places, it does not present the end of the world as imminent and, in fact, makes it clear that the last things are many generations away. It can, however, be read as apocalyptic when considered in the nineteenth-century context of the Book of Mormon's publication because, for readers in this time period, the last days that Nephi describes would have appeared to be very close at hand.

3. Michael Stone, "Lists of Revealed Things in the Apocalyptic Literature," in *Magnalia Dei: The Mighty Acts of God: Essays on the Bible and Archaeology in Memory of G. Ernest Wright*, ed. G. E. Wright, Werner E. Lemke, Frank M. Cross, and Patrick D. Miller (Doubleday, 1976), 443.

4. Timothy P. Weber, "Millennialism," in *The Oxford Handbook of Eschatology*, ed. Jerry L. Walls (Oxford University Press, 2008), 367.

5. Weber, "Millennialism," 367–68.

6. Weber, "Millennialism," 368–69.

7. The term "immanentize the eschaton" was first used by Eric Voegelin in his 1952 work *The New Science of Politics*: "The problem of an eidos in history, hence, arises only when a Christian transcendental fulfillment becomes immanentized. Such an immanentist hypostasis of the eschaton, however, is a theoretical fallacy." *The New Science of Politics* (University of Chicago Press, 1987), 120. Buckley simplified and popularized this as the slogan "Don't immanentize the Eschaton" throughout the 1960s and 1970s in order to critique socialism, communism, and other attempts to create an earthly paradise in the absence of divine intervention. See Gene Callahan, "Know Your Gnostics," *American Conservative* 11, no. 2 (2012): 36–39.

8. Paula Fredriksen, "Apocalypse and Redemption in Early Christianity from John of Patmos to Augustine of Hippo," *Vigilae Christiane* 45 (1991): 151.

9. Albert Schweitzer, *The Quest of the Historical Jesus: A Critical Study of Its Progress from Reimarus to Wrede*, 2nd English ed., trans. W. Montgomery (Adam and Charles Black, 1911), 358.

10. Heather Hardy, "Saving Christianity: The Nephite Fulfillment of Jesus's Eschatological Prophecies," *Journal of Book of Mormon Studies* 23, no. 1 (2014): 30.

11. Hardy, "Saving Christianity," 34.

12. Hardy, "Saving Christianity," 45–50.

13. Hardy, "Saving Christianity," 48.

14. See Christopher J. Blythe, *Terrible Revolution: Latter-day Saints and the American Apocalypse* (Oxford University Press, 2020), 12–49; Grant Underwood, *The Millenarian World of Early Mormonism* (University of Illinois Press, 1999), 25–41.

15. See Underwood, *Millenarian World*, 11–23.

16. "And he did expound all things, even from the beginning until the time that he should come in his glory" (3 Ne 26:3); "Therefore, more blessed are ye; for ye shall never taste of death, but ye shall live to behold all the doings of the Father unto the children of men, even until all things shall be fulfilled according to the will of the Father, when I shall come in my glory with the powers of heaven" (3 Ne 28:7).

17. Grant Hardy, *Understanding the Book of Mormon* (Oxford University Press, 2010), 298, n. 27. Other than the two passages from 3 Nephi that I have quoted, Hardy identifies only two other passages—excluding quotations from the Old Testament—that refer to a Second Coming beyond what is recorded in 3 Nephi: 1 Nephi 22:24–26 and 3 Nephi 29:2, either of which, I believe, could refer to the visit in 3 Nephi.

18. Matthew 27:51–53 reads: "And, behold, the veil of the temple was rent in twain from the top to the bottom; and the earth did quake, and the rocks rent; And the graves were opened; and many bodies of the saints which slept rose and came out of the graves after his resurrection, and went into the holy city, and appeared unto many." The passage mentions an earthquake that did some damage to the temple in Jerusalem, but it does not approach the apocalyptic cataclysms described in the Book of Mormon during the same time period.

19. In the penultimate chapter attributed to him, Mormon states that "three hundred and eighty and four years had passed away" (Morm 6:5) since the signs were given announcing the birth of Christ, according to the Nephite system of reckoning time (3 Ne 2:8). Moroni takes over the record in Mormon 8 and writes that "four hundred years have passed away since the coming of our Lord and Savior" (Morm 8:6).

20. Unlike the Nephite-Lamanite civilization, which can be dated precisely in the text by reference to a known historical event (the fall of Jerusalem in 587/6 BCE), the Jaredite narrative begins in the Bible's primeval history section (Gen 1–11) and belongs to the world of mythic time rather than historical time. The official LDS Church timeline places the arrival of the Jaredites in the New World at 2200 BCE. The anthropologist John Sorensen placed it at 3100 BCE. "The Years of the Jaredites"

(FARMS, 1969). And while most readers agree that the text places the end of the Jaredite civilization soon after the arrival of the Mulekites in the middle of the sixth century BCE, Brant Gardner places it as late as 200 BCE. *Traditions of the Fathers*, 381, n. 3. The text itself gives us no way to fix date of either the beginning or the end of the civilization.

21. Grant Hardy, *Understanding the Book of Mormon: A Reader's Guide* (Oxford University Press, 2010), 231. On pages 231–32 Hardy prints a chart of similarities between Moroni's Jaredite narrative and Mormon's Nephite narrative that shares some of the comparisons that I use in my chart.

22. Rosalynde Frandsen Welch, *Ether: A Brief Theological Introduction* (Maxwell Institute, 2020), 55.

23. Hardy, *Understanding the Book of Mormon*, 222.

24. Jared Hickman, "The Book of Mormon as Amerindian Apocalypse," *American Literature* 86, no. 3 (September 2014): 429–61.

25. Hickman, "The Book of Mormon as Amerindian Apocalypse," 451. The quotation in the article comes from 3 Nephi 20:15–16, 19.

26. Janeice Johnson, "Becoming a People of the Books: Toward an Understanding of Early Mormon Converts and the New Word of the Lord," *Journal of Book of Mormon Studies* 27 (2018): 21–22.

27. Underwood, *Millenarian World*, 8.

28. In a review of *The Millennial World of Early Mormonism*, Mormon historian Marvin S. Hill argues that Underwood "ignores much evidence favoring this view [that Mormons sought to build a political kingdom before the Second Coming] and employs deductive reasoning to contend that the conservative Mormons, being premillennialists and not postmillennialists . . . could not have established an earthly kingdom." See "The Millenarian World of Early Mormonism (Book Review)," *Church History* 65 (March 1996): 120–22.

29. *Times and Seasons* (Nauvoo, Hancock Co., IL) 3, no. 13 (2 May 1842): 776.

30. Marilyn Arnold, *Sweet Is the Word* (Covenant, 1996), 290.

31. Collins, *Apocalyptic Imagination*, 53–107.

32. Michael T. Miller, "The Evolution of the Patriarch Enoch in Jewish Tradition," *Distant Worlds Journal* 1 (2016): 128–41.

33. See Andrei A. Orlov, *The Enoch-Metatron Tradition* (Mohr-Siebeck, 2005); Daphna Arbel, "Enoch-Metatron: The Highest of All Tapsarim? 3 Enoch and Divinatory Traditions," *Jewish Studies Quarterly* 15, no. 4 (2008): 289–320; and Agata Paluch, "*Enoch-Metatron* Revisited: Prayers, Adjurations, and Metonymical Hermeneutics in Premodern Jewish Mystical and Magical Texts," *Entangled Religions* 13, no. 6 (2022), https://er.ceres.rub.de/index.php/ER/article/view/9519.

34. See Clyde R. Forsberg, *Equal Rites: The Book of Mormon, Masonry, Gender, and American Culture* (Columbia University Press, 2004), 61–62.

35. The United Firm was dissolved in April 1834, two years after it was created. See Max H. Parkin, "Joseph Smith and the United Firm: The Growth and Decline of the

Church's First Master Plan of Business and Finance, Ohio and Missouri, 1832–1834," *BYU Studies Quarterly* 46, no. 3 (2007): 5–66.

36. John Dominic Crossan, *The Historical Jesus: The Life of a Mediterranean Jewish Peasant* (HarperCollins, 1992), 292.

37. Crossan, *The Historical Jesus*, 292.

38. Crossan, *The Historical Jesus*, 238–360.

39. John Dominic Crossan, *The Essential Jesus: Original Sayings and Earliest Images* (Castle, 1998), 8.

40. Crossan's dating for these texts, along with his rationale, can be found in the first appendix to his *Historical Jesus*, 427–50.

41. See Marcus Borg, John Dominic Crossan, and Stephen Patterson, "Jesus Was Not an Apocalyptic Prophet," in *The Apocalyptic Jesus: A Debate*, ed. Dale C. Allison and Robert J. Miller (Polebridge, 2001), 31–82; and John Dominic Crossan, "A Future for the Christian Faith," in *The Once and Future Jesus*, ed. Robert W. Funk (Polebridge, 2000), 109–29.

42. Frank Kermode, *The Sense of an Ending* (Oxford University Press, 1967), 6.

43. Kermode, *The Sense of an Ending*, 17.

44. Mircea Eliade, *The Myth of the Eternal Return; Or, Cosmos and History*, trans. Willard R. Trask (Princeton University Press, 1971), 5.

45. The long block of Isaiah quotations in 2 Nephi begins with one of Isaiah's clearest statements about the last days: "And it shall come to pass in the last days, when the mountain of the Lord's house shall be established in the top of the mountains and shall be exalted above the hills, and all nations shall flow unto it. And many people shall go and say: Come ye and let us go up to the mountain of the Lord, to the house of the God of Jacob, and he will teach us of his ways, and we will walk in his paths. . . . And he shall judge among the nations and shall rebuke many people. And they shall beat their swords into plowshares and their spears into pruning hooks. Nation shall not lift up sword against nation, neither shall they learn war any more" (2 Ne 12:2–4/Isa 2:2–4).

46. In 1828 Martin Harris took a copy of some of the characters from the plates to Columbia University and showed them to several scholars of ancient languages, including the famous classicist Charles Anthon. According to Harris, Anthon confirmed the antiquity of the characters and gave him a certificate to that effect, which he then took back and destroyed when Harris said that the book had come from plates delivered by an angel. When Anthon asked to see the plates, Harris refused, saying that they were sealed, and Anthon replied, "I cannot read a sealed book." This account has itself been canonized in the Joseph Smith—History section of the Pearl of Great Price, where it is usually interpreted as a fulfillment of a prophecy in Isaiah 29:11 (JS—H 1:63–65). In subsequent public statements Anthon gave a very different version of events. See Richard E. Bennett, "Martin Harris's 1828 Visit to Luther Bradish, Charles Anthon, and Samuel Mitchill," in *The Coming Forth of the Book of Mormon: A Marvelous Work and a Wonder*, ed. Dennis L. Largey, Andrew H. Hedges,

John Hilton III, and Kerry Hull (Religious Studies Center, Brigham Young University; Deseret Book, 2015), 103–15.

47. This was the interpretation of LDS apostle LeGrande Richards in his 1950 book *A Marvelous Work and a Wonder*, one of the best-selling and most influential LDS books of all time. Nephi uses the phrase two chapters earlier in a similar sense when he prophesies that "the Lord will set his hand again the second time to restore his people from their lost and fallen state. Wherefore he will proceed to do a marvelous work and a wonder among the children of men" (2 Ne 25:17).

Index

Scripture Index

15:33–31   181

Moroni
1–7   181
10   181
10:1   176

DOCTRINE AND
COVENANTS
27:5   99
28:8   204n30
32:2–3   204n30

THE PEARL OF GREAT
PRICE
Moses
3:16–17   45
5:10–11   50
5:11   8

5:21   68
5:29–33   64
5:49   68
5:52   68
6:26–30   185
6:31–32   185
7:8   64
7:18–21   186
7:22   65

Abraham
1:23–24   65

Joseph Smith—History
1:63–65   227n46

Articles of Faith
204n30

MICHAEL AUSTIN is the Provost of Snow College.
His eight books include *Vardis Fisher*, winner of the
Association for Mormon Letters Award for Best
Criticism. He is also a recipient of the Association
of Mormon Letters Lifetime Achievement Award.

The University of Illinois Press
is a founding member of the
Association of University Presses.

———————————————

University of Illinois Press
1325 South Oak Street
Champaign, IL 61820-6903
www.press.uillinois.edu